The Holy Trinity—
God for God and God for Us

Princeton Theological Monograph Series

K. C. Hanson, Charles M. Collier, and D. Christopher Spinks,
Series Editors

Recent volumes in the series:

Myk Habets
Trinitarian Theology after Barth

Jens Zimmermann
Being Human, Becoming Human:
Dietrich Bonhoeffer and Social Thought

Gergely Tibor Bakos
On Faith, Rationality, and the Other in the Late Middle Ages:
A Study of Nicholas of Cusa's Manuductive Approach to Islam

Tracey Mark Stout
A Fellowship of Baptism: Karl Barth's Ecclesiology
in Light of His Understanding of Baptism

Timothy Matthew Slemmons
Groans of the Spirit: Homiletical Dialectics in an Age of Confusion

Friedrich-Wilhelm Marquardt
Theological Audacities: Selected Essays

Christopher L. Fisher
Human Significance in Theology and the Natural Sciences:
An Ecumenical Perspective with Reference to Pannenberg,
Rahner, and Zizioulas

William J. Meyer
Metaphysics and the Future of Theology:
The Voice of Theology in Public Life

The Holy Trinity—
God for God and God for Us

*Seven Positions on the Immanent-Economic Trinity
Relation in Contemporary Trinitarian Theology*

Chung-Hyun Baik

☙PICKWICK *Publications* · Eugene, Oregon

THE HOLY TRINITY—GOD FOR GOD AND GOD FOR US
Seven Positions on the Immanent-Economic Trinity Relation
in Contemporary Trinitarian Theology

Princeton Theological Monograph Series 145

Pickwick Publications
An Imprint of Wipf and Stock Publishers
199 W. 8th Ave., Suite 3
Eugene, OR 97401

www.wipfandstock.com

ISBN 13: 978-1-60608-998-9

Cataloging-in-Publication data

Baik, Chung-Hyun, 1971–

The holy Trinity—God for God and God for us : seven positions on the immanent-economic Trinity relation in contemporary trinitarian theology / Chung-Hyun Baik.

Princeton Theological Monograph Series 145

xiv + 220 p. ; 23 cm. — Includes bibliographical references and index.

ISBN 13: 978-1-60608-998-9

1. Trinity. 2. Trinity—History of Doctrines I. Title. II. Series.

BT111.3 B35 2010

Manufactured in the U.S.A.

Contents

Acknowledgments

"AM I A GOD NEAR BY, SAYS THE LORD, AND NOT A GOD FAR OFF? . . . Do I not fill heaven and earth?" (Jer 23:24–24). God is both a God near by and a God far off; both the immanent God and the transcendent God. God fills the whole cosmos so that it is the theater of the glory of God. And God is the one God who lives together with one another as God the Father, God the Son and God the Holy Spirit. And this God is the God of love who invites and embraces us into God's own fellowship of love. Glory to God who has led my journey of theology to confess who the Triune God is for my faith and life.

I would like to express my sincere appreciation to all those who have helped me on my journey through GTU in Berkeley: Dr. Claude Welch who advised me for the first two years of the doctoral program, Dr. Anselm Ramelow who helped me explore the philosophical aspects of my thesis, Dr. Christopher A. Beeley from Yale Divinity School who guided me in the deep and wide ocean of patristics, Dr. Michael J. Dodds who read my drafts carefully and provided precious comments and critiques, and Dr. Ted Peters who, as the coordinator of my dissertation committee, always encouraged me to pursue my theological projects and also gave me much critical but fruitful advice. A happy memory is one early morning getting an email from Dr. Peters, greatly to my surprise, responding to a draft which I had sent in late on the previous late!

In addition, my deep gratitude to all those to whom I owe so much for the last ten years of theological study: to Elder EarChul Lim and Kwonsa JungSin Park who supported me financially for my study at Presbyterian College & Theological Seminary in Seoul; to Dr. Inseol Song and Kwonsa Soon-Joo Lee who helped me embark on my study at Princeton Theological Seminary; to Elder Mong-Song Kim, to Senior Pastor Jin-Hong Kim, and Dr. Hoe-Kwon Kim who provided financial support for me to continue to study at Yale Divinity School and at GTU in Berkeley. And to Dr. Sou-Young Lee, Senior Pastor of Saemoonan

Presbyterian Church and to its Future Leader Nurture Scholarship Committee, that encouraged and supported me as I completed my dissertation.

Most of all, my special gratitude to my parents (Senior Pastor Il-Bok Baek and Kwonsa Soon-Hee Choi) and to my parents-in-law (Deacon Tae-Cho Jung and Kwonsa Hye-Sook Kim) who prayed for my study in the early morning as well as in the late night every day, and to all my extended family members. Especially my inexpressible joy and thanks to my yoke-fellows who walk together with me in the journey of life and faith: my lovely wife Hyun-Jin Jung and my beloved daughter Joo-Hee Baik who, whenever I was burdened and even exhausted, have guided me into the world of art with comfortable rest and have led me into the world of innocent childhood with refreshing energy, without which I could not have finished this tough and sometimes treacherous journey.

감사의 글

"나 여호와가 말하노라 나는 가까운데 하나님이요 먼데 하나님은 아니냐? . . . 나는 천지에 충만하지 아니하냐?" (예레미야 23장 23-24절). 하나님은 가까운데 하나님이시며 먼데 하나님이시며, 내재의 하나님이시며 초월의 하나님이시고, 천지에 충만하셔서 온 누리가 하나님의 영광의 무대이며, 성부 하나님, 성자 하나님, 성령 하나님으로서 한 분 하나님이 되시는 삼위일체의 하나님이시며, 우리를 하나님 자신의 사랑의 사귐으로 초대하시고 불러주시는 사랑의 하나님이십니다. 이러한 삼위일체의 하나님이 나의 삶과 신앙에 어떠한 분이신지를 고백할 수 있도록 신학의 여정을 인도해주신 하나님께 영광을 돌려드립니다.

버클리 연합신학대학원에서의 신학여정을 도와주신 여러분들에게 진심으로 감사를 드립니다. 박사과정의 첫 두 해를 지도해주신 끌로드 웰치 교수님, 논문의 철학적인 관점들을 탐구하도록 도움을 주신 안셀름 레믈로우 교수님, 교부학의 넓고 깊은 대양을 안내해주신 예일신학대학원의 크리스토퍼 빌리 교수님, 논문초안을 꼼꼼하게 읽으시고 귀중한 조언을 해주시고 비판해주신 마이클 다즈 교수님, 그리고 신학연구계획들을 추진하도록 항상 용기를 북돋워주시고 날카로우면서도 많은 열매를 맺을 수 있도록 조언을 해주신 논문지도교수인 테드 피터스 교수님께 깊은 고마움을 전합니다. 기억할수록 행복한 순간이 있었습니다. 논문을 한창 써가는 때 어느 이른 아침 일찍 일어나서 피터스 교수님의 전자우편을 열어본 순간 깜짝 놀랐습니다. 전날 밤 늦게 보낸 논문초안에 관하여교수님께서 보내주신 조언의 이멜이었습니다.

그리고, 지난 십 여 년의 신학연구를 지속할 수 있도록 도와주신 분들께 심심한 사의를 표합니다. 장로회신학대학원에서 수학하는 동안 재정적으로 후원해주신 임의철 장로님과 박정신 권사님, 프린스턴신학교에서의 유학의 첫 발걸음을 내디딜 수 있도록 도와주신 송인설 교수님과 이순주 권사님, 예일신학대학원과 버클리 연합신학대학원에서의 신학연구를 지속할 수 있도록 지원해주신 김몽송 장로님과 두레연구원의 김진홍 목사님과 김회권 교수님, 그리고 논문을 완성할 수 있도록 격려해주시고 든든한 뒷받침이 되어주신 새문안교회의 이수영 목사님과 미래지도자육성장학위원회에 깊은 감사를 드립니다.

무엇보다도, 매일 이른 새벽마다 깊은 밤마다 본인의 신학공부를 위하여 기도해주신 부모님(백일복 목사님 최순희 권사님)과 장인 장모님(정태조 집사님 김혜숙 권사님)께, 그리고 모든 가족들에게 특별한 감사의 마음을 드립니다. 특히, 인생과 신앙의 여정을 함께 걸어가는 동행자이며 동역자인 사랑하는 아내 정현진과 사랑스런 딸 백주희에게 형언할 수 없이 기쁘고 고마운 마음을 전합니다. 논문으로 인하여 힘들고 지칠 때마다, 푸근한 예술의 세계에서 편안한 쉼을 누릴 수 있도록 안내해주고, 그리고 순진무구한 동심의 세계에서 마음껏 웃고 새로운 힘을 얻도록 해주었기에, 힘든 여정을 끝까지 걸어갈 수 있었습니다.

Abbreviations

ACW	*Ancient Christian Writers.* 60 vols. Westminster: Newman, 1946–2004.
ANF	*The Ante-Nicene Fathers: Translations of the Writings of the Fathers down to AD 325.* 10 vols. Edited by Alexander Roberts and James Donaldson, eds. Grand Rapids: Eerdmans, 1996–2001.
CD	Karl Barth. *Church Dogmatics.* Translated by Geoffrey W. Bromiley. Edinburgh: T. & T. Clark, 1975.
EDT	*Evangelical Dictionary of Theology.* 2nd ed. Edited by Walter A. Elwell. Grand Rapids: Baker Academic, 2001.
EEC	*Encyclopedia of Early Christianity.* 2nd ed. Edited by Everett Ferguson. New York: Garland, 1997.
FC	*The Fathers of the Church.* 110 vols. Washington, DC: The Catholic University of America Press, 1947–.
KD	Karl Barth. *Die Kirchliche Dogmatik.* Zollikon: Evangelischer, 1947–1970.
LCC	*The Library of Christian Classics.* 26 vols. Philadelphia: Westminster, 1953–1966.
NPNF(1st)	*A Select Library of Nicene and Post-Nicene Fathers of the Christian Church* (1st series). 14 vols. Edited by Philip Schaff and Henry Wace. Grand Rapids: Eerdmans, 1989–1997.
NPNF(2nd)	*A Select Library of Nicene and Post-Nicene Fathers of the Christian Church* (2nd Series). 14 vols. Edited by Philip Schaff and Henry Wace. Grand Rapids: Eerdmans, 1989–1997.

OCCT   *The Oxford Companion to Christian Thought*. Edited by Adrian Hastings. Oxford: Oxford University Press, 2000.

PG   *Patrologiae cursus completus*. Series Graeca. Edited by J. P. Migne. Paris, 1857–1866.

PL   *Patrologiae cursus completus*. Series Latina. Edited by J. P. Migne. Paris, 1844–1855.

ST   Thomas Aquinas, *Summa Theologica*. 5 vols. Translated by the Fathers of the English Dominican Province. Westminster: Christian Classics, 1981.

TDNT   *Theological Dictionary of New Testament*. Edited by G. Kittel. Grand Rapids: Eerdmans, 1985.

TRE   *Theologische Realenzyklopädie Band I–XXXVI*. Edited by Gerhard Müller. Berlin: Walter de Gruyter, 1977–2004.

INTRODUCTION

Ontology, Epistemology, and Mystery in the Contemporary Renaissance of Trinitarian Theology

Scope and Nature

THIS BOOK CENTERS ON CONTEMPORARY DISCUSSIONS ON THE RE-
lationship between the immanent Trinity and the economic Trinity
from the perspective of both ontology and epistemology. The *immanent
Trinity* generally refers to the inner relationships within the Trinity;
whereas the *economic Trinity* broadly denotes the Trinity active and
revealed in creation, redemption, and consummation.

This book places itself within the recent rediscovery and renaissance of Trinitarian theology. The contemporary renewal of Trinitarian
theology was initiated by Karl Barth and Karl Rahner; it has been nur-
tured by the Eastern Orthodox theologians such as Vladimir Lossky and
John D. Zizioulas; it has been further advanced by Jürgen Moltmann,
Wolfhart Pannenberg, and Robert W. Jenson; it has been extended by
some process theologians such as William Norman Pittenger, Joseph
A. Bracken, and Marjorie Hewitt Suchocki, and by some others such as
feminist theologian Catherine Mowry LaCugna, liberation theologian
Leonardo Boff, and Asian-American theologian Jung Young Lee.

I will identify seven different positions on the relationship between the immanent and the economic Trinity: Barth's mutual correspondence; Rahner's identity; Moltmann, Pannenberg, and Jenson's
eschatological unity; Boff and Pittenger's "much more than"; Bracken's

"immersing"; Suchocki and LaCugna's "absorbing"; and Lee's mutual inclusiveness.

This book locates the contemporary issue of the relation between the immanent and the economic Trinity within a more comprehensive framework of the historical discussions of Trinitarian theology, where the terms used for this distinction are consonant, though not identical. The distinction between the immanent Trinity and the economic Trinity is traced back to some other parallel distinctions in the history of theology: the immanent *Logos* [λόγος ἐνδιάθετος]—the expressed *Logos* [λόγος προφορικός]; procession [*processio*]—mission [*missio*]. In addition, the immanent-economic distinction is interwoven with some other important theological terms such as dispensation [*dispositio, dispensatio*], economy [οἰκονομία (*oikonomia*)], and operation or activity [ἐνέργεια (*energeia*)]. Though *dispositio* and *oikonomia* are mostly interchangeable with each other, this book makes a differentiation between them mainly due to some incompatible differences, and uses both the Latin term *dispositio* and the Greek term *oikonomia* [οἰκονομία] in order to highlight the differences.

Centering on the issue of the relation between the immanent and the economic Trinity, I approach the contemporary discussions of the issue primarily in terms of ontology and epistemology. In so doing, I show that ontology and epistemology are indispensably woven into the issue and that each theologian has had to come to grips with certain tensions: ontological, epistemological, or both. For example, Barth starts with the reality of revelation attested in the Scripture, proceeds through an analysis of revelation, and then leads to the concepts of God's Triunity in revelation, which point to God's Triunity in Godself. Thus Barth has to come to grips with an epistemological tension. The main question, then, for this book is how each theologian has dealt with the tensions in each one's own treatment of the relation between the immanent and the economic Trinity.

I further show that a concept of divine mystery is intimately involved in ontological or epistemological tensions, and that a concept of divine mystery has functioned to resolve the tensions. For example, despite the strength to hold fast to the sameness and unity in content between the economic and the immanent Trinity, Barth's position of mutual correspondence implies unavoidably the ontological independence or priority of the immanent Trinity, which, in turn, inevitably evokes an epistemological tension. Thus, in order to resolve the tension, Barth makes a further distinction between God's primary objectivity and God's secondary objectivity, and then finally resorts to a concept of mystery as *ignoramus*.

In addition, for Rahner, though his rule of identity strongly affirms that God whom we experience is Godself, because the economic *Logos* is the immanent *Logos* and the Holy Spirit in history is the Spirit within God, nonetheless Rahner's rule has an inherent ontological tension. Thus he makes a further distinction between the immanent *Logos* as the inward symbol and the economic *Logos* as the outward symbol in an ontological sense, which ultimately rests on the notion of the incomprehensible mystery of God. Furthermore, Boff contends that there is a close link, correlation, and correspondence between the immanent Trinity and the economic Trinity by saying that the latter is an epistemological gateway to the former and the former is an ontological ground of the latter. However, Boff does not go so far as to affirm the full identity of the immanent and the economic Trinity mainly on the basis of his strong focus on the eternal mystery of the immanent Trinity. Thus this book also inquires into the ways in which a concept of divine mystery has been used by each theologian, a question inseparably linked to the main question of the book.

Though this book treats a number of contemporary theologians, nevertheless it does not expand on each theologian's doctrine of the Trinity itself. Instead, it approaches them primarily from the perspective of both ontology and epistemology, and simultaneously in terms of the function of a concept of divine mystery. In addition, though I approach the issue in terms of the general philosophical perspectives of ontology and epistemology, nonetheless I do not explore the ontology or epistemology of any particular philosopher.

Thesis: The Need for a More Integrative Relation between the Immanent Trinity and the Economic Trinity

While considering eleven contemporary theologians and identifying seven different positions with regard to the relationship between the immanent and the economic Trinity, this book shows that ontology and epistemology are indispensably woven into the issue of how that relationship is conceived. While each position displays certain tensions:

ontological, epistemological, or both, each position attempts to resolve these tensions by using a concept of divine mystery. Taking these critical analyses into consideration, this book argues that, for a more fully integrative relationship between the immanent and the economic Trinity, it is necessary to put a concept of mystery in the foreground. This mystery is Jesus Christ. Christ as mystery is not merely a device for resolving epistemological or ontological tensions; but rather the mystery revealed in Christ is the very mystery of the Triune God, which is to be determinative of ontology and epistemology.

Method: Philosophical, Historical, and Critical-Analytical

First of all, this book is both theological and philosophical. That is, it approaches the contemporary theological topic of the relation between the immanent Trinity and the economic Trinity in terms of the philosophical perspectives of ontology and epistemology. Here ontology is used broadly as an inquiry into the reality of being [ὄν], and epistemology refers generally to knowledge [ἐπιστήμη], how we know or perceive reality. In employing these perspectives, this book takes into consideration the fact that philosophy itself has moved historically from its focus on ontology (for example, Aristotle, for whom metaphysics is the first philosophy) to its focus on epistemology (for example, Descartes, for whom epistemology is the first philosophy; and Husserl, for whom phenomenology is the first philosophy).

Secondly, this book addresses this theological topic historically and systematically, by retrieving the relevant historical treatments of the related issues and by establishing the connections between these historical discussions and contemporary discussions in systematic theology.

Finally, this book delves into the contemporary systematic-theological issue analytically, critically, and constructively. It analyzes how each theologian mentioned above has dealt with tensions: ontological, epistemological, or both. At the same time, it critiques each approach with regard to how effectively each theologian resolves these tensions. Lastly, it provides a constructive suggestion on how viewing the issue from an ontological-epistemological framework may further the discussion of the relation between the immanent and the economic Trinity.

Significance

This study is very significant in several ways: First, it provides an insightful perspective which views contemporary theological discussions on the immanent-economic Trinity relation within a wide philosophical and historical context. Second, it analyzes salient contemporary theological discussions in terms of ontology and epistemology and identifies seven different positions on the relation. Last, by showing through a critical analysis that each of these positions expose certain tensions: ontological, epistemological, or both, and has used a concept of mystery to resolve the tensions, though in a restricted way, this book offers a constructive proposal which may provide a way forward in future discussions.

Contemporary Renaissance of Trinitarian Theology

The Eclipse in the Late Eighteenth and Nineteenth Centuries

Since the explicit formulation of the doctrine of the Trinity by the Council of Nicea in 325 and the Council of Constantinople in 381, it has been believed, taught, and confessed throughout the whole history of Christianity. However, the doctrine of the Trinity has been challenged, criticized, and attacked, as well. This was especially the case during the late eighteenth and nineteenth centuries, when the doctrine was severely called into question throughout the range of theological thought such as biblical, philosophical, systematic, and historical theology.

BIBLICAL THEOLOGY   *This effect Exile directly*

First, in the area of biblical theology, Johann Salomo Semler (1725–1791), inaugurated this trend in his four-volume *Treatise on the Free Investigation of the Canon [Abhandlung von freier Untersuchung des Canon]* (1771–1775) in which he claimed that the Word of God and Holy Scripture are not at all identical,[1] and that not all parts of the Bible were inspired. Thus he questioned one of cornerstones of the Reformation, the principle, *Sola Scriptura* (by Scripture alone), which entailed the hermeneutical principle of *Scriptura sui ipsius interpres* (The Scripture interprets itself). Shortly thereafter, Johann Philipp Gabler (1753–1826),

---

1. Hasel, *Old Testament Theology*, 14.

in a lecture at the University of Altdorf in 1787, presented biblical theology as a purely historical discipline and thus completely independent of dogmatics.[2] This position criticized the earlier view of the Bible as providing proof-texts for dogmatic themes including the doctrine of the Trinity. Thus Semler and Gabler inaugurated the historical-critical method in the study of the Bible. As a consequence, the modern critical study of the Bible called into question the authenticity of the biblical texts which had been considered to be inspired and to support the doctrine of the Trinity.

PHILOSOPHICAL THEOLOGY   *This is directed at Trinity*

Second, in the area of philosophical theology, Immanuel Kant (1724–1804), in his book *Critique of Pure Reason* [*Kritik der reinen Vernunft*] (1781 [1st edition], 1787 [2nd edition]), distinguished between *phenomena*, referring to objects present in experience, and *noumena*, denoting objects lying beyond experience. Then Kant restricted our knowledge to *phenomena* alone. This means that we can have no knowledge of an object in itself [*Ding an sich*], and this further implies that we can have no authentic knowledge of God through our pure reason.[3] In his later book *Critique of Practical Reason* [*Kritik der praktischen Vernunft*] (1788), Kant acknowledged three metaphysical realities as postulated by practical reason, which are God, immortality, and freedom.[4] However, in his 1798 essay *The Conflict of Faculties* [*Der Streit der Fakultäten*], Kant did not attribute any practical value to the doctrine of the Trinity: "From the doctrine of the Trinity, taken literally, nothing whatsoever can be gained for practical use, even if one believed that one comprehended it—and less still if one is conscious that it surpasses all our concepts."[5]

SYSTEMATIC THEOLOGY

Third, in the area of systematic theology, Friedrich Schleiermacher (1768–1834), generally regarded as the founder of liberal theology, disputed the traditional ecclesiastical doctrine of the Trinity in terms of his new approach to religion and faith. In his 1799 book *On Religion: Speeches*

2. Hasel, *Old Testament Theology*, 15–16.
3. Kant, *Critique of Pure Reason*, 264–69.
4. Kant, *Critique of Practical Reason*.
5. Kant, *Der Streit der Fakultäten*, 34.

to its *Cultured Despisers* [*Über die Religion. Reden an die Gebildeten unter ihren Verächtern*], Schleiermacher argued that the essence of religion is neither thinking nor acting, but intuition and feeling [*Gefühl*].[6] And he claimed that one can be a fully religious person without coming into contact with concepts such as revelation and inspiration.[7] Then, in his *magnum opus*, *The Christian Faith* [*Der christliche Glaube*] (1821–1822 [1st edition], 1830–1831 [2nd edition]), Schleiermacher affirmed that piety is neither knowing nor doing, but a modification of feeling, or of immediate self-consciousness,[8] and reduced the idea of God to nothing more than the expression of the feeling of absolute dependence.[9] And what is more remarkable in this book is that Schleiermacher not only deferred discussion of the doctrine of the Trinity to the end of his thick two-volume book,[10] but also assigned no real value to the traditional ecclesiastical doctrine of the Trinity. Furthermore, he relegated it to the second rank, when he stated that the traditional ecclesiastical doctrine of the Trinity is "not an immediate utterance concerning the Christian self-consciousness, but only a combination of several such utterances."[11]

Historical Theology

Lastly, in the area of historical theology, Adolf von Harnack (1851–1930), in his *History of Dogma* [*Lehrbuch der Dogmengeschichte*] (1885[1st edition]), provided his main thesis that dogma from its conception to its construction was the result of the Greek spirit on the soil of the Gospel. For Harnack, dogma, mainly referring to the doctrine of the Trinity and Christology, was the product of the gradual Hellenization of the Christian Gospel. As a consequence, he contended that the doctrine of the Trinity is neither essential nor necessary to the gospel.[12] Such a position was fully expressed in his 1899–1900 lectures at the University of Berlin, the result of which was the publication of his book *What is*

6. Schleiermacher, *On Religion*, 22.

7. Ibid., 44.

8. Schleiermacher, *Christian Faith*, I, 3.

9. Ibid., I, 5.

10. Schleiermacher, *Christian Faith*, II, 170–72.

11. Ibid., II, 170.

12. Harnack, *History of Dogma*.

Christianity? [*Das Wesen des Christentums*] in 1900. In these lectures, Harnack summarized Jesus' own teaching under three headings: first, the kingdom of God and its coming; second, God the Father and the infinite value of the human soul; and last, the higher righteousness and the commandment of love.[13] It is noteworthy that in this book Harnack put a great focus on God the Father to the exclusion of God the Son and God the Holy Spirit and with no mention of the Triune God. He understood the term 'the Son of God' simply as indicating Jesus' own consciousness of being the Son of God, which is, in turn, nothing but a practical consequence of Jesus' knowing God as his Father.[14] And he considered the Holy Spirit merely as an individual's immediate and living connection with God the Father.[15]

All these factors in the areas of biblical, philosophical, systematic, and historical theology, which are intimately related to major intellectual movements characteristic of modern culture, called into question the importance of the doctrine of the Trinity in the late eighteenth and nineteenth centuries. Though there were, of course, those who continued to adhere to the doctrine of the Trinity, nevertheless these revisionist accounts were much more influential and pervasive; all of them converging on the eclipse of the doctrine of the Trinity.

The Rediscovery in the Twentieth and Early Twenty-First Centuries

Against the trajectory suggested by the theological work of the previous two centuries, however, the twentieth and early twenty-first centuries have witnessed a considerable rediscovery of the doctrine of the Trinity. Though this effort encompassed all areas of Christian theology, the most remarkable came from the area of systematic theology.[16]

---

13. Harnack, *What is Christianity?*, 51.

14. Ibid., 128.

15. Ibid., 165.

16. The British Council of Churches (BCC), in the report of the Study Commission on Trinitarian Doctrine Today in 1989, picked up the three theological works which have exerted considerable influence on the rediscovery of the doctrine of the Trinity in the twentieth century: first, Karl Barth's first volume of *Church Dogmatics* [*Die kirchliche Dogmatik*] in 1932 on the Protestant Church side; second, Vladimir Lossky's *The Mystical Theology of the Eastern Church* in 1944 on the Eastern Orthodox Church side; and last, Karl Rahner's *The Trinity* in 1967 on the Roman Catholic Church side. The British Council of Churches, *The Forgotten Trinity*, vols. 1–3.

SYSTEMATIC THEOLOGY

In the area of systematic theology, Karl Barth (1886–1968) was the first to initiate a renewal of theological interest in the doctrine of the Trinity. While serving as a pastor in the small town of Safenwil from 1911 to 1921 and witnessing the outbreak of the First World War (1914–1918), Barth discussed what should be the right starting point of theology and then found it in the Bible. As a result, Barth wrote a provocative commentary *The Epistle to the Romans* in 1918 with the publication of the first German edition in 1919 and its sixth German edition in 1928. The heavily revised second edition, written in 1921, published in 1922, and translated into English in 1933, was much more sensational. Indeed as Karl Adam described it, Barth's *Römerbrief* fell like "a bombshell on the playground of the theologians."[17]

In this work, Barth attacked liberal theology's anthropological understanding of God which originated from Schleiermacher. Drawing heavily on Kierkegaard's talk of "the infinite qualitative difference between God and man,"[18] he put a great stress on God's being the wholly other, on the freedom of God, and on the lordship of God. He emphasized that human efforts to reach God are certain to fail. In his 1923–1924 lectures at Göttingen, Barth further criticized Schleiermacher on the grounds that he had made man the subject of theology and God merely its predicate.[19]

Thus Barth's *Church Dogmatics* published in 1932, began, as the starting point of theology, not with the human consciousness of God, but with the Word of God.[20] He distinguished three different forms of the Word of God: written (the Scripture), revealed (revelation), and preached (Church proclamation). He argued that the three forms of the Word of God are in unity, because the Scripture attests to revelation and Church proclamation is fulfilled by revelation.[21] Then Barth analyzed the biblical concept of revelation which denotes that God reveals Godself as the Lord, and he proceeded to affirm that God who reveals Godself in the Bible is also God's revealing and God's being

---

17. As quoted in Mueller, *Makers*, 23; and in Ahlstrom, *Religious History*, 934.
18. Barth, *Epistle to the Romans*, 355.
19. Barth, *Theology of Schleiermacher*.
20. Barth, *CD*.
21. Barth, *CD* I, 1, 121.

revealed. God is Revealer (subject), Revelation (predicate, event), and Revealedness (object, effect). In this way, Barth arrived at the doctrine of the Trinity, and calls revelation attested by the Scripture as the root or basis of the doctrine of the Trinity.[22] Such a starting point of theology enabled Barth to put the doctrine of the Trinity at the head of all dogmatics, a position which, of course, was contrasted starkly with that of Schleiermacher. This is not merely a matter of the position of the discussion of the Trinity in the whole dogmatics. It is, rather, that for Barth to put the doctrine of the Trinity first indicates that the doctrine of the Trinity is constitutive of his whole approach to dogmatics. As he says: "The doctrine of the Trinity is what basically distinguishes the Christian doctrine of God as Christian, and therefore what already distinguishes the Christian concept of revelation as Christian, in contrast to all other possible doctrines of God or concepts of revelation."[23]

Second, Vladimir Lossky (1903–1958) and John D. Zizioulas introduced the Eastern Orthodox theology of the Trinity and stimulated the Western Church theologians. Lossky, a Russian Orthodox theologian, after being expelled from Russia in 1922, lived with Russian refugees in Paris and worked there until his death in 1958. Zizioulas, a Greek Orthodox theologian, studied in Athens and taught in Edinburgh, Glasgow, and London. These Orthodox theologians introduced the Eastern Orthodox theology of the Trinity into the Western Church.

In his 1944 book *The Mystical Theology of the Eastern Church*, drawing heavily on the apophatic or negative way of doing theology, the most distinctive characteristic of Eastern orthodox theology, Lossky affirmed both God's absolute incomprehensibility and God's self-revelation as the Trinity in the incomprehensibility.[24] Lossky goes on to argue that the revelation of God the Holy Trinity is the basis of all Christian theology, and that the Trinity is the sole ground of all reality and all thought. In this sense, Lossky reinvigorates the ontology of the Trinity as the ultimate reality together with the epistemology of apophaticism which is required for human understanding of the incomprehensible mystery of the Trinity.

22. Barth, *CD* I, 1, 296–333.

23. Ibid., 301.

24. Lossky, *Mystical Theology*, 64.

Another contribution of Lossky's is his account of the effort of the Greek Fathers, such as Gregory of Nyssa, Basil the Great, and Gregory of Nazianzus to distinguish between the term ousia [οὐσία] (substance, essence) and *hypostasis* [ὑπόστασις] (person). Lossky emphasized that the genius of the Greek Fathers made the creative use of the two synonyms to distinguish in God between that which is common (*ousia*) and that which is particular (*hypostasis*). In this sense, Lossky's objective here was to argue that the doctrine of the Trinity is not the product of the Hellenization of the Christian gospel, but rather the purification of the Hellenistic thought and the transformation of rational speculation into a contemplation of the mystery of the Trinity.[25]

Zizioulas, while noting the Greek Fathers' creative appropriation of the terms *ousia* and *hypostasis*, went further than Lossky in emphasizing the ontology of personhood and the *perichoresis* [περιχώρησις] (mutual indwelling) of the three persons. Unlike the Western Church, which started with the essence of God as unity and then proceeded to the three persons of the Trinity, the Eastern Church started with the *hypostasis* of the three persons, especially the person of the Father, and then proceeded to their unity through *perichoresis*. For the Greek Fathers, as Zizioulas explains: "the unity of God, the one God, and the ontological 'principle' or 'cause' of the being and life of God does not consist in the one substance of God but in the *hypostasis*, that is, the person of the Father . . . who is the 'cause' both of the generation of the Son and of the procession of the Spirit."[26] This Greek Orthodox account of personhood ontology and *perichoresis* enables us to understand being as *koinonia* [κοινωνία] (communion), and their views come to exercise considerable influence on current Western Trinitarian theologians such as Moltmann and Pannenberg.

Third, Karl Rahner (1904–1984), in his 1967 essay on the Trinity, pointed out that, though Christians confess the orthodox doctrine of the Trinity, they are almost mere monotheists in their practical life.[27]

25. Lossky, *Mystical Theology*, 50–51.

26. Zizioulas, *Being as Communion*, 40–41.

27. Rahner, *Trinity*, 10. This book was translated from his 1967 essay, "The Triune God as the Transcendental Ground of Salvation History" [*Der dreifaltige Gott als transzendenter Urgrund der Heilsgeschichte*], which was listed in the second volume of *Mysterium Salutis* [*The Mystery of Salvation*]. And this essay was actually based on his 1960 essay, "Remarks on the Dogmatic Treatise *De Trinitate*" [*Bemerkungen zum*

Rahner judged that this problem traced back to the conventional separation in the Western Church between the treatise dealing with the one God and that dealing with the Triune God, especially in Thomas Aquinas and Augustine.[28] In order to resolve this issue, Rahner suggests that it is necessary to reconnect the treatise on the one God and the treatise on the Triune God, and to present the Trinity as a mystery of salvation. To this end he formulated his famous "basic thesis," or "basic axiom [*Grundaxiom*]" as follows: "The 'economic' Trinity is the 'immanent' Trinity and the 'immanent' Trinity is the 'economic' Trinity."[29] By the basic axiom, Rahner specifically means that the immanent *Logos* and the economic *Logos* are strictly the same and that the *Logos* with God and the *Logos* with us are strictly the same. In addition, Rahner's rule of identity firmly avers that the economic *Logos* expresses exactly what the immanent *Logos* is within the inner life of the Trinity, that the hypostatic union of the economic *Logos* is the very constitutive way of expressing the immanent *Logos*, and that mission has the sameness with procession. Furthermore, Rahner's rule implies that the God who comes to us in salvation history is no other than the God who is eternally God. The God whom we experience in salvation history is the very God who is eternally God. To put it simply, God communicates Godself to us and God is the God of self-communication to us. In other words, what is communicated in the divine self-communication is precisely Godself.

God's threefold relationship to the world is "not merely a copy or an analogy of the inner Trinity,"[30] but exactly the Triune personal God, because the divine self-communication occurs only in the intra-divine manner of the two communications of the divine essence by the Father to the Son and the Spirit. Only in that way, God can communicate Godself. As he puts it: "God has given himself so fully in his absolute self-communication to the creature, that the 'immanent' Trinity becomes the Trinity of the 'economy of salvation,' and hence in turn the Trinity of salvation which we experience *is* the immanent Trinity. This means

---

dogmatischen Traktat «De Trinitate»], which was included in the fourth volume of *Schriften zur Theologie*.

28. Rahner, *Trinity*, 16–17.

29. Ibid., 22. The basic thesis or axiom is also called "the guiding principle," or "the methodical principle" by Rahner himself, and it is widely known as "Rahner's Rule." For more information regarding it, see n. 28 and n. 30 in chapter 3. Rahner's own italics.

30. Ibid., 35.

that the Trinity of God's relationship to us *is* the reality of God as he is *in himself*: a trinity of persons."[31] This principle of identity between the immanent and the economic Trinity became a powerful momentum to evoke much further discussions concerning the doctrine of the Trinity.

According to Sanders, interpreters of Rahner's rule are divided into two groups, the radicalizers and the restricters: The former group argues for a strong identity between the economic Trinity and the immanent Trinity, and it includes Piet J. A. M. Schoonenberg, Hans Küng, Jürgen Moltmann, Wolfhart Pannenberg, Robert W. Jenson, and Catherine Mowry LaCugna. The latter group asserts that Rahner goes too far and calls for a restriction of Rahner's rule. Yves Congar, Walter Kasper, Hans Urs von Balthasar, T. F. Torrance, and Paul Molnar belong to this group.32

Fourth, Stanley J. Grenz (1950–2005) wrote a very informative and well-organized book in 2004 in which he picked up the eleven representative theologians who have made the most significant contributions to the rediscovery of the doctrine of the Trinity over the course of the twentieth century. He begins with Karl Barth, whose attention to the divine act of God's self-revelation is essential to the renewed interest in the Trinity, and with the work of Karl Rahner for whom the key is the divine act of God's self-communication. Next, he deals with Jürgen Moltmann, Wolfhart Pannenberg, and Robert Jenson, who emphasize the historical and economic character of the three divine persons of the Trinity. Then, he proceeds to Leonardo Boff, John Zizioulas, and Catherine Mowry LaCugna, whose focus is on the relational character of the Triune God. Lastly, he summarizes the Trinitarian views of Elizabeth A. Johnson, Hans Urs von Balthasar, and Thomas F. Torrance, who returned to the importance of the immanent Trinity.

However, the significance of Grenz's book does not lie in this well-organized summary, but in its own suggestion of a future direction for the Trinitarian theology. Grenz organized the eleven Trinitarian theologians into four groups according to the "golden thread" which he discerned weaving its way through their works. The golden thread is "the question as to how theology can conceptualize the relationship between God-in-eternity [the immanent Trinity] and God-in-salvation

---

31. Rahner, "Concept of Mystery," 69. Rahner's own italics.
32. Sanders, "Image of the Immanent Trinity," 108–98.

[the economic Trinity] in a manner that takes seriously the importance of the latter to the former and avoids collapsing the former into the latter or compromising the freedom of the eternal God."[33]

The most remarkable contribution of Grenz comes from his grand project on the Trinitarian theology, namely *The Matrix of Christian Theology* which would have consisted of six volumes: anthropology, theology (proper), christology, pneumatology, ecclesiology, and eschatology. At the heart of this series was to be the explication of the Triune God. Unfortunately, however, the whole project did not see the light of day due to his early death from a brain hemorrhage in 2005, except the first volume on a theological anthropology in 2001 and the second volume on a Trinitarian ontology in 2005. Nonetheless, even these two volumes are highly noteworthy for the future development of contemporary Trinitarian theology. The second volume will be touched in the area of philosophical theology.

In the first volume, dealing with a Trinitarian theology of the *imago Dei*,[34] Grenz maintains that it is required to restore the social and relational aspects of the *imago Dei* in the contemporary loss of the centered self. According to the Bible, humankind is created in the image of God, but the image of God is Jesus Christ who is the visible manifestation of the divine reality. New humanity in the Holy Spirit, that is, "the ecclesial self—the self constructed *extra se in Christo* by the Holy Spirit"[35] is to bear the image of Christ and to participate in the very life of the Triune God. This is ontologically possible, because the biblical God, as a dynamic life of persons-in-relationship or persons-in-communion, is not only the community of love throughout all eternity, but also readily responds to the world in accordance with the essential divine love. Here, drawing on Moltmann, Pannenberg, and Zizioulas, he treats the imago dei not only as an anthropological concept, but also as a theological, ecclesiological, and eschatological concept. In this way, Grenz aims to construct "an eschatologically determined, social conception of the image of God and, in turn, a trinitarian depiction of the relational self."[36]

33. Grenz, *Rediscovering the Triune God*, 222.

34. Grenz, *Social God*.

35. Ibid., 332.

36. Ibid., 18.

BIBLICAL THEOLOGY

In the second place, in the area of biblical theology, the historical-critical method in the study of the Bible had been so pervasive in the nineteenth and early twentieth centuries since Semler and Gabler, that it called into question the authenticity of the biblical texts which had been considered to be inspired and to support the doctrine of the Trinity. Nevertheless, there was also a strong undercurrent of conservative Protestant thought which adhered to the doctrine of the Trinity based on the Bible against the subjectivist, speculative and agnostic attitudes towards the Trinity.[37] First, Benjamin B. Warfield (1851–1921), in his 1915 article "The Biblical Doctrine of the Trinity," argued that "the doctrine of the Trinity is given to us in Scripture, not in formulated definition, but in fragmentary allusions."[38] Though the mystery of the Trinity is not revealed in the Old Testament, nevertheless the mystery of the Trinity underlines it. And the whole New Testament is Trinitarian to the core and all its teachings are built on the assumption of the Trinity.39 Thus the use of non-biblical terms such as Trinity, substance, person and so on for the doctrine of the Trinity is justifiable, in that they preserve the truth of the Scripture.

Second, G. A. F. Knight, in his 1953 monograph *A Biblical Approach to the Doctrine of the Trinity*,[40] tried to gather together from the Old Testament some of the concepts which lie behind the doctrine of the Trinity. Considering the uses of Hebrew terms such as "Name of God," "Face of God," and "Wisdom of God," Knight argued that there are some distinction and differentiation within God. And the Shema in Deut 6:4 ("Hear, O Israel: The LORD our God, the LORD is one" [NIV]) uses the Hebrew word *'eḥādh* for one, not the word *yahidh*. The latter means the unique one, namely, the only one of a class, whereas the former means an organic unity which is used for one flesh between a man and a wife in Gen 2:24. In this way, Knight concludes

---

37. Welch, *In This Name*, 34–41.

38. Warfield, "Biblical Doctrine of the Trinity," 22. This article first appeared as "Trinity," in *The International Standard Bible Encyclopedia*, ed. James Orr, 3012–22. Chicago: Howard-Severance, 1915.

39. Warfield, "Biblical Doctrine," 30–32.

40. Knight, *Biblical Approach*.

that "the Hebrew Scriptures reveal to us as lying behind the words: 'The Holy Blessed Trinity.'"[41]

Third, Arthur W. Wainwright in his 1962 book *The Trinity in the New Testament*,[42] affirms that the New Testament acknowledges both the divinity of Jesus Christ and the divinity of the Holy Spirit. In addition, a variety of triadic pattern passages in the New Testament such as Matt 28:19 (baptismal formula), 2 Cor 13:14 (benediction formula), 1 Cor 12:4–6, 2 Thess 2:13–14 and so on, show that the early Christians believed in the Father and the Son and the Spirit. Wainwright concludes that although the writers of the New Testament were unschooled in systematic methods, they were nevertheless able to give an account of the work of God through Christ, in the Spirit, which must provide the basis for Christian thought about the Triune God.

Lastly, these above-mentioned works in the area of biblical theology are very helpful in defending the biblical doctrine of the Trinity against the other positions. For example, R. G. Crawford, drawing heavily on Knight and Wainwright in his 1967 article, especially criticizes the positions of the Unitarians who hold fast to the one God, that is, God as the Father, and who contend that, for example, Matt 28:19 does not say anything about the equality of the three in essence and thus does not support the doctrine of the Trinity.[43] On the other hand, James R. White, a Reformed Baptist Church theologian, in his 1998 book *The Forgotten Trinity*, effectively disputes the Jehovah's Witnesses' interpretation of the word "God" in the last clause of John 1:1 ("In the beginning was the Word, and the Word was with God, and the Word was God [θεός ἦν ὁ λόγος]"). They contend that, as there is no Greek article prior to the word "God," the word should be translated into "a god," not "God." Against them, White argues that the anarthrous θεός can be translated only in a qualitative sense which means that the Word shared the nature and being of God. He went further to pinpoint that John is very careful to differentiate between the Father and the Son here, because, if John put an article before "God," then it would mean modalism which says

---

41. Knight, *Biblical Approach*, 78.

42. Wainwright, *Trinity*.

43. Crawford, "Is the Doctrine of the Trinity Scriptural?," 282–83.

that there is only one person who sometimes acts like the Father and sometimes like the Son.[44]

PHILOSOPHICAL THEOLOGY

In the third place, as for the area of philosophical theology, there have been some reactions against Kant's distinction between *phenomena* and *noumena* and his attempt to restrict our knowledge to *phenomena* alone. This restriction implies that we can have no authentic knowledge of an object in itself [*Ding an sich*]—including God—through our pure reason. As a result, on the one hand, Kant's transcendental focus on *phenomena* led some subsequent thinkers to direct their attention to the human subjective side, which was mainly expressed through Romanticism. For example, Schleiermacher attempted to reach God through human consciousness of absolute dependence. And we noted above that this kind of subjective method by Schleiermacher was harshly criticized by Barth.

On the other hand, Kant's position on *noumena* led some others to agnostic, and finally atheistc attitudes toward God. Against these consequences there have been some reactions. For example, Hegel (1770–1831), though influenced by Kant's transcendental turn, reacted against the limits placed upon divine knowledge by Kant's critique. The point of Hegel's thought was to overcome Kant's *noumena*, and to secure the knowledge of the essence of God. Thus in his 1807 book *The Phenomenology of Spirit/Mind*, he considered God as the Absolute Spirit (Father) who achieves consciousness finitely (as Son) and unites all differences in himself (as Spirit). God is essentially the Triune God in God's absolute idea.

In the contemporary period, Eberhard Jüngel reacted against the atheistic consequence of modern rationalistic philosophy originating from Kant's position on *noumena* and further lurking in the Cartesian methodic doubt of the thinking self. In his magisterial book *God as the Mystery of the World* in 1977, Jüngel attempted to defend and support the possibility of talk about God on the ground of the death of Jesus Christ on the cross, which is *the* Trinitarian event. In that event, God, who is love, is differentiated between the one who loves (the Father), the beloved (the Son), and the chain or event of love (the Spirit).

---

44. White, *Forgotten Trinity*, 52–58.

In this sense, the epitome of the story of Jesus Christ is the doctrine of the Trinity.[45]

Grenz goes further than Jüngel to propose a Trinitarian theo-ontology in the second volume of *The Matrix of Christian Theology*.[46] From his analysis of the history of onto-theology, he points out that Christian thinkers have tended to understand the God of the Bible in accordance with a metaphysical framework of being. As a result, their efforts brought about an onto-theology in which God is made to fit within classical ontology, and which finally led to the death of onto-theology. Then, Grenz notes that the self-naming of the Triune God unfolds in the narratives of the Bible. The unfolding story starts with the revelation of the "I AM" name to Moses (Exod 3:14), through the incarnation of the "I AM" in Jesus Christ (John 6:35; 8:12; 10:9; 10:11–14; 11:25; 14:6; 15:1), to the exaltation of Jesus as the eternal "I AM" in the Holy Spirit (Rev 1:8; 1:17; 21:6). Based on this biblical point, Grenz pursues the deeper question of ontology from a thoroughgoing Trinitarian perspective. Rather than asking about the implications of ontology for theology, he ascertains the implications of the Christian conception of God as Triune for the questions of ontology.

HISTORICAL THEOLOGY

In the last place, in the area of historical theology, against Harnak's thesis of the Hellenization of the gospel in his book *History of Dogma*, there have been persistent responses, especially nowadays combined with the contemporary renaissance of the doctrine of the Trinity. First, John Norman Davidson Kelly (1909–1997) in his 1958 *Early Christian Doctrines* traced the overall development of the doctrine of the Trinity in the light of both the internal integration of the fresh data of revelation and the outward infiltration of secular thoughts.[47] Second, Jaroslav Pelikan (1923–2006), in his 1971 book *The Christian Tradition: A History of the Development of Doctrine*, argued that the dogma of the Trinity was a proper formulation, because it was already enshrined in liturgy and also documented in the Bible.[48] Third, Edmund J. Fortman,

45. Jüngel, *God as the Mystery*, 344.

46. Grenz, *Named God*.

47. Kelly, *Early Christian Doctrines*, 84, 87.

48. Pelikan, *Christian Tradition*, 1:223.

in his 1972 book *The Triune God: A Historical Study of the Doctrine of the Trinity*, approached the development of the doctrines in terms of "the Christianization of the Hellenism" to some extent.[49] Last, William J. Hill, in his 1982 book *The Three-Personed God: The Trinity as a Mystery of Salvation*, acknowledged that although the entire historical development was unquestionably a process of Hellenizing the *kerygma*, nonetheless it was a *kerygma* already enriched by the inspired theologizing of John and Paul. At the same time, he strongly affirmed that there had been a controlling and corrective process continually at work, in which a faith-confession "appropriated Hellenistic categories and transformed them" in the process.[50]

For all of these scholars, it was not the doctrine of the Trinity but the position of Arius that perfectly fitted Harnack's thesis. For Arius, there is only one God who alone is uncreated, unbegotten, and un-originated [ἀγένητος (*agenetos*)]. If the Son is begotten [γεννητός (*gennetos*)] by the Father, then the Son is not God but a creature. Thus Arius said, "And before he was begotten or created or defined or established, he was not."[51] Here Arius wrongly identified the biblical term *gennetos* [γεννητός] (begotten) with the Greek term *genetos* [γενητός] (created). What is more, Arius held fast to the Greek principle of simplicity. For him, if the begotten Son is not created, then the Son would be unbegotten like the Father or at least a portion of the Father. Then the Father would be "compounded, divided, mutable and a body,"[52] which Arius could not accept. Thus the position of Arius is the perfect instance of Hellenization. Considering the new developments in the area of historical theology, Harnack's thesis that the dogma of the Trinity is the product of the Hellenization of the gospel is no longer persuasive, but is to be regarded as an oversimplification.

The Renaissance of Trinitarian Theology

As we have shown in the above, the twentieth and early twenty-first centuries have witnessed a rediscovery of the doctrine of the Trinity in

---

49. Fortman, *The Triune God*, 44. This book was originally published by Hutchinson in London in 1972.

50. Hill, *Three-Personed God*, 50.

51. Arius, *Letter to Eusebius*, 30.

52. Ibid., 32.

all the four areas of theology. However, this contemporary rediscovery not only restores the importance of the doctrine of the Trinity from its eclipse, but also goes further to exercise a more considerable influence than ever before on all areas and all aspects of theology. Christopher Schwöbel calls this new interest in the doctrine of the Trinity "the renaissance or revival of Trinitarian theology" and rightly summarizes the point of the contemporary rediscovery as follows:

> A characteristic feature of this increased engagement with the doctrine of the Trinity is that it is not restricted to specific issues of the Christian doctrine of God while leaving other aspects of theology unchanged. Reflection on the Trinity, so it seems, inevitably has repercussions for the whole project of Christian theology and its relation to the cultural situation of the times. Trinitarian theology therefore appears to be a summary label for doing theology that effects all aspects of the enterprise of doing theology in its various disciplines.[53]

In the contemporary renaissance of Trinitarian theology, all theological loci and themes are approached in the light of the Trinity. They include creation, anthropology, christology, soteriology, atonement, pneumatology, spirituality, ecclesiology, eschatology, ministry, worship, sacraments, mission, prayer, family life, society, diverse culture, world religions, and so on. As the God who we believe and worship is no other than the Triune God, we could not think all things in other than a Trinitarian way for our faith and life. In this sense, the importance of the doctrine of the Trinity cannot be overemphasized.

---

53. Schwöbel, "Renaisssance," 1.

2

Philosophical and Historical Context

An Overview of Ontology and Epistemology in the History of Western Philosophy

AS THE "LOVE OF WISDOM," PHILOSOPHY [φιλοσοφία] NATURALLY includes a broad range of concerns: ontology, epistemology, ethics, logic, and so on, but the first two of these, however, are those which determine the main characteristics of each philosophy. Ontology is an inquiry into the reality of being [ὄν] and epistemology is an inquiry into the knowledge [ἐπιστήμη] of the reality of being. Here ontology is considered to be a discipline which explores fundamental principles of physical beings. Despite a distinction between ontology and epistemology, however, both always interact with each other. Epistemology strives to understand the "reality" postulated by ontology, while ontology requires some account from epistemology as to how one can *know* (or form reliable beliefs about) the nature of "being." Thus both ontology and epistemology are correlative to each other.

A history of western philosophy shows that the focus of philosophy has moved from ontology or metaphysics which was the first philosophy for Aristotle, through epistemology which Descartes regarded as the first philosophy and through phenomenology which Husserl considered as the first philosophy, to contemporary anti-metaphysical tendencies as seen in some contemporary philosophers such as Heidegger, Levinas, Foucault, and Derrida. For example, the first philosophy for Levinas is the ethics of love.

Pre-Socratic Philosophers

Among pre-Socratic philosophers who sought to investigate *arche* [ἀρχή], namely, the first principle of all things, Heraclitus of Ephesus[1] (530–470 BC) claimed that all things flow and expressed it in his epigram that no one can step into the same river twice.[2] All things are in process and in change, but Heraclitus supposed that there is an underlying common constituent of things, which is termed the *Logos* [λόγος]. Thus reason penetrates into the *Logos* of all things, whereas sense, which looks at appearances, does not comprehend the *Logos*.

Unlike Heraclitus who noted change of all things, Parmenides (520–440 BC) put a stress on the unchanging-ness of reality. His positions are well expressed in the following argument: first, "What is is; and nothing else is at all"; second, "What is is both uncreated and indestructible;" third, "What is is unchanging;" lastly, "What is is indivisible."[3] Reality, for him, is what is uncreated, unchanging, immovable, and indivisible. In addition, Parmenides offered a contrast between truth and opinion, between knowledge and error, between reality and appearance, and between intellect and sense, which would be repeated in history of western philosophy.

Plato

Plato (427–347 BC) provided an ontology of *eidos* [εἶδος] (idea or form) and an epistemology of recollection, which are remarkably characterized by the dualistic division between the world of *phenomena* [φαινόμενα] and the world of *eidoi* (ideas or forms).[4] *Phenomena* are visible and sensible particulars, while *eidoi* are invisible and intelligible universals. *Phenomena* are changeable and temporal, whereas *eidoi* are unchangeable and eternal. *Phenomena* are the imperfect copies of the perfect *eidoi*. For example, this table or that table in the world of *phenomena* is a certain copy of the *eidos* of table. Or, in other words, this table or that table participates in the *eidos* of table. As particulars of the world of *phenomena* are changeable, temporal, and imperfect, only

---

1. Kirk et al., *Presocratic.*

2. Lamprecht, *Brief History*, 13.

3. Ibid., 14.

4. Allen, *Philosophy*, 47.

eidos is "real" in the sense that it is only "that which is" or "that which truly is."

Such an ontology of *eidos* determines its corresponding epistemology of recollection. According to Plato, we cannot acquire knowledge [ἐπιστήμη] of *phenomena*, because they are changeable and imperfect. We can have only *doxa* [δόξα] (opinion) of *phenomena*. Neither can we attain to knowledge of *eidos* by generalizing from its particulars, because they are, though approximate, not perfect. Instead, we can have knowledge of *eidos* through *anamnesis* [ἀνάμνησις] whereby we recollect *eidoi* which we had known before our soul came into the prison of the body. Plato's ontology and epistemology are well illustrated in his work *Republic* with his three famous images: the image of the sun, the image of divided line, and the image of cave.

Aristotle

Aristotle (384–322 BC) proposed an ontology of *ousia* [οὐσία] (substance), which was translated into Latin as *substantia* by Cicero. Primary *ousia* refers to each concrete, individual being, and secondary *ousia* denotes genera or species of *ousia*. For example, this red table or that wooden chair belongs to primary *ousia*, and table or chair is secondary *ousia*. Remarkably, Aristotle insisted that *ousia* is always a union of *eidos* and matter, despite their stark difference that *eidos* is eternal and unchangeable, whereas matter is temporal and changeable. Aristotelian insistence is in a sharp contrast to Platonic dualistic division between the world of *phenomena* and the world of *eidoi*. And such a contrast implies that, unlike Plato's world of *eidoi* which is independent of the world of *phenomena*, Aristotle's *eidoi* are always present in *phenomena* because *eidoi* are instantiated in matter.[5] For Aristotle, *eidos* is the principle of individuality and matter is the principle of particularity.[6] Thus the distinction between *eidos* and matter leads Aristotle to maintain that *ousia* is an individual particular being and is a subject of the nine other categories, which are basic concepts whereby we analyze this world: quality, quantity, relation, place, time, position, condition, action, and passion. In addition, the distinction between *eidos* and matter enables

5. Moser and Nat, *Human Knowledge*, 31.

6. Lamprecht, *Brief History*, 70.

him to explain change as a movement from potentiality [δύναμις] to actuality [ἐγέργεια (*energeia*), ενδελέχεια (*entelecheia*)].

Such an ontology of *ousia* determines its corresponding epistemology which supposes that knowledge of an individual, particular *ousia* is possible and this knowledge is our first and most certain knowledge. Thus Aristotle placed a high value on physics such as natural science and mathematics. However, what is "the first philosophy" for him is metaphysics, the study of being *qua* being, because physics studies beings that are material and changeable and mathematics studies beings which are not changeable but inseparable from matter, whereas metaphysics studies beings that can be said to be, namely, beings that are neither changeable nor inseparable from matter, but eternal. In brief, Aristotelian epistemology starts with beings which are "better known to us" and then arrives at beings that are "better known in themselves."[7]

Plotinus

Plotinus (205–270) suggested an ontology of *hypostasis* [ὑπόστασις], by which he means an intelligible transcendent world that stands above the physical world, and upon which the finite and visible world depend.[8] There are many transcendent *hypostaseis*, but thee main *hypostaseis* are the One [ἐν], the *Nous* [νοὑς] (the Mind) and the *Psyche* [ψυχή] (the Soul), all of which form a graded divine Triad.[9] The most supreme *hypostasis* is the One, from which emanates the *Nous*, from which emanates the *Psyche*, and from which emanates the physical world. The One, as the unknowable and ineffable source of all things, overflows by necessity, and the *Nous*, as the image of the One is the eternal, unchangeable, archetypal world of divine thoughts like Platonic *eidoi*,[10] and lastly, the

7. Aristotle, *Metaphysics* Z.3, 1029 b3–12; *Posterior Analytics* 71b32; *Prior Analytics* 68b35–37; *Physics* A.1, 184 a16–20; *Topics* Z..4, 141 b2–142 a12. As cited in S. Marc Cohen, "Aristotle's Metaphysics" (2008), in *Stanford Encyclopedia of Philosophy*: http://plato.stanford.edu/entries/aristotle-metaphysics.

8. Lamprecht, *Brief History*, 101.

9. There have been many scholars, including Harnack, who puts a more emphasis on the influence of Plotinus' notion of the Triad on Augustine's doctrine of the Trinity. Against this strong steam, Jong Sung Rhee, while acknowledging similarities, nonetheless stresses the fundamental differences between Plotinus and Augustine. Rhee, *Augustine's Doctrine*, 394–412. This book is based on his 1963 ThD dissertation in San Francisco Theological Seminary.

10. Plotinus, *Enneads*, V. 2, 372.

Psyche, as the author of life which breathes life into all things, creates the sensible material world.[11] Plotinus, like Plato, makes a sharp distinction between the intelligible transcendent world and the sensible material world. But it is also noteworthy that Plotinus, like Aristotle, closely links the sensible material world to the intelligible transcendent world.

Such an ontology of *hypostasis* elicits its own epistemology of contemplation towards the union of the One. As all things ontologically emanate by necessity from the three *hypostaseis*, all things, including matter in the lowest, are in ceaseless contemplation and aspiration to return to the highest One. While the *Psyche* starts with the sensible material world, passes through the *Nous*, and arrives at the union with the One, the *Psyche* undergoes some higher degrees of contemplation. In the first place, with temperance, the *Psyche* is released from desires for particular ends. With courage, the *Psyche* remains firm against the lure of particularity. With justice, the *Psyche* comes to have no desire for any personal acquisitions. With wisdom, the *Psyche* is absorbed in contemplation of pure divine thoughts. Then, in the second place, the *Psyche* passes through art, friendship and logic. Through art, the *Psyche* is concerned with divine thoughts which are expressed with sensible particular materials. Through friendship, the *Psyche* experiences a higher unity in which distinction of persons is lost in aspiration for the good. And through logic, the *Psyche* is solely concerned with the eternal interrelationship of pure divine thoughts. And in the last place, the *Psyche* would be completely purified from the contaminations of finitude and materiality.[12]

Thomas Aquinas

Thomas Aquinas (1225–1274) was much influenced by Aristotle in his affirming that *substantia* (substance, *ousia*) is a composition of *forma* (form, *eidos*) and *materia* (matter). However, Aquinas realized that the Aristotelian ontology of *ousia*, though it explains material substances, does not deal well with immaterial substances such as angels and God. For example, Aquinas understood that God is pure act [*purus actus*] and so does not have any potentiality [*potentia*]. God has nothing to

11. Ibid., V. 2, 370.

12. Lamprecht, *Brief History*, 104–5.

do with matter, because matter implies potentiality.[13] Thus Aquinas complemented the Aristotelian ontology of *ousia* with his own ontology of *essentia* (essence) and *esse* (existence), according to which, material substances are a composition of *forma* and *materia*, and have a distinction between *essentia* and *esse*. Angels are not a composition of *forma* and *materia*, but have a distinction between *essentia* and *esse*. God is not a composition of *forma* and *materia*, and has an identity of *essentia* and *esse*.[14]

The ontology of *essentia* and *esse* leads Thomas to preserve a distinction between *essentia* and *esse* in his own corresponding epistemology, which fundamentally maintains a sharp differentiation between what is knowable to us and what is knowable in itself. The differentiation is subtly recognized in his well-known five ways to God, all of which start from the world to God. Notably, Aquinas finally arrives not at *Dei esse* (the being of God) or *Dei essentia* (the essence of God), but merely at the truth *Deum esse* (that God is).[15] In addition, the distinction between *essentia* and *esse* lays the foundations of another differentiation between *res significata* (the thing signified) and *modus significandi* (the mode of signification),[16] which implies that our knowledge of something is always a mode of our mind's knowing it and thus our knowledge of something is different from something itself. This is more so with regard to our knowledge of God. In this sense, we cannot comprehend God, but God understands Godself through Godself.[17]

Descartes and Lock

René Descartes (1596–1650), searching for certainty of knowledge, provided an epistemology of ideas. In his 1637 book *Discourse on Method* in French, and in his 1641 book *Meditations on First Philosophy* in Latin, Descartes began with his method of doubt in which he determined to doubt anything about which he could not be certain. Having peeled back the layers of spurious "knowledge" Descartes found one

---

13. Aquinas, *Summa Theologica*, I, Q.3, a.2, co. Hereafter cited as *ST*.

14. Aquinas, *ST*, I, Q.12, a.2, ad.3.

15. Ibid., I, Q.2, a.3, co.

16. Ibid., I, Q.39, a.4, co.

17. Ibid., I, Q.14, a.2, ad.3; For a recent study regarding *esse* and *essentia* in Aquinas, see Wippel, *Metaphysical Thought*; and O'Callaghan, *Thomist Realism*.

thing that he could be certain of: *Cogito ergo sum* [*Je pense, donc je suis*] (I think, therefore I am), which understands the subject to be *res cogitans* (a thinking thing). From this he went further to insist upon innate ideas in the mind, such as an idea of self, an idea of God, an idea of matter as *res extensa* (an extended thing), and so on. They are the ideas which are imprinted on the mind by nature, differing both from adventitious ideas which come from without and from factitious ideas which are fashioned by the mind.[18] On the ground of such innate ideas, Descartes acknowledges three basic ontological realities: the mind, matter as extension, and God. Like Descartes, John Locke (1632–1704) was also concerned with an epistemology of ideas. Unlike Descartes, however, Locke denied the possibility of innate ideas in the mind. Instead, in his 1690 book *An Essay Concerning Human Understanding*, Locke traced all ideas back to their origin in sense experience and argued that all ideas originate from sense experience. With regard to the origin of ideas, Descartes is considered to be a rationalist, whereas Locke is regarded to be an empiricist.

However, both Descartes and Locke contributed so much to an epistemology of ideas, or an epistemological idealism, that the word 'ideas' was widely used and discussed in the seventeenth and eighteenth centuries. Noteworthy, the term "ideas," though originating from Plato's *eidos* (form, idea), acquired a quite different meaning at these times, that is, the contents of the mind. Thus ideas gained something of a quasi-autonomous reality, even apart from sense objects, partly because there are innate ideas in the case of Descartes and partly because ideas are representations of sense experience in the case of Locke.[19] In this way, Descartes and Locke opened the door for modern philosophy which was primarily concerned with epistemology of ideas and its subjectivity of the mind, which would culminate in Kant's transcendental turn to the subject.

Immanuel Kant

Immanuel Kant (1724–1804) argued for an epistemology of transcendental idealism. In his book *Kritik der reinen Vernunft* (*Critique of Pure Reason*) (1781, 1st edition, 1787, 2nd edition), Kant made a distinction

18. Lamprecht, *Brief History*, 224–25.
19. Allen, *Philosophy*, 181.

of all objects into *phenomena* and *noumena*. While *phenomenon* refers to an object of our sense experience, *noumenon* denotes an object beyond our sense experience, namely, *Ding an sich* (a thing in itself).[20] Then Kant restricted our knowledge to *phenomena* alone and regarded *noumena* as unknowable. It is here noteworthy that Kant's *phenomena* are not objects in themselves, but objects given to our *Sinnlichkeit* (sensibility) which receives objects through two pure forms of sensible intuition: space and time. And Kant's *phenomena* are objects which continue to be thought by *Verstand* (understanding) through twelve basic concepts, namely, categories.

Hence Kant's *phenomena* are not objects in themselves but their modes or ways in which objects are received by intuition and then necessarily conceived by concepts. In this sense, Kant entitled all such knowledge of *phenomena* transcendental, because mind imposes *a priori* conditions on objects through intuition and concepts,[21] both of which, Kant maintains, constitute the elements of all our knowledge.[22] What is the most important for Kant is neither an object nor experience, but *a priori* conditions of mind. Thus Kant called his epistemology of transcendental idealism the Copernican revolution in philosophy. As Copernicus radically changed a view of the movements of the sun and the earth, Kant completely changed a view of a relation between mind and object. Kant made objects move around the mind and made them conform to *a priori* conditions of mind, not the other way around.[23] In this way, Kant fully completed a transcendental turn to the subject in philosophy.

Hegel and Husserl

Kant's postulation of unknowable *noumena* led some subsequent philosophers to hold an agnostic attitude and to reject ontology. On the other hand, Kant's transcendental turn to the subject with regard to *phenomena* led others to place the focus on consciousness. Georg Wilhelm Friedrich Hegel (1770–1831) was influenced by Kant's transcendental turn to the subject and thus a starting point of his philosophy was con-

---

20. Kant, *Critique of Pure Reason*, 266–67, 271.

21. Ibid., 59, 298–99.

22. Ibid., 92.

23. Lamprecht, *Brief History*, 365.

sciousness. However, in contrast to Kant's focus on human inner subject, Hegel regarded consciousness as a process of realization of the Absolute Being as the Subject in history. In his 1807 book *Phänomenologie des Geistes* [*Phenomenology of Spirit/Mind*],[24] Hegel analytically traced the manifold consciousness of the Absolute Being, such as sensuous consciousness, self-consciousness, reason, spirit, religion, and lastly, absolute knowledge. Here it is noteworthy that Hegel adhered to a possibility of attaining to absolute knowledge [*Wissenshaft*], which is contrasted to Kant's postulation of unknowable *noumena*.

Though Edmund Husserl (1859–1938) was much influenced by the Cartesian epistemology of ideas and the Kantian epistemology of transcendental idealism, he argued against a psychologism which attempted to reduce all *phenomena* to a mere mental state. To establish philosophy as a rigorous science, Husserl, following his teacher Franz Brentano (1838–1917), put a great focus on a main characteristic of human consciousness, that is, intentionality of consciousness, which indicates that every act of consciousness is directed toward an object and consequently consciousness is essentially consciousness *of something*.[25] In his Göttingen lectures from 1905–1907,[26] Husserl realized through his methods such as *epoché* (bracketing) of ontological questions about the world, phenomenological reduction, and transcendental subjectivity, that a peculiar act-object structure is a *noesis-noema* structure of intentional acts. *Noema* is object presented in consciousness, while *noesis* is the intentional acts by which we intend objects such as perception, judgment, remembrance, etc. Through such phenomenological methods, Husserl aimed to acquire knowledge about the essence of consciousness and then to attain to the things themselves [*zu den Sachen selbst*], and thus phenomenology became the first philosophy for Husserl.

Contemporary Philosophers: Heidegger, Levinas, Foucault, Derrida

In areas of ontology and epistemology, contemporary philosophy has witnessed not only anti-metaphysical or non-ontological positions,

24. Hegel, *Phenomenology of Spirit*.
25. Sokolowski, *Introduction*, 8–9.
26. Husserl, *Ideas Pertaining*.

but also non-transcendental epistemological positions. They are either a logical result of previous ontological concerns or a reaction against prior transcendental epistemologies.

First, with regard to ontology, Martin Heidegger (1889–1976), taught and influenced by Husserl, started his 1927 book *Sein und Zeit* (*Being and Time*) with an exhortation to reawaken the question of the meaning of being [*Sinn von Sein*] from its awful forgetfulness.[27] The question was asked again in his 1953 book *An Introduction to Metaphysics*: "Why are there beings at all instead of nothing?"[28] These questions indicate that Heidegger hoped to restore *Dasein* back to the power of being. However, his philosophical concern with beings is very different from traditional ontological concerns which hold fast to essence as well. Heidegger, appropriating Husserl's phenomenological method, focused on examining *Existenz* (existence) alone, which is also referred to as *Dasein* (Being-There) or *Das In-der-Welt-sein* (Being-in-the World).

Such a tendency is found as well in Immanuel Levinas (1906–1995), especially in his 1949 book *En découvrant l'existence avec Husserl et Heidegger* (*Discovering Existence with Husserl and Heidegger*).[29] Levinas went further than his immediate predecessors to work on what was the first philosophy to him, being devoted to a phenomenological description of an existence of the face-to-face encounter with the other, but to the exclusion of the question of being or essence. This point was clearly reflected in his 1974 book *Autrement qu'être ou au-delà de l'essence* (*Otherwise than Being, or Beyond Essence*).[30] In this way, essence came to be completely separated from existence and to be finally excluded from contemporary philosophical discussions.

Second, with regard to epistemology, Michel Foucault (1926–1984) was not only anti-metaphysical but also attempted a non-idealistic understanding of knowledge, in that he considered knowledge as being constructed primarily by external historical factors. In his 1966 book *Les Mots et les choses. Une archéologie des sciences humaines* (*The Order of Things: An Archaeology of the Human Sciences*), and in his 1969

27. Heidegger, *Being and Time*, 1.

28. Heidegger, *Introduction to Metaphysics*.

29. Levinas, *Discovering Existence*. This book is a truncated version of the original collection of essays in French.

30. Levinas, *Otherwise than Being*.

book *L'archéologie du savoir* (*The Archaeology of Knowledge*), Foucault claimed that knowledge is constituted by *episteme* [*épistémè*] by which he means certain underlying conditions of truth in each period, and also maintained that these conditions have changed in each period of history. Hence there is no such thing as disinterested knowledge. Rather, knowledge is produced and sustained by power.[31] This position enabled him to denounce the Cartesian epistemology of innate ideas, Kantian transcendental idealism, and Husserlian phenomenological idealism.

Like Foucault, Jacques Derrida (1930–2004) held an anti-metaphysical attitude and also a non-idealistic attitude towards knowledge. He went so far as to deconstruct any system of knowledge, in that he insisted that there is no knowledge as such. More specifically, Derrida strived to deconstruct an opposition between essence and existence, between reality and appearance, between the signified and the signifier, and so on, by showing that such kinds of oppositions are an arbitrary construction. For example, Derrida argued that the signifiers of language cannot refer to the transcendental signified in mind, since the signified is itself created by the conventional and hence arbitrary signifiers of language. To pinpoint such ambiguities of language, Derrida coined the word *différance* which sounds no different from *différence*, the latter of which has a double meaning of difference and deferral.[32] The method of deconstruction led Derrida in his 1967 book *De la grammatologie* (*Of Grammatology*)[33] to be opposed to logocentrism sustained by western philosophy.

As we have explored above, the changing focus of western philosophy has moved from an ontology of *eidos*, an ontology of *ousia*, an ontology of *hypostasis*, and an ontology of *essentia and esse*, through the Cartesian epistemology of innate ideas, the Kanian epistemology of transcendental idealism, and the Husserlian epistemology of phenomenological idealism, and finally to contemporary anti-metaphysical and non-idealistic tendencies.

31. Foucault, *Power/Knowledge*, 133.
32. Baird and Kaufmann, *Twentieth-Century Philosophy*, 344–45.
33. Derrida, *Of Grammatology*.

Related Historical Discussions

The ditinction between the immanent Trinity and the economic Trinity can be traced back to some other parallel distinctions in the history of theology: the immanent *Logos* [λόγος ἐνδιάθετος] / the expressed *Logos* [λόγος προφορικός]; procession [*processio*] / mission [*missio*]. In addition, the immanent-economic distinction is interwoven with some other important theological terms such as dispensation [*dispositio, dispensatio*], economy [οἰκονομία (*oikonomia*)], and operation or activity [ἐνέργεια (*energeia*)]. Though *dispositio* and *oikonomia* are mostly exchanged with each other, this book makes a differentiation between them mainly due to some incompatible differences, and uses both the Latin term *dispositio* and the Greek term *oikonomia* [οἰκονομία] in order to highlight the differences. Thus the current section of chapter 2 examines some related distinctions and terms historically and theologically, which is conducive to understanding the issue of the relation between the immanent and the economic Trinity within a wider context.

The Immanent Logos—*The Expressed* Logos

The New Testament writers understood Jesus Christ as "God," "Lord," "Son of God," "Son of Man," "Wisdom," and "*Logos*" [Λόγος] (the Word)."[34] The origin of the concept of *Logos*, as found in the New Testament texts such as John 1:1–18 and Revelation 19:13, on the one hand, can be traced back, through Philo of Alexandria (20 BC—50 AD) who was influenced by Jewish, Greek and Stoic thoughts and who regarded *Logos* as God's creative principle, to the Old Testament writers' notion of *dabar* (Word). On the other hand, the concept of *Logos* in the New Testament continued to be used and was developed by subsequent theologians now known as the Apostolic Fathers and Apologists, especially with respect to its relation to God.

For example, Ignatius of Antioch (35–107) considered Jesus Christ as the *Nous* [νοῦς] (Mind) of God the Father[35] and the *Logos* proceeding from God.[36] And Justin Martyr (100–165) stated that the *Logos* is from the unbegotten and ineffable God the Father,[37] and that God has begot-

---

34. Wainwright, *Trinity in the New Testament*, 53; Fortman, *Triune God*, 10–33.

35. Ignatius of Antioch, *To the Ephesians*, 3.

36. Ignatius of Antioch, *To the Magnesians*, 8.

37. Justin Martyr, *Second Apology*, 13.

ten a certain power as the *arche* [ἀρχή] (the governing principle), one title of which is *Logos*.[38] Jesus Christ is the *Logos* who is the God begotten from the Universal Father, and the *Logos* was with God the Father and talked with God the Father before all creation.[39] Tatian of Assyria (110-180) regarded Jesus Christ as the *Logos* coming forth from the *Logos*-power of the God the Father.[40] Athenagoras of Athens (133–190) understood that God is the eternal *Nous* [νοῦς] (Mind), having *Logos* in Godself from the beginning, and being instinct with *Logos* from eternity.[41] Theophilus of Antioch (later 2nd century) remarked that God has God's own *Logos* internal within his own bowels, and begot the *Logos* and emitted the *Logos* before all things, and regarded the *Logos* as the *arche* [ἀρχή] (the governing principle).[42] Finally, Tertullian (160–220) held that Jesus Christ is the original first-born *Logos* and the Word of God by which God fashioned this whole world.[43]

These observations indicate that Jesus Christ as the *Logos* of God the Father has an intimate relationship with God the Father. Both Justin Martyr and Tatian of Assyria went further to hint that the *Logos* has the same *ousia* [οὐσία] (substance) as God the Father. Justin Martyr stated that the *Logos*, which is indivisible and inseparable from God the Father, was generated from the Father by the power and will of God the Father, "but not by abscission, as if the *ousia* of the Father were divided."[44] Justin Martyr provided an analogy of human speech, by which it is meant that, though we beget and utter a word, our power of uttering words would not be diminished. He offered another analogy of a fire kindled from a fire; an enkindled fire is distinct from the original fire, but the original fire remains the same undiminished fire even after it ignites another.[45] Tatian of Assyria stated that the *Logos* was in God the Father and came into being "by participation, not by abscission."[46] For him, abscission implies a separation of the *Logos* from the original *ousia* of God, while

38. Justin Martyr, *Dialogue with Trypho*, 61.

39. Ibid., 62.

40. Tatian of Assyria, *Address to the Greeks*, 5 and 6.

41. Athenagoras of Athens, *Plea for the Christians*, 10.

42. Theophilus of Antioch, *To Autolycus*, II, 10.

43. Tertullian, *Apology*, XXI, 10 and 17.

44. Justin Martyr, *Dialogue with Trypho*, 128.

45. Ibid., 61, 128.

46. Tatian of Assyria, *Address to the Greeks*, 5.

participation presupposes no deficiency of the *Logos* in the original *ousia* of God. He illustrated this point by the analogy of a torch. Though one torch lights another fire, nevertheless the light of the first torch is not lessened by lighting another fire.[47]

Thus the concept of *Logos* primarily refers to an indivisible and inseparable relation of Jesus Christ to God the Father. However, the concept of *Logos* is not restricted exclusively to the relationship between Jesus Christ and God the Father. It is also extended and applied to the relationship towards the world. Ignatius of Antioch considered Jesus as the mouth through which God the Father truly spoke to the world,[48] and as the written *Logos*, by which he meant cross, death and resurrection.[49] The *Logos* enables us to be perfect, because anyone who is really possessed of the *Logos* of Jesus can listen to Jesus.[50] Justin Martyr regarded Jesus Christ as the *Logos* of whom all human beings partake.[51] As the *Logos* is in every human being, or the engrafted seed of the *Logos* is implanted in every human being, even Socrates had a vague, though not full, knowledge of Jesus Christ.[52] Tatian of Assyria mentioned that the *Logos*, begotten from God the Father, begat in turn our world.[53] This implies that the *Logos* is not merely a helper in the creation of all things by God the Father, but also an active creator of all things together with God the Father. Athenagoras of Athens affirmed that the *Logos* works in the operation of God the Father as well as in the idea of God the Father, by which he means that all things were made after the pattern of the *Logos*.[54] Theophilus of Antioch confirmed that the *Logos* is a helper in the creation of God the Father, and also affirmed that the *Logos* is the *arche* of all things, because the *Logos* rules all things.[55]

We have seen that the above-mentioned earliest theologians made a distinction between the relation of the *Logos* to God the Father and the relation of the *Logos* to the world. Such a distinction became more

---

47. Ibid.

48. Ignatius of Antioch, *To the Romans*, 8.

49. Ignatius of Antioch, *To the Philadelphians*, 8.

50. Ignatius of Antioch, *To the Ephesians*, 15.

51. Justin Martyr, *First Apology*, 46.

52. Justin Martyr, *Second Apology*, 10 and 13.

53. Tatian of Assyria, *Address to the Greeks*, 5.

54. Athenagoras of Athens, *Plea for the Christians*, 10.

55. Theophilus of Antioch, *To Autolycus*, 2:10.

prominent with Theophilus of Antioch, who made a differentiation between the immanent *Logos* [λόγος ἐνδιάθετος] and the uttered or expressed *Logos* [λόγος προφορικός].[56] The former refers to the *Logos* in relation to God the Father, whereas the latter denotes the *Logos* in relation to the world. This distinction draws heavily on the work of the Stoics, for whom the immanent *Logos* [λόγος ἐνδιάθετος] refers to the rational thought within the human mind, whereas the expressed *Logos* [λόγος προφορικός] denotes the word which is uttered without human mind. In addition to this distinction, the Stoics spoke of another distinction between the seminal *Logos* [λόγος σπερματικος], that is, the seed of *Logos*, through which individual things come into being and which dwells in individual things, and the supreme, universal *Logos* which contains the seeds of *Logos* within itself.[57] The immanent *Logos* and the expressed *Logos* are the same *Logos*, though the former remains within human mind, whereas the latter comes without human mind. Both the immanent *Logos* and the expressed *Logos* are possible, as far as the seminal *Logos* of the universal *Logos* is implanted in each human mind.

Taking into consideration all these aspects mentioned above, the first point to be noted with regards to the earliest theologians, is that the immanent *Logos*, that is, the *Logos* in relation to God the Father, is no other than the expressed *Logos*, that is, the *Logos* in relation to the world. They are not two different *Logoi*. The *Logos* that is with God the Father and talks with God the Father on the one hand, is the same *Logos* that, on the other hand, works with God the Father towards the world in creation, providence, incarnation, and so on. For this reason, the so-called twofold stage theory which some scholars maintain that the apologists held, may have only a limited significance, because it draws undue attention to what is only an apparent difference between the immanent *Logos* and the expressed *Logos*. For example, Edmund J. Fortman argued that Justin attempted to explain the mystery of the Trinity by a twofold stage theory of the *Logos*: "In the first stage the Logos had an eternal and probably personal existence with the Father as Someone with whom the Father could commune. In the second stage this Logos was generated as

---

56. Theophilus of Antioch, *To Autolycus*, 2:10. This point is confirmed by Fortman, *Triune God*, 49; by Kelly, *Early Christian Doctrines*, 99; and by Hill, *Three-Personed God*, 32.

57. Kelly, *Early Christian Doctrines*, 18–19.

Son pre-creationally but not eternally by the will of the Father for the purpose of creation."[58] However, the twofold stage theory has caused an inappropriate impression that the immanent *Logos* looks somewhat different from the expressed *Logos*. In addition, the expressed *Logos* is not restricted exclusively to the incarnation of the *Logos* in Jesus Christ. The expressed *Logos* works not only in the incarnation, but also in creation and providence even prior to the incarnation. The expressed *Logos* worked even before it manifested itself in Jesus Christ.

Dispositio / Dispensatio (*Dispensation*)

Dispositio, or *Dispensatio* (*dispensation*) is a Latin term which is mostly translated from οἰκονομία (*oikonomia,* economy) in Greek, which is based on Eph 1:9–10[59] and 3:8–9[60] in the New Testament. *Dispositio* plays a central role in the work of Irenaeus of Lyons, Hippolytus of Rome, and Tertullian. For these theologians, *dispositio* does not merely refer to the incarnation of the Son of God in Jesus Christ, but also points to all the co-workings of the Father, the Son and the Spirit, and even all the co-existence of the three from all eternity.

Irenaeus of Lyons

Irenaeus of Lyons (115–202)[61] understood that *dispositio* is primarily concerned with the Son of God as Jesus Christ. Irenaeus remarked that

---

58. Fortman, *Triune God*, 230. In addition, the twofold stage theory of apologists is mentioned in 45–48, 60, 68, 100, 150.

59. "9 ut notum faceret nobis sacramentum voluntatis suae secundum bonum placitum eius quod proposuit in eo 10 in *dispensationem* plenitudinis temporum instaurare omnia in Christo quae in caelis et quae in terra sunt in ipso" (Vulgate).

60. "8 mihi omnium sanctorum minimo data est gratia haec in gentibus evangelizare ininvestigabiles divitias Christi 9 et inluminare omnes quae sit *dispensatio* sacramenti absconditi a saeculis in Deo qui omnia creavit" (Vulgate).

61. There are a few reasons for this book to include Ireneaus in this section on *dispositio*, not in the next section on *oikonomia*. First, though Irenaeus was from Asia Minor of the East, he pursued his pastoral and theological work in Lyons in the West. Second, he wrote many works in his native Greek, only two of which are extant. Most parts of the extant works are preserved in a translated old Latin. Finally, most of all, Irenaeus' notion of *dispositio* or *oikonomia* fits better with Tertullian and Hippolytus. Fortman, *Triune God*, 101; Berthold Altaner, *Patrology*, 150–52. This translation was based on its original German *Patrologie* (5th ed.). Freiburg: Herder, 1958.

people, who are outside of Christian *dispositio*,[62] understand that Jesus is one, but Christ is another, and know that the Only-Begotten Son of God or the Word of God is one, but the Savior is another. The remark implies that *dispositio* refers to the point that the Son of God or the Word of God is Jesus Christ and the Savior.[63] Irenaeus stated that Jesus Christ came to us by means of the whole dispensational arrangements [*per universam dispositionem*][64] connected with him,[65] and that the Son of God became human in the dispensations [*dispositiones*][66] connected with him.[67] It is worth noting that Irenaeus' *dispositio* is not solely restricted to the incarnation of the Son of God in Jesus Christ. Rather, it goes further to include all the other works of the Son of God such as the creation of all things, the revelation of God to us, the presentation of us to God, the salvation of us,[68] the recapitulation of all things,[69] and so on. For example, as Irenaeus states that the Son of God made great dispensations [*tantas dispositiones*][70] for us, by revealing God to us and also by presenting us to God. To put it simply, the Son of God reveals God to us through many dispensations.[71]

These observations show that Irenaeus' notion of *dispositio* is not limited to the incarnation, but it is applied to all the other works of the Son of God, as well. This is one reason why Irenaeus used its plural form *dispositiones* much more frequently than its singular form *dispositio*. In addition, Irenaeus' *dispositio* is related to the Holy Spirit, as well. The Holy Spirit proclaims the dispensations of God through the prophets.[72] The Spirit of God is present in all the *dispositiones* of God for us, by narrating past things, revealing present things, and announcing future

---

62. *PG* 7, 926C.

63. Irenaeus of Lyons, *Against Heresies*, III, 16, 8 in *ANF*, I.

64. *PG* 7, 925C.

65. Irenaeus of Lyons, *Against Heresies*, III, 16, 6.

66. *PG* 7, 1077A.

67. Irenaeus of Lyons, *Against Heresies*, IV, 33, 7.

68. Ibid., I, 10, 13.

69. Ibid., V, 20, 2; V, 21, 1–2.

70. *PG* 7, 1037B.

71. Ibid.; Irenaeus of Lyons, *Against Heresies*, IV, 20, 7.

72. Irenaeus of Lyons, *Against Heresies*, I, 10, 1.

things.[73] The Spirit of God has set forth the *dispositiones* of the Father and the Son, whereby the Holy Spirit dwells with us.[74]

Most of all, Irenaeus' *dispositio* is ultimately related to the one God in such a way that all *dispositiones* can be called the *dispositio* of God the Father. In this sense, Irenaeus mentioned that the Son of God is the dispenser of the grace of God the Father [*dispensator paternae gratiae*][75] for the sake of us.[76] In addition, when Irenaeus proved that the Son of God accomplished the whole *dispositio,* he claimed to show that the God of the Scriptures is none other than God the Father.[77] Actually, for Irenaeus, the one God has two hands: the Word and the Wisdom, or the Son and the Holy Spirit. God the Father always works by and in the two hands.[78] Thus all *dispositiones* which are worked through the Son and the Spirit can be said to be principally grounded in God the Father.

We have called attention to the fact that Irenaeus' notion of *dispositio* is not restricted exclusively to the incarnation of the Son of God, but also it is applied to all the other works of the Son of God. More importantly, it is also extensively used with regards to the Holy Spirit, and ultimately to God the Father. Therefore it might be an oversimplication to assert that *dispositio* refers exclusively to the incarnation. It is more appropriate to hold that the notion of *dispositio* for Irenaeus refers to all works of the one God through the Son and the Spirit for the sake of us.

The one God always works together with the Son and the Spirit,[79] but there is an order among the three persons: first, God the Father approves; next, the Son ministers; and then the Spirit works for the accomplishment of salvation. And such an order of workings among them hints at some kind of subordinationism. However, it does not imply any *ontological* subordination among the Persons of the Trinity. For Irenaeus insists that the Son and the Spirit are always present with God the Father, even before all creation, and also intimates that the Son and

73. Ibid., IV, 33, 1.
74. Ibid., IV, 33, 7.
75. *PG* 7, 1037B.
76. Irenaeus of Lyons, *Against Heresies,* IV, 20, 7.
77. Ibid., IV, Preface, 4.
78. Ibid., IV, 20, 1–6.
79. Olson and Hall, *Trinity,* 28.

the Spirit freely and spontaneously participate in the works of God the Father.[80] Thus it might be a gross exaggeration to assert from the order of their co-workings that the Son and the Spirit are ontologically subordinate to God the Father. In brief, the notion of *dispositio* for Irenaeus refers primarily to the co-workings of God the Father, the Son, and the Spirit, and also, though implicitly, to the co-existence of the three. *Dispositiones* of the co-workings of the three enable us to see the face of God epistemologically, and *dispositiones* of the co-workings of the three are ontologically grounded in the co-existence of the three. God is through *dispositions* presented to us, revealed to us, and manifested to us, and we are through *dispositiones* presented to God, enabled to see God, saved by God, and recapitulated in God.

Hippolytus of Rome

Like that of Irenaeus, the notion of *dispositio* for Hippolytus of Rome (170–236) is not solely restricted to the incarnation of the Son of God. Rather, it includes all the other works of the Son of God, including the creation of all things. This characteristic is well shown in his disputation against Noetus who maintained that the unbegotten God the Father Himself became the begotten Son of God, when God the Father Himself was born, suffered, and died.[81] Hippolytus argued against Noetus that it is the Son of God who became Jesus Christ, and in this way he maintained in the incarnation a distinction between God the Father and the Son of God. However, this does not mean that the distinction between God the Father and the Son of God originated from the time of the incarnation. Rather, the incarnation of the Son of God in Jesus Christ is a consequence of a more fundamental distinction between God the Father and the Son of God, which started from all eternity.

Hippolytus cites John 1:1 as a paradigmatic account of *dispositio*,[82] which says, "In the beginning was the Word, and the Word was with God, and the Word was God."[83] Here Hippolytus argued for one God, not for two gods. And simultaneously he argued for two persons or two *dispositiones*, by which God the Father and the Son of God are distinct

---

80. Irenaeus of Lyons, *Against Heresies*, IV, 20, 1 and 3.

81. Hippolytus of Rome, *Refutation of All Heresies*, X, 23.

82. Michel R. Barnes, "*Oeconomia*," in *EEC*, 825.

83. Hippolytus of Rome, *Against Heresy of One Noetus*, 14.

from each other. In addition, he mentioned a third *dispositio*, namely, the grace of the Holy Ghost.[84] Thus Hippolytus stated that, while the one God exists alone in the sense that there is nothing besides God and nothing contemporaneous with God, the one God exists in plurality in the sense that there are three persons or three *dispositiones*.[85] Hence, for Hippolytus, the Monarchy of one God is not incompatible with the Trinity of *dispositiones*. Under *dispositio*, God the Father, the Son of God, and the Holy Spirit exist and work together in harmony from all eternity. The Father decrees, the Son executes, and the Holy Spirit gives understanding. The Father is above all, the Son is through all, and the Holy Spirit is in all. And the *dispositio* of harmony is, in turn, led back to the one God. Thus Hippolytus states: "we cannot otherwise think of one God, but by believing in truth in Father and Son and Holy Spirit."[86]

Therefore Hippolytus' notion of *dispositio* refers not only to the incarnation of the Son of God in Jesus Christ, but also includes all the other co-works which the Father, the Son, and the Holy Spirit complete in harmony, and even all the co-existence which the three enjoy from all eternity.

Tertullian

At a first glance, Tertullian's notion of *dispensatio* seems to primarily refer to the incarnation of the Son of God in Jesus Christ. Against Praxeas, who held that God the Father himself was born, suffered, and became Jesus Christ, Tertullian definitely insists that it is under the dispensation [*sub hac dispensatione*][87] that the Son of God was born, suffered, and became Jesus Christ.[88] For him, *dispensatio* points to the fact that the Son of God was born, suffered, and became Jesus Christ, and thus *dispensatio* becomes a theological ground to maintain a distinction between God the Father and the Son of God. In this way, Tertullian's notion of *dispensatio* comes to refer primarily to the incarnation of the Son of God in Jesus Christ.

---

84. Ibid., 14.
85. Ibid., 10.
86. Ibid., 14.
87. *PL* 2, 456B.
88. Tertullian, *Agaisnt Praxeas*, 2.

It would, however, be a severe misunderstanding to think that, for Tertullian, the incarnation of the Son of God in Jesus Christ is itself the ground of a distinction between God the Father and the Son of God. Instead, the incarnation of the Son of God is the most important ramification, which is still one of many ramifications, of another foundational theological stance, that is, that the Son of God is the Reason, Word, and Power of God from all eternity.[89] As Tertullian definitely affirmed that the Son of God is also God on account of the unity of substance or nature, and that what proceeds from God is God,[90] his foundational theological stance involves an inherent distinction between God the Father and the Son of God, which is, in turn, a theological foundation for the incarnation of the Son of God in Jesus Christ.

Careful analysis reveals that Tertullian's notion of *dispensatio* is not merely concerned with the incarnation of the Son of God in Jesus Christ, but ultimately with the eternal distinction between God the Father and the Son of God, which means that, while both have the one same substance, they are "two separate persons" or "two different beings."[91] This stance is true of the Spirit of God, too. Against Praxeas who asserted that the Father, the Son, and the Spirit are the very self-same person, Tertullian maintained that the Father, the Son, and the Spirit, while having the one same substance, are three different persons.[92] These three persons are inseparable from each other in their substance, whereas they are distinct from each other in their persons.[93]

Thus Tertullian's notion of *dispensatio* does not merely refer to the incarnation of the Son and the descent of the Sprit, but also points to all the other co-working and co-existence, even prior to all creation, of the three inseparable but distinct persons of one God. In this sense, Tertullian stated that the Son of God proceeded [*processerit*][94] from God the Father and the Spirit of God proceeded from God the Father through the Son,[95] and also that it is from God's own dispensation [*ab*

---

89. Tertullian, *Apology*, I, 1, 10–11.
90. Ibid., I, 12–13.
91. Tertullian, *Against Praxeas*, 4.
92. Ibid., 2:8.
93. Ibid., 9.
94. *PL* 2, 456B.
95. Tertullian, *Agaisnt Praxeas*, II, 4.

ipsa Dei dispositione][96] that the Son existed before the creation of the world. For this reason, Tertullian states that God was not alone. While God was alone in the sense that there was nothing external to God, God was not alone in that God the Father had the Son and the Spirit with himself, whom God the Father possessed in himself.[97] In this regard, Tertullian wrote, "The Trinity [*trinitas*], flowing from the Father, does not at all disturb the Monarchy [*monarchia*], while the Trinity at the same time guards the state of economy [*et oeconomiae statum protegit*].[98]"[99]

In brief, Tertullian's notion of *dispensatio* denotes the co-existence of the three distinct persons of the one God from all eternity and also the co-workings of the three distinct persons such as creation, incarnation, revelation, and so on.[100]

Oikonomia *(Economy)*

Oikonomia [οἰκονομία] (economy) plays a central role in the teachings of Athanasius (293–373) and of Gregory of Nazianzus (330–390). Unlike *dispositio* which refers not only to the co-workings of the thee divine persons, but also the co-existence of them from all eternity, *oikonomia* generally points to the outward works of the Son or God. For Athanasius, *oikonomia* primarily refers to all the works and ministries of Jesus Christ on the earth, and more focally to the incarnation of the Logos in Jesus Christ. And for Gregory of Nazianzus, though *oikonomia* focally refers to the incarnation of the *Logos* or the Son in Jesus Christ, it is extended to include all the life and the works of the incarnated Son on the earth, and even more extensively all the works of God towards the world.

---

96. *PL* 2, 460A.

97. Tertullian, *Agaisnt Praxeas*, 5.

98. *PL* 2, 464A.

99. Tertullian, *Agaisnt Praxeas*, 8.

100. This point is also confirmed by Studer, *Trinity and Incarnation*, 70. Here Studer states: "[F]or Tertullian there already existed an *oikonomia* in God before there was one in creation, the Old Testament and finally in the incarnation."

ATHANASIUS

Athanasius' notion of *oikonomia* exclusively refers to the incarnation of the *Logos* (the Word) in Jesus Christ, who is the Son of God. He used the term *oikonomia* together with some other words such as visitation in the flesh, ministry, and ministry of covenant.[101] For example, when Paul wrote that the *Logos* was so much better than angels (Heb 1:4), Athanasius interpreted that, as the *Logos* cannot be compared, Paul in the passage alluded to "the *Logos*' visitation in the flesh, and the *oikonomia* which He then sustained[102] (the incarnate sojourn of the *Logos* and the *oikonomia* effected by him)."[103] In addition, Athanasius, referring to the incarnation of the *Logos*, used some expressions such as "His human *oikonomia* and fleshly presence,"[104] "The *Logos*' human *oikonomia*,"[105] "the human *oikonomia*,"[106] and "His manhood."[107] Furthermore, Athanasius' notion of *oikonomia* is directly connected to restoration[108] salvation,[109] and deification.[110]

Athanasius' notion of *oikonomia* arises out of his disputation against Arius and his followers who claimed that, unlike the Father who is alone unbegotten, the Son is not unbegotten and that the Son was not before the Son was begotten or created or defined or established.[111] The point of Arius' position is that "the Son was not before he was begotten,"[112] and the point was based on his presupposition of the Monad, namely, that there is the one God who is alone unbegotten, everlasting, without beginning, immortal, immutable and unchangeable.[113] Thus Arius contended that, although the one unbegotten God had an

101. Athanasius, *Orations against the Arians*, I, 13, 58–64.

102. Ibid., I, 13, 59.

103. Ibid.

104. Athanasius, *Orations against the Arians*, II, 14, 6.

105. Ibid., II, 14, 9.

106. Ibid., II, 15, 12.

107. Ibid., II, 15, 12.

108. Ibid., II, 20, 51.

109. Ibid., II, 22, 75.

110. Athanasius, *Orations against the Arians*, III, 27, 38.

111. Arius, *Letter to Eusebius of Nicomedia*, 4–5.

112. Arius, *Letter to Alexander of Alexandria*, 4.

113. Ibid., 2.

only-begotten Son even before eternal times, the Son is not God but a creature. Otherwise, the one God would be compounded, divided, mutable, and corporeal[114] which would violate the principle of the Monad. Arius held that some passages in the Scripture, such as "Having become better than the angels," "He has become," and "So much more has Jesus become a better surety," may confirm his contention.

Athanasius firmly rebutted the Arian contention, by arguing that the Son is "true God and *homoousios* [ὁμοούσιος] with the true Father,"[115] and that, because the Father is everlasting, the Son is everlasting and thus the Son always was and is and never was not.[116] Thus, for Athanasius, the one God is not the Monad. Rather, the one God is the Triad from all eternity consisting of God the Father, God the Son and God the Spirit.[117] Then, regarding some biblical expressions such as "Having become better than the angels," "He has become," and "So much more has Jesus become a better surety," which the Arians claimed to support the subordination of the Son to God the Father, Athanasius sharply made a distinction between *ousia* (substance, essence) and *oikonomia*. While *ousia* refers to being and existence, *oikonomia* denotes acts and works. The Son or the *Logos* is the same *ousia* as the Father and the *eidos* [εἶδος] (form) of the Father, whereas *oikonomia* refers to the ministry and works of the Word, which came into existence. And those seemingly subordinational texts do not signify the *ousia* of the Word, because the Word is also unoriginated. Instead, they signify the incarnation of the *Logos* in Jesus Christ who works and ministers for our salvation on the earth.[118]

In brief, Athanasius' notion of *oikonomia* exclusively refers to the incarnation of the *Logos* in Jesus Christ, and, extensively at the most, to all the works and ministries of Jesus Christ on the earth.

GREGORY OF NAZIANZUS

Like Athanasius, Gregory of Nazianzus used *oikonomia* primarily to refer to the incarnation of the Son in Jesus Christ. In his *Oration on the*

---

114. Ibid., 5.
115. Athanasius, *Orations against the Arians*, I, 3, 9.
116. Ibid.
117. Ibid., I, 5, 15–16; I, 6, 17–18.
118. Ibid., I, 13, 64.

Theophany, or Birthday of Christ, which focuses on Christ in the flesh, Gregory of Nazianzus specified the subject of the oration as *oikonomia*[119] which denotes the incarnation of the Son, but not as *theologia* [θεολογία] (theology)[120] which signifies the deity of the Son.[121] However, for Gregory of Nazianzus, *oikonomia* is not exclusively restricted to the incarnation of the Son in Jesus Christ, but it includes his entire life and works which the bodily form of the eternal Son in Jesus Christ lived and performed for us. When Gregory of Nazianzus talks about the feast of Pentecost, namely, the coming of the Holy Spirit, he explains that the bodily things of Christ are over, whereas the bodily advent of the Spirit is beginning.[122] Here Gregory of Nazianzus epitomized the bodily things of Christ as follows:

> The Virgin, the Birth, the Manger, the Swaddling, the Angels glorifying Him, the Shepherds running to Him, the course of the Star, the Magi worshipping Him and bringing Gifts, Herod's murder of the children, the Flight of Jesus into Egypt, the Return from Egypt, the Circumcision, the Baptism, the Witness from Heaven, the Temptation, the Stoning for our sake, . . . the Betrayal, the Nailing, the Burial, the Resurrection, the Ascension.[123]

119. *PG* 36, 320B.

120. Ibid.

121. Gregory of Nazianzus, *Oration on the Theophany, or Birthday of Christ*, 38, 8. Here *oikonomia* and *theologia* are contrasted to each other, because the former refers to the incarnation of the Son in Jesus Christ on the earth, whereas the latter denotes the deity of the Son in eternity. Only in this sense, LaCugna's thesis that the Cappadocians, including Gregory of Nazianzus, contributed to the further separation of economy (God for us) and theology (God in Godself) can be understandable. Catherine Mowry LaCugna, *God for Us*, 44.

However, LaCugna's thesis is merely a one-sided exaggeration of the position of the Cappadocians, and, at least, of Gregory of Nazianzus. In contrast to LaCguna, Beeley argues for an intimate connection between them, by saying that, though *oikonomia* and *theologia* are distinct from each other, nevertheless *theologia* is always located within *oikonomia* and *theologia* always points to *oikonomia*. Thus there is no such thing as extra-*oikonomia theologia*. Beeley, "Gregory of Nazianzus," 235–36; and also, Beeley, *Gregory of Nazianzus*, 197–98.

122. Gregory of Nazianzus, *Oration on Pentecost*, 41, 5.

123. Ibid.

Then he continues to explain that these are the divine *oikonomia*, with which Christ orders wisely all that concern us.[124] In this way, we find that Gregory of Nazianzus' notion of *oikonomia* refers to the incarnation of the Son in Jesus Christ, but is also inclusive of all life and works which the bodily form of the Son as Jesus Christ lived and did.

Furthermore, Gregory of Nazianzus' notion of *oikonomia* goes further to include all works of God toward us, which are common to the Father, the Son, and the Spirit. When he discusses the titles of God just before exploring the titles of the Son, he makes a distinction between the titles of authority [ἐξουσίας] and the titles of *oikonomia* towards the world. The Almighty, the King of Glory, the King of the Ages, the King of Powers and so on belong to the former. On the other hand, the God of salvation, the God of vengeance, the God of peace, the God of righteousness, and the God of Abraham, Issac, Jacob and all the spiritual Israel, are all the titles of *oikonomia*.[125] Then he holds that all these two kinds of titles are common to the Godhead, which implies that *oikonomia* is connected not only to the Son but also to the Father and the Holy Spirit. Therefore *oikonomia* is a very inclusive term which signifies all the works of the Father, the Son, and the Holy Spirit.

For Gregory of Nazianzus, such an inclusive notion of *oikonomia* is a result of his refutation of Eunomius and his followers, who argued for the absolute unlikeness between the Father and the Son, by saying on the ground of the absolute Monarchy that the generation of the Son of God is not eternal but has a beginning. In contrast to the Eunomians, Gregory of Nazianzus argued that he himself honored the Monarchy, but that the Monarchy is from the beginning the Trinity, being composed of the Father, the Son, and the Holy Spirit who have an equality of nature and substance.[126] On the one hand, like Athanasius, Gregory of Nazianzus regards some seemingly subordinational biblical passages as pointing to the human nature in the *oikonomia* of the incarnation of the Son in Jesus Christ. On the other hand, he made sure that, as God is the Triune God from all beginning and from all eternity, *oikonomia* is connected to Son, and also to the Father and the Holy Spirit.

---

124. *PG* 36, 436C; Gregory of Nazianzus, *Oration on Pentecost*, 41, 5.

125. *PG* 36, 128B; Gregory of Nazianzus, *Fourth Theological Oration*, 30, 19.

126. Gregory of Nazianzus, *Third Theological Oration*, 29, 2.

In this way, Gregory of Nazianzus' notion of *oikonomia* refers most broadly to all the works of God towards the world, and more broadly to all the life and works of the incarnated Son on the earth. And in the narrowest sense, his notion of *oikonomia* primarily points to the incarnation of the Son in Jesus Christ.

Energia *(Activity, Operation)*

Energeia [ἐνέργεια] (activity, operation) refers to all divine activities in relation to the world. While *oikonomia* comes to be gradually narrowed down to the incarnation of the Son in Jesus Christ, *energeia* always refers to all the works of the Triune God, namely, those of the Father, the Son, and the Holy Spirit.

Gregory of Nyssa

Gregory of Nyssa (335–395) frequently used *energeia* especially in his disputation against Eunomius who claimed the absolute unlikeness among the Father, the Son, and the Holy Spirit on the ground of a difference in *energeia* among them. Alluding to the Father, the Son, and the Holy Spirit respectively, Eunomius maintained that there is the supreme and absolute *ousia*,[127] from which the second *ousia* and the third *ousia* come into existence. Each *ousia* is followed by its own *energeia*[128] which, in turn, commensurately produces its own works. From the fact that some works are more honorable than other works it follows, he argued, that one *energeia* is greater than another, and also that one *ousia* is superior to another.[129] The point of Eunomius' position is that different work and *energeia* show different nature [φύσις] and *ousia* [οὐσία]. In addition, Eunomius went so far as to assert that the first *ousia* by its *energeia* made the second *ousia*, which, in turn, by its *energeia* made the third *ousia*.[130]

Gregory of Nyssa was, first, opposed to Eunomius' newly invented appellation: a supreme and absolute *ousia* for the Father, the second *ousia* for the Son, and the third *ousia* for the Holy Spirit. Instead, Gregory of Nyssa stuck to the scriptural names which he maintained convey the

---

127. *PG* 45, 298A.
128. *PG* 45, 298A–298B.
129. Gregory of Nyssa, *Against Eunomius*, I, 13.
130. Ibid., 17–18.

mystery of Christian faith,[131] because the scriptural names convey well the idea of the proper and natural relationship among the Father, the Son, and the Holy Spirit.[132] A philosophical reason against Eunomius' appellation is that Gregory of Nyssa judged that the ascription of the supreme and highest *ousia* to the first alone would lead to a complete denial of the *ousia* of the second and of the third, which, in turn, secretly and gradually effaces all real belief in their *hypostaseis* [ὑποστάσεως].[133] Thus he made a distinction between *ousia* and *hypostasis* and then suggested that we should not use the term *ousia* but the term *hypostasis* for each of the three persons.[134]

Second, Gregory of Nyssa refuted Eunominus' contention of a hierarchical plurality of *ousia* in the Trinity, which asserts that the second *ousia* is the *energeia* of the first *ousia*, and the third *ousia* is the *energeia* of the second *ousia*. In this regard, Gregory of Nyssa criticized Eunomius for having made a gap wider between *ousia* and *energeia* in the sense that the one follows the other only externally. Instead, he argued that we cannot separate *energeia* and *ousia* in the Trinity. He provided an analogy for the point. According to him, when we say that a man works in wood, this single expression conveys at once the idea of activity and the idea of the artificer, so that, if we withdraw the one, the other has no existence. Here both *energeia* and the one who exercises *energeia* inseparably co-exist.[135]

Third, Gregory of Nyssa, on the one hand, agreed with Eunomius that different work and *energeia* show different nature and *ousia*, because Gregory of Nyssa himself maintained that *energeia* and *ousia* are inseparable. This point is clearly reflected in his own theological method, which is to investigate the divine nature through its *energeiai* (operations).[136] Following the theological method, he examined two possible cases as follows:

131. Ibid., 13.

132. Ibid., 14.

133. *PG* 45, 300D.

134. Gregory of Nyssa, *On the Difference Between Ousia and Hypostasis*, 31–35. This was once regarded as a letter of Basil the Great, but its authorship is now ascribed to Gregory of Nyssa.

135. Gregory of Nyssa, *Against Eunomius*, I, 17.

136. *PG* 32, 692D; Gregory of Nyssa, *On the Holy Trinity*, 6.

If, then, we see that the operations [*energeiai*] which are wrought by the Father and the Son and the Holy Spirit differ one from the other, we shall conjecture from the different character of the operations [*energeiai*] that the natures which operate are also different . . . If, on the other hand, we understand that the operation [*energeia*] of the Father, the Son, and the Holy Spirit is one, differing or varying in nothing, the oneness of their nature must needs be inferred from the identity of their operation [*energeia*].[137]

Then Gregory of Nyssa took the second option, because the Father, the Son, and the Holy Spirit are one in their *energeia*. No activity is not divided to the *hypostaseis* of the Father, and the Son and the Holy Spirit.[138] For him, the Father, the Son, and the Holy Spirit alike give sanctification, life, light, comfort, power, guidance, the change to immortality, the passage to liberty, and every other grace and gift.[139] Therefore he concluded that Eunomius' elaborate account of the differences and degrees in *energeia* among the Father, the Son, and the Holy Spirit is absurd: "To suppose that within the Holy Trinity there is a difference as wide as that which we can observe between the heavens which envelope the whole creation, and one single man or the star which shines in them, is openly profane."[140] In brief, Gregory of Nyssa held that *ousia* and *energeia* in the Trinity are inseparable to each other,[141] while the former could be investigated only though the latter. In addition, he asserted that *energeia* among the Father, the Son, and the Holy Spirit is not different but one in the sense that every *energeia* which proceeds from God to creation starts off from the Father, goes through the Son, and is completed by the Holy Spirit.[142] Thus the holy Trinity works every *energeia*, proceeding from the Father, through the Son, to the Holy Spirit.[143]

137. *PG* 32, 692D–693A; Gregory of Nyssa, *On the Holy Trinity*, 6.

138. Gregory of Nyssa, *On Not Three Gods*, 18.

139. *PG* 32, 693A–693C; Gregory of Nyssa, *On the Holy Trinity*, 6.

140. Gregory of Nyssa, *Against Eunomius*, I, 24.

141. According to Anthony Meredith's interpretation, Gregory of Nyssa draws a distinction between the divine *ousia* and the divine *energeiae*, the latter of which are themselves distinct both from the inner divine *ousia* and from the effects of the divine action. Meredith, *Cappadocians*, 60.

142. Gregory of Nyssa, *On Not Three Gods*, 15.

143. Ibid., 17.

Processio—Missio

A distinction between *missio* (mission) and *processio* (procession) is more prominent in Augustine of Hippo (354–430) and in Thomas Aquinas (1225–1274). While Augustine began with *missio* and then went to *processio*,[144] Aquinas started from *processio* and then proceeded to *missio*.

AUGUSTINE OF HIPPO

The literal meaning of *missio* (mission) is being sent. From the outset in his book *De Trinitate*, Augustine affirmed the *missio* of the Son and the *missio* of the Holy Spirit on the basis of scriptural passages such as Galatians 4:4[145] and John 15:26.[146] Then Augustine set limits on the concept by confining *missio* to being sent visibly in time, namely, a visible manifestation to the world. He explained it by means of a distinction between outer expression and inner design which refers to invisible substance.[147] The Son, while remaining the form of God [*forma Dei*], was sent to be made visible in the form of flesh, or in the form of a servant [*forma servi*].[148] Likewise, the Holy Spirit was sent to be presented to human eyes as a bodily appearance: a dove in Matthew 3:16, a sound of a violent gust bearing down, and divided tongues of fire in Acts 2:2.[149] In this way, Augustine affirmed both the *missio* of the Son and that of the Holy Spirit, despite his acknowledgment of a difference in which the former takes on and becomes the flesh, while the latter employs created forms, but does not becomes themselves.

Then Augustine dealt with a difference between the visible manifestations of the Son and the Holy Spirit, and the divine manifestations

---

144. Augustine, *De Trinitate*.

145. "Cum autem venit plenitudo temporis, *misit* Deus Filium suum, factum ex muliere, factum sub Lege, ut eos qui sub Lege erant redimeret." (When the fullness of time had come, God *sent* his Son, made of woman, made under law, to redeem those who were under law). *PL* 42, 849; Augustine, *De Trinitate*, II, 2, 8.

146. "Cum autem venerit Paracletus quem ego *mittam* vobis a Patre, Spiritum veritatis qui a Patre procedit, ille testimonium perhibebit de me." (When the advocate comes whom I will *send* you from the Father, the Spirit of truth who proceeds from the Father, he will bear testimony about me). *PL* 42, 848; Augustine, *De Trinitate*, II, 1, 5.

147. Augustine, *De Trinitate*, II, 2, 8.

148. *PL* 42, 851; Augustine, *De Trinitate*, II, 2, 9.

149. Augustine, *De Trinitate*, II, 2, 10.

in the Old Testament, because he considered that even in the latter, the Son, the Holy Spirit, or even the Father appeared to people in various created forms and sometimes through angels.[150] Immediately after investigating the Son's mediatorship between God and man at chapters 1–4 in Book IV, Augustine provided a central key to his notion of *missio* by mentioning its purpose: "There you have what the Son of God has been sent for; indeed, there you have what it is for the Son of God to have been sent."[151] The purpose of the Son's *missio* is to be the mediator between God and the world, and the accomplishment of this purpose requires the Son of God to be incarnated into the world.[152] Accordingly, we can infer that, for Augustine, the Son of God cannot be said to have been sent until he began to accomplish the purpose of *missio*. And the theophanies of the Old Testament are regarded as preparatory to the *missio* of the Son and that of the Holy Spirit.[153] In this regard, Augustine's notion of *missio* centers around the Son's incarnation and the Spirit's descent in the New Testament, and it is a soteriological notion with a great emphasis on incarnation and salvation.

Finally, Augustine arrived at his complete definition of *missio* at chapter 5 of Book IV, where he finalized his concept of *missio* as being sent into the world as making known to the world that the Son and the Spirit proceed from the Father in eternity. Thus *missio* reveals in time the eternal *processio* of the divine persons. As he puts it:

> Just as the Father, then, begot and the Son was begotten, so the Father sent and the Son was sent ... *And just as being born means for the Son his being from the Father, so his being sent means his being known to be from him. And just as for the Holy Spirit his being the gift of God means his proceeding from the Father, so his being sent means his being known to proceed from him.* Nor, by the way, can we say that the Holy Spirit does not proceed from the Son as well; it is not without point that the same Spirit is called the Spirit of the Father and of the Son.[154]

150. Ibid., II, 7, 32.

151. Augustine, *De Trinitate*, IV, 5, 25.

152. In order to explain the requirement of the Son's incarnation, Augustine appeals to harmony and justice. That is, Christ observes the basic harmonious proportion of 1 to 2, and the Son of God became a just man to intercede for sinful man with God. Augustine, *De Trinitate*, IV, 5, 25.

153. Augustine, *De Trinitate*, IV, 2, 11.

154. Ibid., IV, 5, 29; Hill's own abridgement of procession is: "Briefly, it is that the

Here *missio* signifies that the Son was sent to be born and that the Holy Spirit was sent to be the gift of God, while *processio* refers to the point that the Son was begotten from the Father in eternity and that the Holy Spirit proceeded from the Father and also from the Son in eternity.

Regarding a relationship between *missio* and *processio*, it is notable that Augustine maintained that *missio* reveals *processio*. The *missio* of the Son means that the Son is from the Father, and the *missio* of the Holy Spirit means that the Holy Spirit is from the Father and the Son as well. This is an epistemological connection between *missio* and *processio*,[155] because *missio* reveals *processio*. According to Augustine, the purpose of the Son's mediatorship between God and man is to purify people by faith and thereby to enable them to contemplate the truth of eternal things, which is the eternal *processio* within the Trinity. In this regard, the significance of *missio*, the purpose of which is the reconciliation of us to God and the purification of us towards God, is to enable people to epistemologically realize that the *missio* of the Son and that of the Spirit reveal that the Son and the Holy Spirit are from the Father. In addition to the epistemological connection, a meticulous analysis shows that there is also an ontological relation between *processio* and *missio*, because Augustine mentions that, just as the Father begot the Son, so the Father sent the Son, and also insinuates that, just as the Father and the Son let the Holy Spirit proceed, so the Father and the Son sent the Holy Spirit.[156] Here *missio* is ontologically grounded in *processio*.

Son is eternally begotten by the Father in total equality of nature, or that he proceeds eternally by way of generation as the Word of the Father; and that the Holy Spirit eternally proceeds from the Father and the Son as from one principle or origin. All this is no more, really, than a rigorous conclusion from the revealed data of scripture."

155. This interpretation regarding epistemological connection is confirmed by Edmund Hill. According to him, the definition of mission as revealing procession does not contradict his long description of the Son's mission as mediating between God and man. The reason is that the object of the mediation is, through reconciling people to God, to give them access to eternal life, which means to know God and Jesus Christ. That is, by knowing that the Son is from the Father, we have eternal life and we benefit from the mediating mission of the Son. Edmund Hill, "Introductory Essay on Book IV," in *De Trinitate*, 148.

156. Augustine, *De Trinitate*, IV, 5, 29; Hill's own abridgement of procession is: "Briefly, it is that the Son is eternally begotten by the Father in total equality of nature, or that he proceeds eternally by way of generation as the Word of the Father; and that the Holy Spirit eternally proceeds from the Father and the Son as from one principle or origin. All this is no more, really, than a rigorous conclusion from the revealed data of scripture."

What about the Father with respect to *missio*? Augustine mentions that, even though God the Father sent the Son and the Spirit, the Father alone is nowhere said to have been sent.[157] And he added that, though God the Father is known by someone in time, the Father is not said to have been sent, because the Father has not got anyone else to be from or to proceed from, but the Father is from no one.[158] For Augustine, God the Father is the source of all godhead.[159] Such a notion of God the Father as source is one of Augustine's characteristic emphases. However, it should not be understood to imply any subordination within the Trinity, taking into consideration the unity and equality of the Trinity which Augustine insistently bolstered in Book I. Actually, Augustine himself argues for the unity and equality of the Trinity from the beginning of *De Trinitate*. From the outset in Book I, Augustine clarifies that "the Father is God and the Son is God and the Holy Spirit is God, and yet this threesome is not three gods but one God, ... the Trinity works inseparably in everything that God works."[160] This principle is related with his distinction between the form of a servant and the form of God, with which he interpreted several scriptural passages which seem to imply something of subordination: "In the form of God the Son is equal to the Father, and so is the Holy Spirit, ... In the form of a servant, however, he is less than the Father, because he himself said the Father is greater than I (John 14:28); he is also less than himself, because it is said of him that he emptied himself (Phil 2:7)."[161] This principle is applied to his understanding of the *missio* of the Son and that of the Holy Spirit, because *missio* does not mean that the sent is less than the sender, but only that one is from the other. It does not imply any lack of equality, but only an origin in eternity.[162]

To sum up, Augustine's notion of *missio* centers around the Son's purpose which is the soteriological mediation between God and man. He started from mere *missio* as being sent, and proceeded through *missio* as being visibly manifested in time, and came to *missio* as being sent

157. Augustine, *De Trinitate*, II, 2, 8.
158. Ibid., IV, 5, 28.
159. Ibid., IV, 5, 19.
160. Augustine, *De Trinitate*, I, 2, 8.
161. Ibid., I, 4, 22.
162. Augustine, *De Trinitate*, II, 1, 3.

with reference to the Son's purpose, and finally ended with *missio* as revealing *processio*. Here *missio* reveals *processio* epistemologically, while *missio* is ontologically grounded in *processio*. In this sense, *missio* and *processio* are inseparably related to each other.

THOMAS AQUINAS

For Aquinas, *processio* and *missio* are in an intimate relationship with each other. But, unlike Augustine who started from *missio* and then went to *processio*, Aquinas began with *processio* and then proceeded to *missio*. According to Aquinas, on the basis of inner divine actions, there are two processions [*processio*] within one God, the procession of the Word [*processio verbi*] and the procession of the Will [*processio voluntatis*]. The former is called generation [*generatio*],[163] and the latter is called spiration [*spiratio*].[164] These two processions give rise to four real relations in God, which are paternity or fatherhood (Begetter to Begotten, Father to Son), filiation or sonship (Begotten to Begetter, Son to Father), spiration (Spirator to Spirated, Father and Son to Holy Spirit), and procession (Spirated to Spirator, Holy Spirit to Father and Son). In turn, three of these four relations: paternity, filiation and procession are constitutive of divine person and give rise to three persons: the Father, the Son, and the Holy Spirit. The Father is the One who begets, the Son is the One who is begotten, and the Holy Spirit is the One who is spirated. Besides, the three persons have five notions or characteristics which distinguish each person from the others. The five notions are innascibility or ingenerateness, paternity, filiation, spiration, procession.[165]

As mentioned in the above, *processio* has several meanings as shown in the table below:

---

163. Aquinas, *ST*, I, 27, 2.
164. Ibid., I, 27, 5, ad 3.
165. LaCugna, *God for Us*, 179–80.

5-4-3-2-1[166]

5 notions (characteristics)	① innascibility (ingeneratedness)
	② paternity (fatherhood)
	③ filiation (sonship)
	④ spiration
	⑤ *procession*
4 relations	① paternity
	② filiation
	③ spiration
	④ *procession*
3 persons	① the Father (paternity)
	② the Son (filiation)
	③ the Holy Spirit (spiration)
2 processions	① *generation* (being begotten)
	② *spiration* (being given)
1 essence (nature)	① one God

Here we find four different concepts of *processio*.[167] However, here we put more focus on two processions, namely, the *processio* of the Son from the Father and the *processio* of the Spirit from the Father and the Son, while we will be less concerned with the other meanings of *processio*. It is noteworthy that, for Aquinas, *processio* is not an outward act outside God, but an inward act within God. In this sense, Aquinas criti-

---

166. A mnemonic device for retaining the essential elements of the Augustinian-Thomistic doctrine of the Trinity says that God is 5 notions, 4 relations, 3 persons, 2 processions, and 1 nature: (1) five notions: ① innascibility (ingeneratedness), ② paternity (fatherhood), ③ filiation (sonship), ④ spiration, ⑤ procession; (2) four real relations: ① paternity (fatherhood), ② filiation (sonship), ③ spiration, ④ procession; (3) three Persons: ① the Father, ② the Son, ③ the Holy Spirit; (4) two processions ① being begotten, ② being spirated; (5) one God (essence, nature). LaCugna, *God for Us*, 179-80.

167. According to Ceslaus Velecky, procession has five meanings in Aquinas: firstly, a generic name for the relatedness of something to its source, having origin from something or being from it; secondly, a specific name for the second procession, i.e. that of the Holy Ghost, coming forth as Love; thirdly, one of the relations which is the personal relation of the Holy Ghost; fourthly, the notion or characteristic property of the Holy Ghost; and lastly, the coming forth from God and the being produced of creatures. Thomas Aquinas, *Summa Theologiae*, vol. 6, 161.

cized both Arius and Sabellius, for the former understands *processio* as an effect proceeding from its cause, and for the latter considers *processio* to be the cause proceeding to the effect.[168] In contrast, for Aquinas, *processio* exists in God and remains within God. *Processio* usually refers to the inner movements within God and thus to the inner relationship within God.

On the other hand, *missio* literally means being sent. According to Aquinas, *missio* implies that the one who is sent either begins to exist where he was not before, or begins to exist where he was before but in a new way. The first case is characteristic of creatures, whereas the second case is ascribed to divine persons.[169] The divine person who is sent does not begin to exist where he did not previously exist, and does not cease to exist where he was.[170] According to Aquinas, for God, there are two missions [*missio*]: the mission of the Son and the mission of the Spirit. The former is called mission [*missio*], and the latter is called giving [*datio*].

In addition, according to Aquinas, we can distinguish between the visible mission [*missio visibilis*] and the invisible mission [*missio invisibilis*]. For the Son was sent by the Father into the world and began to be in the world in a visible way by taking flesh. However, this does not mean that there was once a time when the Son was not in the world. Rather, Aquinas affirms, on the basis of John 1:1, that the Son was already in the world, but in an invisible way. As regards the Spirit, the Spirit was given invisibly by dwelling in the soul through grace. And the Spirit was visibly given on the day of Pentecost. A difference between the Son's visible mission and the Spirit's visible mission is that the Son has been sent visibly as the author of sanctification or holiness, and the Spirit has been sent visibly as the sign of sanctification or holiness.[171]

In any case, for Aquinas, divine *missio* does not mean that the Son and the Spirit who are sent, begin to exist where they did not previously exist, and cease to exist where they were.[172] *Missio* means that the Son or the Spirit begins to exist where he was before, but in a new visible

168. Aquinas, *ST*, I, 27, 1.
169. Ibid., I, 43, 6.
170. Ibid., I, 43, 1, ad 2.
171. Ibid., I, 43, 7.
172. Ibid., I, 43, 1, ad 2.

way. In this sense, though *missio* mainly refers to the outwardly visible movements outside God, *missio* is not exhaustively restricted to temporal visible movements. *Missio* presupposes a kind of succession between an invisible way of existence and a visible way of existence.

What is, then, Aquinas' understanding of the relation between *processio* and *missio*? At a first glance, *missio* and *processio* seem to be quite different from each other, and seem to have no intimate relation. *Processio* is the inner movements within God, whereas *missio* is the outward movements outside God. *Processio* refers to the inner relations between three persons, whereas *missio* points to the outward relations between God and creatures. The generation of the Son and the spiration of the Spirit are exclusively eternal, whereas the mission of the Son and the giving of the Spirit are temporal. These seemingly differences give an impression that there are two separate and isolated movements for God.

However, there are several points to be taken into consideration regarding the intimate relation between *processio* and *missio*. In the first place, though it is sure that *missio* is exclusively used for God's outward actions, whether invisible or visible, *processio* is not exclusively used for divine inner movements. *Processio* in Aquinas is used for the outward movements of God, as well. For example, Aquinas stated, "The Son proceeds [*processit*] in eternity so as to be God, and the Son goes forth [*processit*] in time so as to be man by reason of His visible *missio* and so as to be in man by reason of his invisible *missio*."[173] Here *processio* is used not only for the eternal action within God, but also for the temporal movement outside God. This linguistic observation indicates that *processio* is related to *missio* in some way.

In the second place, the very idea of *missio* does not only refer to the temporal effects of divine persons towards creatures, but also means going forth [*processit*] from another, and in other words, procession [*processit*] according to origin.[174] Sending [*missio*] and giving [*datio*] connote a term in time, but also imply a relationship with their principle.[175] That is to say, *missio* includes procession of origin [*processio originis*], and going forth through an origin. *Missio* not only determines

173. Ibid., I, 43, 2.
174. Ibid., I, 43, 4.
175. Ibid., I, 43, 2.

the temporal term of *processio*, but also signifies *processio* from the principle. *Missio*, though with an addition of a temporal effect, has a link up to eternal *processio*. Thus *missio* and *processio* are linked to each other in terms of the principle of origin. In this regard, Aquinas explained that *processio* may be called a twin procession [*gemina processio*], eternal and temporal [*aeterna et temporalis*], not that there is a double relation to the principle but that there is a double term, temporal and eternal.[176] In other words, inner divine *processio* is eternal procession, and outward divine *missio* is temporal procession.[177]

In the third place, an intimate relation between *processio* and *missio* is confirmed by Aquinas' understanding of God the Father with regard to *processio* and *missio*. Unlike the Son and the Spirit who both proceed in God and are sent outside God, the Father does not proceed and is not sent by another. *Processio* means an inward action from the principle of origin. The Son proceeds from the Father as the principle, and the Spirit proceeds from the Father and the Son as the principle of origin. However, the Father does not proceed. In addition, with regard to *missio*, the Son is sent by the Father, and the Spirit is sent by the Father and the Son. However, the Father is not said to be outwardly sent, mainly because the Father is not inwardly from another. Though he admitted that the Father abides in us through grace, as the Son and the Spirit abides in us, nevertheless he insisted that to be sent [*missio*] is not applied to the Father, mainly because the Father is not from another. This point implies an inner link between *processio* and *missio*. To put it in other words, as giving [*datio*] means a generous communication, the Father does give Himself in the sense that the Father generously bestows Himself as the source of happiness for creatures. However, while giving is the giver's origination of the gift, nevertheless giving [*datio*] is not applied to the Father. In this sense, Aquinas' understanding of the Father as the principle of origin is the same, whether inwardly or outwardly. This point also implies that *missio* and *processio* are linked to each other in a certain way.

---

176. Ibid., I, 43, 2, ad 3.

177. On this point, LaCugna admits that the missions of being sent [*missio*] and being given [*datio*] are temporal, but they are rooted in the eternal processions of generation [*generatio*] and spiration [*spiratio*]. She continues to state that this is what it means to say that the Son and the Spirit proceed and go forth in both time and eternity. LaCugna, *God for Us*, 157.

In the last place, the temporal effects of divine missions are intimately related with divine inner processions. Divine processions refer to the *processio* of the Word which is derived from the action of the intellect, and to the *processio* of Love which is derived from the action of the will. The *processio* of the Word in God is called generation and the Word proceeding is called the Son. The *processio* of Love in God is called spiration and the Love is called the Spirit. The Son's *missio* and the Spirit's *missio* are distinguished in terms of the effects of grace. The Son's *missio* effects the illumination of the intellect, and the Spirit's *missio* effects the kindling of the affection.[178] Here the Son's *missio* by the Father corresponds to the *processio* of the Word from the Father, and the Spirit's *missio* by the Father and the Son corresponds to the *processio* of the Love from the Father and the Son. As nothing can be loved by will unless it is conceived in the intellect, so nothing can be kindled by the Spirit unless it is not understood by the Son.

So far we have examined the intimate relationship between *processio* and *missio* in God: Firstly, *processio* is used for the temporal movement outside God as well as for the eternal action within God. Secondly, *missio* is rooted in the eternal *processio* in terms of the principle of origin. Thirdly, the understanding of the Father as the principle of origin is the same whether inwardly or outwardly. As the Father does not proceed, so the Father is not sent. Finally, the temporal effects of *missio* correspond to the eternal *processio*. Taking these points into consideration, we find that *processio* and *missio* are intimately related to each other for Aquinas. The *missio* of the Son and the *missio* of the Holy Spirit are rooted in the eternal *processio* of generation and the eternal *processio* of spiration.

There is one more thing not to be ignored. According to Aquinas, God is in all things by his power, inasmuch as all things are subject to the power of God. God is by divine presence in all things, as all things are bare and open to the eyes of God. God is in all things by divine essence, inasmuch as God is present to all as the cause exists in the effects.[179] This is the common mode of God's presence in all things.[180] In addition to this mode, there is another special mode of God's presence.

---

178. Aquinas, *ST*, I, 43, 2, ad 3.

179. Ibid., I, 8, 3.

180. Ibid., I, 43, 3.

According to it, God is said to be present as the object known is in the knower, and the beloved in the lover. This is God's presence by grace, according to which God is said not only to exist in the rational creature but also to dwell therein as in his own temple.[181]

Notably, the special mode of divine presence is based on divine processions and includes divine missions. In this sense, divine *missio* is an appropriate bridge to the next treatise *De Deo Creante*.[182] Therefore, God's inner *processio* is linked to the making of creatures through divine *missio*. The name of God the Father pertains to the Father's relation to the Son, not to the Father's relationship to the creature. However, the Father is the Father to us as well as the Father of the Son. In addition, the Word is an analogy for the procession of Son from the Father. The Father knows Himself and speaks Himself in the Word. However, the name Word also contains a reference to creatures. The Father utters not only Himself but also every creature by begetting the Word. Furthermore, for Aquinas, the processions of Word and Love indicate, though secondarily, a reference to creation, inasmuch as the divine truth and goodness are the grounds of God's knowing and loving of creatures.[183]

Besides, Aquinas says explicitly that the eternal processions of the divine persons ground the production of creatures. The processions of Son and Spirit within God, that is, the being begotten of the Son and the being spirated of the Spirit, give rise to the divine missions such as the sending forth of the Son and the Spirit into creation and salvation in history. The divine persons as proceeding exercise causality in relation to creation. The processions of the divine persons serve as a model for the procession of creatures.[184]

Therefore Aquinas holds that the Father speaks Himself and his creatures. The Father and the Son love each other and love us. Of course, this is not in a univocal way, because Creator and creatures do not have the same nature. However, this does not mean that God and we are totally different from each other. Rather, it means that there is a secure guarantee of an intimate relationship between God and us,

---

181. Ibid.

182. LaCugna also admits that the production of creatures is the exterior effect of the divine procession. LaCugna, *God for Us*, 142.

183. Aquinas, *ST*, I, 37, 2 and 3.

184. Ibid., I, 45, 6.

between God in Godself and God for us. To be brief, for Aquinas, God the Father utters not only Himself but also us. God the Father loves not only the Son but also us by the Holy Spirit. Therefore, God in Godself is not different from God for us.[185]

185. There are many recent scholars who grasp an inseparably intimate relationship between *processio* and *missio*, or between the immanent and the economic Trinity. For example, Anselm K. Min argues that, for Aquinas, "the doctrine of the immanent Trinity is essential to the doctrine of the economic Trinity." Min, *Paths to the Triune God*, 170. Also see pages 207–8, 216, 238; Emery, using the terms "the immanent Trinity" and "the creative Trinity," maintains that, for Aquinas, "the study of the divine Trinity in its immanent life [the immanent Trinity] is not separated from the study of creation or of the economy of salvation [the creative Trinity]." Emery, "The Doctrine of the Trinity," 49–50.

3

Contemporary Discussions on the Immanent-Economic Trinity Relation I

ONE OF THE MAJOR ISSUES ANIMATING CONTEMPORARY DISCUSSIONS of Trinitarian theology is the relation between the immanent Trinity and the economic Trinity. In chapter 3 and chapter 4 I make an attempt to identify seven different positions on the immanent-economic Trinity relation: Barth's mutual correspondence; Rahner's identity; Moltmann, Pannenberg, and Jenson's eschatological unity; Boff and Pittenger's "much more than"; Bracken's "immersing"; Suchocki and LaCugna's "absorbing"; and Lee's mutual inclusiveness. In so doing, I explicate each of these seven positions in turn by examining each one's uses of the two terms: the immanent and the economic Trinity. These explications in chapters 3–4 will form the basis for chapter 5, which critically analyzes each of the positions in terms of ontology, epistemology and a concept of mystery.

Barth: Mutual Correspondence

Barth's Use of the Immanent Trinity and the Economic Trinity

Karl Barth employs the term "the immanent Trinity" seven times[1] and uses the term "the economic Trinity" four times[2] in the entire *Church Dogmatics*. And both "the economic Trinity" and "the immanent Trinity"

---

1. Barth, *CD*, I/1, 172, 173, 333, 479, 481 (twice), 485. A term "The eternal Trinity" appears as well in I/1, 486; According to Benjamin C. Leslie, Barth is reluctant to use the terms "the immanent Trinity" and "the economic Trinity," because the immanent-economic distinction tends to imply an essential distinction within God. Benjamin C. Leslie, *Trinitarian Hermeneutics*, 213 n.50.

2. Barth, *CD*, I/1, 333, 358, 479, 481.

appear together only three times in the whole *Church Dogmatics*. Some
of these passages bring to light what Barth means by "the economic
Trinity" and "the immanent Trinity."

In the first place, when Barth argues for the free grace of God's
Word against Erich Przywara's criticism that the Trinity for Barth dis-
solves into revealer, revealing, and revealedness, Barth makes a distinction between the immanent Trinity and the economic Trinity as
follows:

> In the thinking necessary in correlating God and man we must
> not think away the free basis that this correlation has in God,
> . . . If we are not to do this, then it is not just good sense but
> absolutely essential that along with all older theology we make
> a deliberate and sharp distinction between *the Trinity of God
> as we may know it in the Word of God revealed, written, and
> proclaimed*, and *God's immanent Trinity*, i.e., between *"God in
> Himself"* and *"God for us,"* between *the "eternal history of God"*
> and *His temporal acts.* In so doing we must always bear in mind
> that the *"God for us"* does not arise as a matter of course out of
> the *"God in Himself,"* . . . [3]

Here the economic Trinity refers to God for us—the Trinity known in
the revealed, written, and proclaimed Word of God. On the other hand,
the immanent Trinity refers to God in Godself. The criterion of the immanent-economic distinction is the Word of God which is revelation.[4]
In another aspect, the immanent Trinity signifies the eternal history
of God, whereas the economic Trinity points to God's temporal acts.
The immanent-economic distinction is parallel to the eternal-temporal
distinction.

In the second place, when Barth analyzes the biblical concept of
revelation and leads to the concepts of God's Triunity, he insinuates that
the Trinity can be understood not only as the economic Trinity but also
as the immanent Trinity. He states his position as follows:

> Our concepts of unimpaired unity and unimpaired distinction,
> the concept of the one essence of God and of the three persons
> or modes of being (*Seinsweisen*) to be distinguished in this es-
> sence, and finally the polemical assertion, which we touched on
> only briefly, that *God's triunity* is to be found not merely *in His*

3. Ibid., I/1, 172.

4. Ibid., I/1, 117.

> *revelation* but, because in His revelation, *in God Himself* and in
> Himself too, so that the Trinity is to be understood as *"imma-
> nent"* and not just *"economic"*—none of this is directly biblical,
> i.e. explicitly stated in the Bible; it is Church doctrine. We have
> established no more than that the biblical doctrine of revelation
> is implicitly, and in some passages explicitly, a pointer to the
> doctrine of the Trinity.[5]

Here the immanent Trinity refers to the Trinity in Godself, whereas the
economic Trinity denotes the Trinity in God's revelation. The immanent-economic distinction centers on revelation.

In the third place, when he discusses the *Filioque* issue (siding
with the Western Church tradition over that of the Eastern Orthodox
Church), Barth defines a relation between the immanent Trinity and
the economic Trinity as follows:

> [W]e have consistently followed the rule, which we regard as
> basic, that statements about *the divine modes of being anteced-
> ently in themselves* cannot be different in content from those
> that are to be made about *their reality in revelation*. All our
> statements concerning what is called *the immanent Trinity* have
> been reached simply as confirmations or underlinings or, mate-
> rially, as the indispensable premises of *the economic Trinity*.[6]

Here the immanent Trinity refers to the divine modes of being antecedently in themselves, whereas the economic Trinity denotes the divine
modes of being in revelation. The criterion of making a distinction between the immanent Trinity and the economic Trinity is revelation.

In the last place, Barth goes further to apply the immanent-economic distinction to the *Filioque* and makes a differentiation between
"the immanent *Filioque*"[7] and the economic *Filioque*. The immanent
Filiqoue is that in the being of God antecedently in Godself, whereas
the economic *Filioque* is that in God's revelation. The economic *Filioque*
means that the Holy Spirit is the Spirit of both the Father and the Son in
God's revelation, whereas the immanent *Filioque* means that the Holy
Spirit is the Spirit of both the Father and the Son to all eternity. In other
words, the immanent *Filioque* means that the Spirit is the Spirit of both

5. Ibid., I/1, 333.

6. Ibid., I/1, 479.

7. Ibid., I/1, 481. Barth uses the term "the immanent *Filioque*," which implies a corresponding term "the economic *Filioque*," though he himself does not use it.

the Father and the Son in God's work *ad intra*, whereas the economic *Filioque* means that the Holy Spirit is the Spirit of both the Father and the Son in God's work *ad extra*.

As has been mentioned above, the immanent-economic distinction centers around revelation. And the immanent-economic distinction is in accord with the eternal-temporal distinction and with the *ad intra–ad extra* distinction. All these distinctions center around God's revelation. The economic Trinity is the Trinity in God's revelation, the Trinity in God's temporal acts, and the Trinity in God's work *ad extra* and God's work for us. On the other hand, the immanent Trinity is the Trinity antecedently in Godself, the Trinity in God's eternal history, and the Trinity in God's work *ad intra* and God's work within Godself.

Specifically with regard to each person of the Trinity, the economic Trinity is concerned with God our Father and our Creator who is the Lord of our existence, whereas the immanent Trinity is related to the eternal Father who is the Father of the Son of God. The economic Trinity is concerned with God our Reconciler who reconciles us to the Father, whereas the immanent Trinity is related to the eternal Son who is the Son of God the Father. And the economic Trinity is concerned with God our Redeemer who sets us free, whereas the immanent Trinity is related to the Holy Spirit who is the Spirit of the love of the Father and the Son. In addition, more specifically with regard to the *Filioque*, the economic Trinity is concerned with the economic *Filioque*, whereas the immanent Trinity is related to the immanent *Filioque*.

Mutual Correspondence

With regard to the relation between the immanent Trinity and the economic Trinity, Barth argues that there is a corresponding relation between the Trinity in God's revelation and the Trinity in Godself, between the Trinity in God's temporal acts and the Trinity in God's eternal history, and between the Trinity in God's work *ad extra* and for us and God's work *ad intra* and within Godself. In addition, with regard to each person of the Trinity, Barth holds that there is a corresponding relation between God our Creator and the eternal Father, between God our Reconciler and the eternal Son, and between God our Redeemer and the eternal Holy Spirit. Furthermore, Barth asserts that there is a corresponding relation between the immanent *Filioque* and the economic *Filioque.*

It comes as no surprise that several passages in *Church Dogmatics* advocate the correspondence of the economic Trinity to the immanent Trinity. It is so, because Barth starts with the reality of revelation, proceeds through an analysis of revelation, and leads to the recognition of the economic Trinity and then that of the immanent Trinity. Firstly, Barth states that the unity and distinction of the three modes of being in God's revelation point to the corresponding difference and unity among the three modes of being in Godself.[8] The unity and distinction of the economic Trinity correspond to those of the immanent Trinity. Secondly, Barth remarks that the unity of the Father, the Son, and the Holy Spirit *ad extra* corresponds to the unity of the Father, the Son and the Holy Spirit *ad intra.*[9] Thirdly, Barth mentions that the involution and convolution of the three modes of being in God's work exactly corresponds to those of the three modes of being in God's essence.[10] Fourthly, with regard to each person of the Trinity, which is, for Barth, each "mode or way of being" [τρόπος ὑπάρξεως, *modus entitativus*],[11] Barth maintains that the content of creation in the economic Trinity refers back to a corresponding inner possibility in the immanent Trinity. This point means that God our Creator and God our Father of the economic Trinity corresponds to the eternal Father of the immanent Trinity.[12] Likewise, for Barth, God our Reconciler and God our Redeemer corresponds to the eternal Son and the eternal Spirit respectively. Fifthly, with regard to the *Filioque*, Barth asserts that the love in reconciliation corresponds to the eternal Spirit as the love of the Father and the Son.[13] All these passages affirm a correspondence of the economic Trinity to the immanent Trinity.

In addition, there are some passages as well, which support the converse direction of correspondence, that is, the correspondence of the immanent Trinity to the economic Trinity. For instance, firstly, with

8. Ibid., I/1, 362.

9. Ibid., I/1, 371.

10. Ibid., I/1, 374.

11. Ibid., I/1, 359.

12. Ibid., I/1, 392.

13. Ibid., I/1, 483.

regard to God the Father, Barth argues that the eternal Father corresponds to our Creator and our Father.[14] For Barth, God the Father is our Creator and our Father in Jesus Christ. Thus he maintains that it follows from this point that God the Father is already the eternal Father who corresponds to our Creator and our Father. Secondly, with regard to the *Filioque*, Barth states that the full consubstantial fellowship between the Father and the Son as the essence of the Holy Spirit corresponds to the fellowship between God and human beings as the work of the Holy Spirit, with the former being the prototype of the latter.[15]

These observations show that Barth holds a position of mutual correspondence between the economic Trinity and the immanent Trinity. The economic Trinity corresponds to the immanent Trinity, and the immanent Trinity corresponds to the economic Trinity. Such a position is clearly disclosed with regard to God the Son, for Barth states both that God the Son is our Reconciler, "because He [the Son] is so antecedently in Himself as the Son or Word of God the Father,"[16] and that "as Christ is in revelation, so He is antecedently in Himself."[17] This is the same of the Holy Spirit, as well. Barth clearly states as follows: "What He [the Holy Spirit] is in revelation He is antecedently in Himself. And what He is antecedently in Himself He is in revelation."[18] These remarks obviously advocate the mutual correspondence between the economic Trinity and the immanent Trinity.

For Barth, the mutual correspondence is grounded in his understanding of the unity between essence and work, and of the oneness between being and act. God's essence is God's work, and God's work is God's essence.[19] God's being and God's act are not twofold but one.[20] God's revelation is God in Godself and God in Godself is God's revela-

---

14. Ibid., I/1, 391; Karl Barth, *Kirchliche Dogmatik*, I/1, 412. ". . . Aber daraus, daß er in Jesus und nur in Jesus als Schöpfer und also als unser Vater offenbar wird, geht hervor, daß er das Entsprechende schon zuvor und an sich ist, nämlich in seinem Verhältnis zu dem, durch den er offenbar wird, also in seinem Verhältnis eben zu Jesus." Hereafter cited as *KD*.

15. Barth, *CD*, I/1, 482.

16. Ibid., I/1, 399.

17. Ibid., I/1, 428.

18. Ibid., I/1, 466.

19. Ibid., I/1, 371.

20. Ibid., I/1, 428.

tion, because God does and reveals that which corresponds to God's divine essence, and because God's work is grounded in God's divine nature.[21]

The Content of Mutual Correspondence

However, Barth's mutual correspondence does not mean that the economic Trinity and the immanent Trinity are exactly identical both in content and in form. If so, it would, then, be the case, either that the economic Trinity is immersed into the immanent Trinity, or that the immanent Trinity is absorbed into the economic Trinity. This is not what Barth intends to affirm. Rather, Barth wants to maintain both the distinction and unity between the immanent and the economic Trinity. In order to do so, Barth holds the unity or sameness of them in content, but he takes the difference between them in form. To put it in other words, Barth's notion of mutual correspondence is asymmetrical, which means that the way in which the economic Trinity corresponds to the immanent Trinity is not the same as the way in which the immanent Trinity corresponds to the economic Trinity.

On the one hand, with regard to the correspondence of the economic Trinity to the immanent Trinity, Barth clearly formulates that the economic Trinity corresponds to the immanent Trinity as its "prototype."[22] More specifically, he adds that the immanent Trinity is the "reason," "way," and "basis"[23] of the economic Trinity. These terms imply an ontological sense of correspondence. In this sense, the economic Trinity ontologically corresponds to the immanent Trinity, but not conversely. For example, with regard to the Holy Spirit, Barth explicates as follows:

> Thus God— . . . God the Holy Spirit—is "antecedently in Himself" the act of communion, the act of impartation, love, gift. *For this reason and in this way and on this basis* He is so in His revelation. Not *vice versa!* We know Him thus in His revelation. But He is not this because He is it in His revelation; [rather]

21. Ibid., IV/1, 187.
22. Ibid., I/1, 482.
23. Ibid., I/1, 471.

because He is it antecedently in Himself, He is it also in His revelation."[24]

God the Holy Spirit is the ontological reason, way, and basis of our Redeemer, because God the Holy Spirit is antecedently in Godself the eternal Spirit of the eternal Father and the eternal Son. Likewise, God the Father is the ontological reason of our Creator and our Father, because God the Father is antecedently in Godself the eternal Father of the eternal Son. God the Son is the ontological way of our Reconciler, because God the Son is antecedently in Godself the eternal Son of the eternal Father. In addition, the immanent *Filioque* is the ontological prototype of the economic *Filioque*.

On the other hand, with regard to the correspondence of the immanent Trinity to the economic Trinity, Barth means that the immanent Trinity corresponds to the economic Trinity which is the epistemological gateway to the immanent Trinity. God our Creator and God our Father epistemologically refers us back to the eternal Father of the eternal Son. Jesus Christ in revelation leads us to perceive the eternal Son of the eternal Father. The Holy Spirit takes us to the recognition of the eternal Spirit of the Father and the Son. In addition, the love which meets us in the economic *Filioque* carries us into seeing the eternal love in the immanent *Filioque*. Thus, for Barth, the immanent Trinity corresponds to the economic Trinity epistemologically.

Therefore Barth's notion of mutual correspondence means that the economic Trinity ontologically corresponds to the immanent Trinity, and simultaneously, that the immanent Trinity corresponds to the economic Trinity epistemologically. What is more important, the intent of Barth in his mutual correspondence is to maintain the unity or sameness in content between the economic Trinity and the immanent Trinity. This point is well exposed in Barth's own statement that whatever is said about the immanent Trinity are "confirmations [*Bestätigungen*]," "underlinings [*Unterstreichungen*]" and "the indispensable premises [*die unentbehrlichen Vordersätze*]" of the economic Trinity.[25] And also, this point is in accord with Barth's "basic rule [*die grundlegende Regel*]," which pervades the whole *Church Dogmatics*. Barth's basic rule says, "statements about the divine modes being antecedently in themselves

24. Ibid., I/1, 471.
25. Ibid., I/1, 479.

cannot be different in content from those that are to be made about their reality in revelation."[26]

In brief, Barth's notion of mutual correspondence means both the ontological correspondence of the economic to the immanent Trinity and the epistemological correspondence of the immanent to the economic Trinity. Most of all, such mutual correspondence is established for Barth to intend to maintain the sameness or unity in content between the economic Trinity and the immanent Trinity, and also to differentiate the economic Trinity and the immanent Trinity in form.[27]

Rahner: Identity

Rahner's Rule

With regard to the relation between the immanent Trinity and the economic Trinity, Karl Rahner formulates his "basic thesis," or "basic axiom [*Grundaxiom*]" in his book *The Trinity* which was translated into English in 1970, as follows: "*The 'economic' Trinity is the 'immanent' Trinity and the 'immanent' Trinity is the 'economic' Trinity.*"[28] The basic thesis or axiom is also called "the guiding principle," or "the methodi-

---

26. Ibid., I/1, 479.

27. There are some scholars who interpret Barth's correspondence not as mutually but as unilaterally. For example, first, Eberhard Jüngel, in his interpretative paraphrase of Barth on the Trinity, one-sidedly summarizes that God corresponds to Godself [*Gott entspricht sich*]. This puts a more focus on the correspondence of God's being *ad extra*, namely, the economic Trinity, to God's being *ad intra*, that is, the immanent Trinity. Eberhard Jüngel, *God's Being*, 36.

Second, Jürgen Moltmann, though acknowledging that Barth breaks through the unilinear view of correspondence only in his account of Christ's death on the cross, asserts that Barth maintains "the Platonic notion of correspondence" in his distinction between the immanent Trinity and the economic Trinity, and thus for Barth, "what God revealed himself as being in Jesus Christ, he is in eternity, 'beforehand in himself.'" Moltmann, *Trinity and the Kingdom*, 159.

Third, Leslie, though admitting that Barth's thought may not be reduced to a Platonic style dualism, adheres to the one part of thesis, by stating that, for Barth, the economic Trinity corresponds to the immanent Trinity. Leslie, *Trinitarian Hermeneutics*, 195, 214 n. 58.

28. Rahner, *Trinity*, 22. Rahner's own emphasis. According to Rahner, the basic axiom was first formulated not by Rahner himself, but by someone else who has not been identified. Rahner confesses that he does not know exactly when and by whom the basic axiom was formulated for the first time. Rahner, "Oneness and Threefoldness of God in Discussion with Islam," in *Theological Investigations*, XVIII, 114.

cal principle" by Rahner himself,[29] and it is widely known as "Rahner's Rule."[30] As a matter of fact, Rahner's book *The Trinity* was translated from his 1967 essay, "The Triune God as the Transcendental Ground of Salvation History" [*Der dreifaltige Gott als transzendenter Urgrund der Heilsgeschichte*], which was published in the second volume of *Mysterium Salutis: Grundriß heilsgeschichtlicher Dogmatik* [*The Mystery of Salvation: The Outline of Salvation History Dogmatics*].[31] Actually, this essay was based on his 1960 essay, "Remarks on the Dogmatic Treatise *De Trinitate* [*Bemerkungen zum dogmatischen Traktat «De Trinitate»*]," which was included in the fourth volume of *Schriften zur Theologie*.[32] In the 1960 essay, Rahner's rule was formulated as follows: "the Trinity of the economy of salvation *is* the immanent Trinity and vice versa."[33] "Thus we have the identity of the immanent Trinity with the Trinity of the economy of salvation."[34] These observations indicate that Rahner's distinction between the immanent Trinity and the economic Trinity entirely hinges on the economy of salvation, or salvation history. For Rahner, the economic Trinity, which is also called "the Trinity of the economy of salvation,"[35] "the Trinity of salvation,"[36] or "the salvific Trinity,"[37] is the Trinity manifested in salvation history. On the other hand, the immanent Trinity is the Trinity apart from salvation his-

29. Rahner, "Divine Trinity," 295–303. This encyclopedia consists of 6 volumes and was published simultaneously in six languages including English and German in 1968–1970; The same entry is listed in *Encyclopedia of Theology*, 1755–64.

30. In his 1993 book on the Trinity, Ted Peters acknowledged that Roger E. Olson coined the term "Rahner's Rule." Ted Peters, *God as Trinity*, 213 n. 33. Peters himself used the term first in his article on the Trinity in 1987; Ted Peters, "Trinity Talk: Part I," 46. On the other hand, in his 1990 article on Pannenberg's Trinity, Olson admitted that Peters first coined the term "Rahner's Rule" in his article on the Trinity in 1987. Olson, "Wolfhart Pannenberg's Doctrine," 178; This point is affirmed both by Sanders, "Image of the Immanent Trinity," 3 n.5; and Grenz, *Rediscovering*, 238 n.126.

31. Feiner and Löhrer, *Mysterium Salutis I, II, III:1, III–2, IV:1, IV:2 and V*.

32. Rahner, "Remarks" 77–102. Rahner's *Theological Investigations*, vols. I–XXIII (1961–1992). For the complete table of contents and abstract of entire volumes, refer to the following book: Pekarske, *Abstracts*.

33. Rahner, "Remarks," 87. Rahner's own italics.

34. Ibid.

35. Ibid., 90.

36. Rahner, "Concept of Mystery," 69.

37. Rahner, "Remarks" 96 and 98; "Concept of Mystery," 70–71.

tory. The economic Trinity is "the Trinity of God's relationship to us,"[38] whereas the immanent Trinity is "the reality of God as he is *in* himself."[39] The economic Trinity is the Trinity "outside the intra-divine life,"[40] whereas the immanent Trinity is the Trinity within the intra-divine life. The economic Trinity is the life of the Trinity *ad extra*, whereas the immanent Trinity is "the life of the Trinity *ad intra*."[41] Thus the point of the Rahner's rule is to affirm the reciprocal identity between the economic Trinity and the immanent Trinity, between the Trinity manifested in salvation history and the Trinity apart from salvation history, between the Trinity outside the intra-divine life and the Trinity within the intra-divine life, and between the life of the Trinity *ad extra* and the life of the Trinity *ad intra*.

The Identity of the Economic Logos and the Immanent Logos

For Rahner, the economy of salvation, or salvation history predominantly refers to the incarnation of the Son and the decent of the Holy Spirit. Actually, Rahner admits that salvation history includes the revelation of the Old Testament as well as that of the New Testament.[42] Moreover, he acknowledges that salvation history has continuity between the revelation of the Old Testament and that of the New Testament.[43] Despite such continuity, however, they are qualitatively different from each other. For Rahner regards the revelation of the Old Testament merely as "the preparation for salvation," "the immediate historical prelude to the Incarnation of the divine Word,"[44] and "an authentic secret prehistory of the revelation of the Trinity."[45] Therefore it is noteworthy that,

38. Rahner, "Concept of Mystery," 69.

39. Ibid.

40. Rahner, *Trinity*, 23.

41. Rahner, "Divine Trinity," 1757.

42. With regard to the relation between salvation history and the world history, Rahner offers three theses: Firstly, salvation history takes place with the history of this world. Secondly, salvation history is distinct from profane history. And lastly, salvation history explains profane history. Rahner, "History of the World and Salvation-History," in *Theological Investigations*, V, 97–114.

43. Rahner, "Divine Trinity," 295.

44. Rahner, "History of the World," 108–9.

45. Rahner, *Trinity*, 42.

whenever Rahner talks about the economic Trinity with regards to his basic axiom, Rahner predominately, though not exclusively, refers to the incarnation of the Son and the decent of the Holy Spirit. In this way, Rahner's discussion on the economic-immanent Trinity relation comes to be, focally but narrowly, concerned with the incarnation of the *Logos* and the decent of the Spirit.

What then, does Rahner mean by the terms "the immanent Trinity" and "the economic Trinity" respectively with respect to his basic axiom? Regarding the incarnation of the Son, Rahner states that Jesus Christ as the incarnated *Logos* is the second divine person, the Son of the Father and the *Logos* of God.[46] "The *Logos* with us" is "the *Logos* with God." "The economic *Logos*" is "the immanent *Logos*."[47] These expressions have an implication that the economic Trinity is related to the economic *Logos* and the *Logos* with us, whereas the immanent Trinity is concerned with the immanent *Logos* and the *Logos* with God. Therefore Rahner's rule of identity specifically means that the economic *Logos* is the immanent *Logos* and the immanent *Logos* is the economic *Logos*. With his basic axiom, Rahner purports to assert that the economic *Logos* and the immanent *Logos* are "the same."[48]

As Rahner explains, the point that the economic *Logos* is the same as the immanent *Logos* means that "the one and the same *Logos* is *himself* in the human reality." And he adds that it is not the sameness of lifeless identity in which both the *Logos* and the human reality are so mingled that nothing can be distinguished. Neither is it just an addition of one to the other, nor merely a juxtaposition of the two. On the contrary, it is the dynamic identity where both are neither confused nor separated, and it is the direct and immediate identity within the Trinity and without the Trinity. And the difference between the two is an inner modality of the unity.[49]

In this way, Rahner's rule of identity comes down to his understanding of a hypostatic union between the *Logos* and the human nature. Notably, Rahner addresses acrid remarks against three lines of understanding of a hypostatic union in the history of theology. The first

---

46. Ibid., 23.
47. Ibid., 33.
48. Ibid.
49. Ibid., and 33 n. 30; "Remarks," 94.

line of thought regards a hypostatic union as an instance of a general situation. In contrast, however, Rahner firmly maintains that a hypostatic union cannot be an example of a general situation, because there is only one hypostatic union of the *Logos*.[50] The second line of thought considers that every divine person might assume a hypostatic union. Being rigidly opposed to this line of thought, however, Rahner asserts that, if a hypostatic union might take place in every divine person, then the incarnation of the *Logos* would reveal properly nothing about the *Logos*, that is, about the *Logos'* own relative specific features within the Trinity.[51] Lastly, the third line of thought understands the human nature assumed by the *Logos* only as something which rests in its separate essence, namely, something as having nothing to do with the *Logos*. On the contrary, Rahner insists that the human nature of the *Logos* is not a mask assumed from without but "the constitutive real symbol" of the *Logos*.[52]

With regard to the last point, Rahner's concept of symbol has further implications on his understanding of the hypostatic union of the *Logos*. According to Rahner, symbol is the supreme and prime representation in which one reality renders another present.[53] The humanity of the *Logos* is the self-disclosure of the *Logos*.[54] In turn, the *Logos* is the symbol of God the Father. Conversely, God the Father is expressed through the immanent *Logos* which is, in turn, expressed through the economic *Logos* in humanity. God can utter Godself outwardly, because God expresses Godself inwardly. It means that, as the immanent *Logos* is the inner constitution of God the Father's image, likeness, reflection, representation and presence, so the economic *Logos* is the outer continuation of the immanent constitution.[55] Furthermore, the immanent self-utterance of God in divine eternal fullness is the condition of the

---

50. Rahner, *Trinity*, 24–28.

51. Ibid., 28–30.

52. Ibid., 31–33.

53. Rahner, "Theology of the Symbol," 225. In this essay, Rahner offers two basic principles of an ontology of symbolism as follows: Firstly, all beings are symbolic by their nature, because they necessarily express themselves in order to attain their own nature. Secondly, the symbol is the self-realization of a being in the other, which is constitutive of its essence.

54. Ibid., 239.

55. Ibid., 236–37.

self-utterance of God outside Godself.[56] The economic *Logos* not only expresses the immanent *Logos* as it is, but also the economic *Logos* is the very constitutive way in which the immanent *Logos* is expressed as it is.

What Rahner intends to advocate through his adamant objection to those three lines of thought can be summarized as follows: First, there is certainly only one hypostatic union of the *Logos*. Only the incarnation of the *Logos* can be considered as a dogmatically certain instance for an economic relation of the divine persons to the world. Second, the economic *Logos* reveals exactly what the immanent *Logos* is within the Trinity and thus what God is. Lastly, the human nature of the *Logos* is the very constitutive way of expressing the immanent *Logos*. In other words, the mission of the *Logos* to the world has the sameness with the procession of the immanent *Logos* within the Trinity. Considering these points, therefore, Rahner's rule of identity, which says that the economic *Logos* is the immanent *Logos* and *vice versa*, firmly avers that the economic *Logos* expresses exactly what the immanent *Logos* is within the inner life of the Trinity, that the hypostatic union of the economic *Logos* is the very constitutive way of expressing the immanent *Logos*, and that mission has the sameness with procession.

In brief, there is certainly only one hypostatic union. Only the *Logos*, who is the Son of the Father within the Trinity, assumes a hypostatic union. And it is inwardly grounded in the proper character which the Son has in relation to the Father and the Holy Spirit within the Trinity. As the Son is by nature the *Logos* and symbol of the Father, the Son could express the Father to the world through the hypostatic union. As the Son is begotten from the Father as image and likeness, the Son could represent the Father properly through the incarnation. The mission of the Son is innerly based on the procession of the Son from the Father.

Grace: God's Self-Communication

Rahner's way of understanding of the incarnation of the Son runs parallel to his way of understanding of the descent of the Holy Spirit. As the economic *Logos* is the immanent *Logos*, the Holy Spirit which we experience in the salvific history is the Holy Spirit within the Trinity.

---

56. Rahner, "Theology of the Incarnation," 115.

As the hypostatic union is innerly grounded in the proper character which the Son has in relation to the Father, the descent of the Holy Spirit is also intrinsically grounded in the proper character which the Spirit has in relation to the Father and the Son. As the Son is begotten from the Father as the image and likeness of the Father and thus the Son represents the Father through the hypostatic union, so the Holy Spirit proceeds from the Father and the Son as the love between the Father and the Son and thus the Holy Spirit communicates God's grace to humans.

Likewise, this way of understanding of the incarnation of the Son and of the descent of the Spirit essentially runs parallel with his way of understanding of the Father. Following the Bible and the Greek Fathers, Rahner regards God [ὁ θεός] as the one unoriginate Father. As the Father is the unoriginate one, from whom the Son is begotten, and from whom the Spirit proceeds from the Son as well, so the Father is the one who reveals and communicates Godself through the Son and in the Holy Spirit. God, whom we experience in the economy of salvation through the Son and in the Holy Spirit, is the unoriginated God the Father who begot the Son and let the Spirit proceed.

Based on this way of understanding of the Father, the Son, and the Holy Spirit, Rahner leads to the doctrine of grace, that is, the grace of God's threefold self-communication. In this threefold self-communication, each of the three divine persons works in and through each one's own relations to the other persons. In other words, the unoriginated Father imparts Godself in two different modes, namely, the Son and the Holy Spirit. Rahner succinctly expounds God's threefold self-communication as follows:

> The Father gives himself to us too as Father, that is, precisely because and insofar as he himself, being essentially with *himself*, utters himself and *in this way* communicates the Son as his own, personal self-manifestation; and because and insofar as the Father and the Son (receiving from the Father), welcoming each other in love, drawn and returning to each other, communicate themselves *in this way*, as received in mutual love, that is, as Holy Spirit.[57]

---

57. Rahner, *Trinity*, 35. Rahner's own emphasis.

God's threefold self-communication takes place according to the proper nature of each of the three divine persons. Firstly, as the Father is the unoriginate one in relation to the Son and the Spirit, the Father imparts Godself to the world as the permanently sovereign God the Father. Secondly, as the Son is begotten from the Father, the Son manifests Godself to the world in the incarnation of the *Logos*. Lastly, as the Spirit proceeds from the Father and the Son as the love between both, the Spirit comes to humans' transcendental heart in the descent of the Holy Spirit.[58] Through the divine threefold self-communication, God relates to the world in the three relative ways in which God subsists.

More importantly, what is communicated in such divine self-communication is precisely what God is in Godself. God's threefold relationship to the world is not merely "a copy or an analogy of the inner Trinity," but exactly the Triune personal God, because the divine self-communication occurs exactly according to the intra-divine manner of the two communications of the divine essence by the Father to the Son and the Spirit. Precisely only in that way, God can communicate Godself. Therefore the point of Rahner's rule is summarized by Rahner himself as follows: "God has given himself so fully in his absolute self-communication to the creature, that the 'immanent' Trinity becomes the Trinity of the 'economy of salvation,' and hence in turn the Trinity of salvation which we experience *is* the immanent Trinity. This means that the Trinity of God's relationship to us *is* the reality of God as he is *in himself*: a Trinity of persons."[59]

To sum up, Rahner's notion of identity between the economic Trinity and the immanent Trinity predominantly means that the economic *Logos* is the immanent *Logos* and *vice versa*, and that the Holy Spirit that we experience in salvific history is the Holy Spirit within the Trinity. Moreover, Rahner's notion of identity fundamentally means that the hypostatic union of the economic *Logos* in the incarnation is the very constitutive way of expressing the immanent *Logos*, and that the descent of the Holy Spirit is the very constitutive way of expressing the Holy Spirit which eternally proceeds from the Father and the Son. Furthermore, all these together mean that, through the incarnation of the Son and the decent of the Holy Spirit, God the Father communi-

---

58. Rahner, "Oneness and Threefoldness," 115.

59. Rahner, "Concept of Mystery," 69. Rahner's own emphasis.

, with an implication that God's relationship with us is the
God as God is in Godself.[60]

Pannenberg, and Jenson: Eschatological

Unity

Despite a difference in their theological method, Jürgen Moltmann, Wolfhart Pannenberg, and Robert W. Jenson converge when it comes to the *eschatological* unity of the immanent and the economic Trinity. First, Moltmann states that the economic Trinity completes and perfects itself to the immanent Trinity eschatologically. Second, Pannenberg maintains that God's activity comes to completion at *eschaton*, and thus the unity of the economic and the immanent Trinity takes places eschatologically. And lastly, Jenson holds that the identity of the economic Trinity and the immanent Trinity is eschatological in the sense that the immanent Trinity is the eschatological reality of the economic Trinity.

Moltmann: Doxological and Eschatological Unity

For Moltmann, the economic Trinity designates the Trinity in the economy of salvation, in which the Triune God is revealed. Thus the economic Trinity is also called "the revelatory Trinity." On the other hand, the immanent Trinity is named for the Trinity as God is in Godself. Thus the immanent Trinity is also called "the substantial Trinity." The economic Trinity refers to God for us, whereas the immanent Trinity denotes God in Godself.[61] While he maintains that the distinction does

---

60. As mentioned at page 17 of this book, Sanders holds that interpreters of Rahner's rule are divided into two groups, the radicalizers who argue for a strong identity and the restricters who contend that Rahner goes too far and thus call for a restriction of Rahner's rule. Sanders, "The Image of the Immanent Trinity," 108–98.

Rahner himself is concerned that his position of identity may jeopardize divine freedom. Thus he tries to keep the balance in his own way: "God's presence by the Word in the Spirit must be different from himself, the eternal mystery: and yet it cannot be other than himself, something that would stand before him and veil him" (Rahner, "Remarks," 100), and "The identity does not of course mean that one denies that the 'economic' Trinity, one with the immanent Trinity, only exists by virtue of the free decree of God to communicate himself (supernaturally). But by virtue of this free decree, the gift in which God imparts himself to the world is precisely God as the triune God, and not something produced by him through efficient causality, something that represents him," (Rahner, *Sacramentum Mundi*, 1758).

61. Moltmann, *Trinity and the Kingdom*, 151.

not mean two different Trinities, Moltmann provides two theological reasons for the distinction and continuity between the economic Trinity and the immanent Trinity.

The first reason is that the distinction and continuity secure authentic freedom and grace for divine love. On the one hand, if the Triune God is love, but is compelled to love by any outward or inward necessity, then divine love would not be free and gratuitous. The Triune God freely and gratuitously loves the world, because the love for the world is the very same love that the Triune God is in Godself. On the other hand, if the Triune God is love, but this love suffices for Godself alone and does not communicate grace and salvation, then the love for the world would be arbitrary. The love of the Triune God is the love which essentially communicates grace to the world.[62]

The second reason for the distinction and continuity is more important, because it clearly shows some of remarkable characteristics of Moltmann's unique understanding of the immanent Trinity and also of the economic Trinity, which are ultimately based on his theological method. Moltmann states as follows: "The other and specific starting point for distinguishing between the economic and the immanent Trinity is to be found in *doxology*. The assertions of the immanent Trinity about eternal life and the eternal relationships of the triune God in himself have their *Sitz im Leben*, their situation in life, in the praise and worship of the church: Glory be to the Father and to the Son and to the Holy Ghost!"[63] Here we can notice that, for Moltmann, the immanent Trinity refers to the eternal inner relationships within the Triune God. But what is unique in him is that he claims that our assertions of the immanent Trinity are doxological. For him, doxology is a responsive expression in thanks, praise, and adoration, to our experience of salvation. He continues to maintain that, in such a doxological expression, we participate in what we perceive, and we participate in the fullness

---

62. In his book on Christian Eschatology, while criticizing the thesis of God's self-glorification, in which there is no divine eschatology, Moltmann argues that only a Trinitarian understanding of God maintains both selfless love and divine completion without contradiction. That is, "the three divine Persons love one another mutually in complete, selfless love. By virtue of their love the Father is wholly in the Son, the Son is wholly in the Father, and the Spirit is wholly in the Father and the Son. Through their mutual self-giving, they together form the perfect and complete divine life which through self-giving communicates itself." Moltmann, *Coming of God*, 326.

63. Moltmann, *Trinity and the Kingdom*, 152. Author's own italics.

of the divine life. Such a doxological understanding implies that, in our doxological response to the experience of salvation in the economic Trinity, we fully participate in the immanent Trinity.[64]

From the economic-immanent distinction in doxology it follows that, for Moltmann, the economic Trinity is essentially concerned with our experience of salvation, and the immanent Trinity is related to something that arises from our experience of salvation in the economic Trinity. This point is well shown in his understanding of *theologia* and *oikonomia*. While reminding us that the early church regards the doxological knowledge of God as *theologia* and the doctrine of salvation as *oikonomia*, Moltmann himself considers the immanent Trinity as the content of doxology, and the economic Trinity as the object of kerygmatic and practical theology.[65]

Such a doxological understanding of the economic Trinity and the immanent Trinity is principally based on his theological method. Moltmann always starts with experience of salvation, which is fully disclosed in the event of the cross of Jesus Christ.[66] This is the same of his doctrine of the Trinity. Paraphrasing Kant, Moltmann states as follows: "The place of the doctrine of the Trinity is not the 'thinking of thought,' but *the cross of Jesus*. 'Concepts without perception are empty' (Kant). The perception of the trinitarian conception of God is *the cross of Jesus*. 'Perceptions without concepts are blind' (Kant). The theological concept for the perception of the crucified Christ is *the doctrine of the Trinity*."[67] Such an inseparable relation between the cross of Jesus Christ and the doctrine of the Trinity leads Moltmann to consider the cross of Jesus Christ as the material principle of the doctrine of the Trinity, and the doctrine of the Trinity as the formal principal of knowledge of the cross.[68] In other words, the real cross of Christ is the content of the

---

64. Moltmann discusses Trinitarian doxology in more detail, and in relation to the Holy Spirit in his book, *Spirit of Life*, 301–6. Its original German text was published in 1991 with the title *Der Geist des Lebens: Eine ganzheitliche Pneumatologie*.

65. Moltmann, *Trinity and the Kingdom*, 152.

66. Moltmann himself confessed that the theology of cross has been the guiding light of his theological thought, which goes back through his 1964 book *Theology of Hope* even to the late 1948. Jürgen Moltmann, *Crucified God*, 1.

67. Moltmann, *Crucified God*, 240–41.

68. Ibid., 241; Moltmann, "Autobiographical Note," 213; Moltmann, *History and the Triune God*, 174. This book was translated from its German text *In der Geschichte des dreieinigen Gottes: Beiträge zur trinitarischen Theologie*, which was published in 1991.

doctrine of the Trinity, and the doctrine of the Trinity is the form of the crucified Christ.[69]

More specifically, Moltmann explains that the cross event on Golgotha is the story of three different subjects in a *perichoretic* unity: Father, Son, and Holy Spirit. The Father delivered up the Son on the cross for us through the Holy Spirit. What is most striking here is that Moltmann sees in this cross event both the economic Trinity and the immanent Trinity. The cross is the event of the economic Trinity, because it is for us that the Father delivered up the Son on the cross through the Holy Spirit. Simultaneously, the cross is the event of the immanent Trinity, for it is the event between God and God in the sense that God distinguished Godself from Godself. To put it differently, it is the event which has both a deep division in Godself and an authentic unity in Godself. It has a deep division, because the Father abandoned the Son on the cross in the Spirit. At the same time, it has an authentic unity, for the Father was at one with the Son through the Spirit.[70] In this way, for Moltmann, the cross of Jesus Christ is a Trinitarian event both for us and in Godself, namely, both the event of the economic Trinity and the event of immanent Trinity.

Moltmann's understanding of the cross event in terms of both the economic Trinity and the immanent Trinity has some significant implications on his discussion of the relation between the economic and the immanent Trinity. In the first place, Moltmann asserts that his own economic-immanent distinction itself is neither metaphysical nor speculative, but that it is very concrete and practical. For his own economic-immanent distinction is completely based on the concrete event of cross of Jesus Christ on the Golgotha for us.

In the second place, Moltmann maintains that the economic-immanent distinction itself is not imposed from outside, but originates from God, for God distinguished Godself from Godself on the cross event. In this regard, he criticizes the patristic tradition which grounds the economic-immanent distinction in the Platonic division between *eidos* (idea or form) and *phenomenon* (appearance). In Moltmann's judgment, such a traditional distinction wrongly imposes misconceptions on the economic-immanent distinction, such as a dichotomy

---

69. Moltmann, *Crucified God*, 246.

70. Ibid., 244–46.

between the world and God: evanescent and non-evanescent, temporal and eternal, passible and impassible, and dependent and independent.

In the third place, as a consequence of the previous points, Moltmann thinks that it is necessary to surrender the traditional distinction, insofar as the tradition sees the cross event as merely related to the economy of salvation alone but not to the immanent Trinity. In this aspect, Moltmann claims to affirm Rahner's rule of identity of the economic Trinity and the immanent Trinity, though he acknowledges that Rahner's rule is still vulnerable to the dissolution of the one in the other. Anyway, Moltmann's intent is to put a focus on the interaction between the economic Trinity and the immanent Trinity.

In the fourth place, Moltmann derives from the cross event a theological possibility of speaking about God "retrospectively."[71] By this he means that we can talk about God only from the perspective of the cross event. His retrospective way of God-talk is starkly contrasted to some traditional ways of God-talk which are dependent on metaphysical or moral presuppositions. According to Moltmann, his Trinitarian theology of the cross no longer interprets the event of the cross in the framework of a metaphysical or moral concept of God which has already been presupposed. Instead, Moltmann claims that his Trinitarian theology of the cross develops God-talk only from the history of cross. Only the story of Jesus Christ on the cross shows who God is and what God is.

In the fifth place, Moltmann goes markedly further in noting that, in the very event of cross, the economic Trinity has "a retroactive effect"[72] on the immanent Trinity. Moltmann's position insight of "a retroactive effect" is grounded in his way of interpreting the cross event as "an event concerned with a relationship between persons in which these persons constitute themselves in their relationship with each other."[73] He states this position as follows: "the surrender of the Son for us on the cross has a retroactive effect on the Father and causes infinite pain. On the cross God *creates* salvation outwardly for his whole creation and at the same time *suffers* this disaster of the whole world inwardly in himself. From the foundation of the world, the *opera trinitatis ad extra* corre-

---

71. Ibid., 247.

72. Moltmann, *Trinity and the Kingdom*, 160.

73. Moltmann, *Crucified God*, 247.

spond to the *passions trinitatis ad intra*."[74] The event of cross constitutes the inner relationship among the Father, the Son, and the Holy Spirit. In this sense, the economic Trinity executes a retroactive effect on the immanent Trinity. To put it differently, the economic Trinity is determinative of the immanent Trinity, for he adds that the pain of the cross determines the inner life of the Triune God from eternity to eternity.[75]

In the last place, most of all, Moltmann discovers an eschatological dimension in the event of cross. According to him, the cross event between the Father who abandoned and the Son who was forsaken is essentially an eschatological event, namely an event among the Father, the Son, and the Holy Spirit, for the Holy Spirit is the love between the Father and the Son and also the love which creates life and salvation. In this way, the cross event contains within itself all human history of guilt and death, takes it up into the history of God, or the history of the Trinity, and integrates it into the future of the history of the Trinity.[76] As the pain of the cross determines the inner life of the Triune God, so our doxological response through the Spirit determines the inner life of the Triune God. As the cross of the Son has a retroactive effect on the inner relations among the Triune God, so our doxological expression through the Spirit constitutes the inner life of the Triune God. On this point, Moltmann states that Christian doxology always ends with an eschatological prospect in which we will praise and adore the Triune God for ever and ever.

So far we have explored Moltmann's doxological understanding of the distinction between the economic Trinity and the immanent Trinity, together with his theological method, which always starts from the event of cross of Jesus Christ. In so doing, we have discovered some creative and even provocative insights: a non-metaphysical, or specifically non-Platonic understanding of an economic-immanent distinction; an inseparable relation between the cross of Jesus Christ and the doctrine of the Trinity; a retrospective way of God-talk in terms of the cross event; a retroactive effect of the economic Trinity on the immanent Trinity; and an eschatological dimension. With these points, Moltmann claims to overcome the traditional dichotomy between the immanent

74. Moltmann, *Trinity and the Kingdom*, 160. Moltmann's own italics.

75. Ibid., 161.

76. Moltmann, *Crucified God*, 246.

Trinity and the economic Trinity, which unduly interprets the cross event "statically as a reciprocal relationship between two qualitatively different natures, the divine nature which is incapable of suffering and the human nature which is capable of suffering."[77]

Regarding his own eschatological understanding of relation between the economic Trinity and the immanent Trinity, Moltmann says: "If it is the quintessence of doxology, then the doctrine of the immanent Trinity is part of eschatology as well. *The economic Trinity* completes and perfects itself to *the immanent Trinity* when the history and experience of salvation are completed and perfected, and also that *the economic Trinity* is raised into and transcended in *the immanent Trinity*."[78] For Moltmann, the economic Trinity is the immanent Trinity eschatologically, and the immanent Trinity is the economic Trinity doxologically.

Pannenberg: Futurist and Eschatological Unity

For Panenberg, the economic Trinity mainly refers to the Trinity of salvation history, or the Trinity of the economy of salvation. It is mostly concerned with "the economy of God's relations with the world."[79] As Pannenberg alludes, it roughly corresponds to something which the phrases "the Trinity of revelation" or "the revelational Trinity"[80] intend to express. On the other hand, the immanent Trinity primarily refers to "the immanent relations in God,"[81] "the intratrinitarian life of God,"[82] and "the immanence of the divine life."[83] Pannenberg suggests that it approximates some other terms in the history of theology such as "the eternal Trinity" or "the essential Trinity."[84] In this way Pannenberg makes a distinction between the economic Trinity and the immanent Trinity. The former is concerned with God's relations with us in the economy of salvation, while the latter is related to the intra-Trinitarian relations within God.

---

77. Ibid., 245.
78. Moltmann, *The Trinity and the Kingdom*, 161.
79. Pannenberg, *Systematic Theology*, 1:5:327 and 331.
80. Ibid., I, 5, 291 and 300.
81. Ibid., I, 5, 294.
82. Ibid., I, 5, 313.
83. Ibid., I, 15, 646.
84. Ibid., I, 5, 291 and 313.

With respect to the relation between the economic and the immanent Trinity, Pannenberg explicates Rahner's rule of identity both positively and critically. In so doing, Pannenberg reveals his own position regarding the economic-immanent Trinity relation. Though Pannenberg evaluates Rahner's rule of identity positively, he also imposes his own interpretation: "This thesis [Rahner's rule] means that the doctrine of the Trinity does not merely begin with *the revelation of God in Jesus Christ* and then work back to *a trinity in the eternal essence*, but that it must constantly link *the trinity in the eternal essence of God* to *his historical revelation*, since revelation cannot be viewed as extraneous to his deity.[85] In Pannenberg's view, Rahner's rule rightly holds fast to a constant link between the revelation of God in Jesus Christ and the eternal essence of God, or between revelation and deity.

However, Pannenberg addresses some critical remarks on Rahner's rule. In the first place, Rahner's rule is narrowly restricted to the instance of the incarnation of the *Logos*. Though he acknowledges with Rahner that the hypostatic union of the divine *Logos* and the human Jesus is unique, Pannenberg suggests that we should extend Rahner's rule and consider it within a wider context of the whole economy of the Triune God in the world.[86] Notably, for Pannenberg, the economy of salvation is not merely the incarnation of the Son and the descent of the Holy Spirit. But it is also extensively concerned with God's relations with the world through the whole works of God's economy.

In the second place, Pannenberg is sympathetic with Walter Kasper's concern that Rahner's rule may be taken to mean that the immanent Trinity is dissolved into the economic Trinity.[87] However, their solutions are quite different from each other. Kasper appeals to the apophatic character of the immanent Trinity, by which he means that the immanent Trinity eludes all language and thought, and thus it is ever a "*mysterium stricte dictum*" in the economic Trinity. Besides, Kasper asserts that it is not possible to deduce the immanent Trinity by a kind of extrapolation from the economic Trinity.[88] Unlike Kasper, Pannenberg,

---

85. Ibid., I, 5, 328.

86. Ibid., I, 1, 328.

87. Ibid., I, 5, 331; Walter Kasper meticulously discusses Rahner's rule of identity: Kasper, *God of Jesus*, 275–76.

88. Kasper, *God of Jesus Christ*, 276. Here Kasper paraphrases Rahner's rule as follows: "[I]n the economic self-communication the intra-trinitarian self-communication

while maintaining persistently a distinction between the immanent Trinity and the economic Trinity, comes to focus on the point that the immanent Trinity cannot be seen in detachment from the economic Trinity.

In the last place, Pannenberg criticizes Rahner and even Kasper in that they presuppose some knowledge of the immanent Trinity from the outset. Pannenberg points out that Rahner himself already presupposes something about the eternal essence of God apart from God's revelation in Jesus Christ: "Rahner did not yet draw the consequence that *the eternal self-identity of God* could not be conceived independently of *the salvation-historical workings of the Son and of the Spirit*; to the contrary, in his view, such independence of *God's eternal self-identity* remained a firm presupposition."[89] In this regard, Pannenberg goes further to point out that Rahner does not provide any conceptual framework for a constant link between the eternal self-identity of God and the revelation of God in Jesus Christ.[90] *or the flow of history.*

Pannenberg's remarks on Rahner's rule, whether positive or critical, can be best understood in terms of his theological method.[91] Notably, Pannenberg in *Systematic Theology* starts with a notion of theology as the quest for the truth of God. Then he asserts that our knowledge of the truth of God is made possible by God and therefore by revelation.[92] Such dependence of our knowledge of God on divine revelation is constitutive for his concept of theology.[93] Pannenberg agrees with Barth that God can be known only as God gives Godself to be known. However, unlike Barth, Pannenberg puts more weight on the indirect character of revelation. According to Thesis I in his 1961 book *Revelation as History*, the self-revelation of God in the biblical witnesses is not of a direct type in the sense of theophany. Rather, it is indirect, for it is brought about

---

is present in the world in a new way, namely, under the veil of historical words, signs and actions, and ultimately in the figure of the man Jesus of Nazareth." In this way, Kasper claims to do justice to the immanent Trinity as well as the kenotic, free, gratuitous character of the economic Trinity.

89. Pannenberg, "Problems of a Trinitarian Doctrine," 251.

90. Ibid., 251.

91. Stanley J. Grenz provides his own compact summary of this whole book, with an overview of each theme and its issues in order. Grenz, *Reason for Hope*.

92. Pannenberg, *Systematic Theology*, I, 1, 2.

93. Ibid., I, 1, 4.

by means of the historical acts of God.[94] As a consequence, Pannenberg rejects any kind of static notion of revelation.

This view of the indirect character of revelation determines some features of Pannenberg's theology. They are seminally expressed in Thesis II in *Revelation as History*, which states that revelation is not comprehended completely in the beginning, but at the end of the revelation history. Thus God's final revelation at the end of history will bring final knowledge of the content and truth of God.[95] On this point, Pannenberg claims that theological statements about God are essentially historical, provisionally hypothetical, and ultimately eschatological.

For Pannenberg, all these features converge on his understanding of the deity of God as rule and lordship, a view which has come to be called "Pannenberg's Principle."[96] The deity of God is revealed, only when God's lordship over the world is visible, that is, when the kingdom of God comes. By implication, God would not be the God of the world, if God does not prove Godself to be its Lord.[97] In this aspect, Pannenberg's Principle radically means that God's deity or essence is dependent on creation in history. In addition, as God is God only in the execution of God's lordship, Pannenberg mentions that the full accomplishment of it is determined as something future, and that, in this sense, God is "futurity as a quality of being [*Seinsbeschaffenheit*]."[98] Furthermore, as God is the power of the future, God always eludes all speech and concept about God.[99]

94. Pannenberg, *Revelation as History*, 125. This book was originally published in 1961 by the so-called "Heidelberg Circle" or "Pannenberg Circle" in which Pannenberg played a central role.

95. Pannenberg, *Systematic Theology*, I, 1, 16.

96. It is Roger E. Olson who first coined the term "Pannenberg's Principle." Olson, "Wolfhart Pannenberg's Doctrine," 199. This point is confirmed by Grenz, *Rediscovering*, 96; Pannenberg's Principle is found in as early as 1967. Wolfhart Pannenberg, "Theology and the Kingdom of God," 6–7. This article is included in *Theology and the Kingdom of God*, ed. Richard John Neuhaus, 51–71.

97. Pannenberg, "God of Hope," II, 242. The book is a translation of Pannenberg's 1967 book, *Grundfragen systematischer Theologie: Gesammelte Aufsätze*, which consists of several lectures and essays in 1959–1965.

98. Pannenberg, "God of Hope," II, 240.

99. Ibid., II, 242.

Following out the implications of this theological method, Pannenberg explicates and develops the doctrine of the Trinity,[100] especially in terms of his understanding of Jesus Christ as the historical self-revelation of God, and whom he regards as "the quintessence of the divine plan for creation and history and of its end-time but already proleptic revelation."[101] It is notable that, for Pannenberg, the story of Jesus Christ as the Son in the mutual self-differentiation from the Father on the one side and from the Holy Spirit on the other side is the "basis" or "starting point" for the doctrine of the Trinity.[102] In other words, the reciprocal self-distinctions of God are, for him, constitutive of the divinity of the Trinitarian persons.[103]

With respect to the reciprocal relation between the Father and the Son, Pannenberg says:

> Precisely by distinguishing himself from the Father, by subjecting himself to his will as his creature, by thus giving place to the Father's claim to deity as he asked others to do in his proclamation of the divine lordship, he [Jesus] showed himself to be the Son of God and one with the Father who sent him (John 10:30). ... As the one who corresponds to the fatherhood of God, Jesus is the Son, and because the eternal God is revealed herein as Father, and is Father everywhere only as he is so in relation to the Son, the Son shares his deity as the eternal counterpart of the Father.[104]

Pannenberg maintains that the self-distinction of Jesus from the Father is not only constitutive of his fellowship with the eternal God, but also of the eternal Son in his relation to the Father. On the Father's part, God as the Father is manifest only in the relation of Jesus to him and thus in the eternal encounter with Jesus as the Son. Here is a genuine mutuality of dependence between the Father and the Son, which is clearly seen

100. For a summary of Pannenberg's doctrine of the Trinity, refers to Olson's article, "Pannenberg's Doctrine of the Trinity."

101. Pannenberg, *Systematic Theology*, I, 4, 257. Here Pannenberg regards the doctrine of the Trinity as the explication of the implication of the self-revelation of God in Jesus Christ as the Word of God.

102. Pannenberg, *Systematic Theology*, I, 5, 272–73.

103. Pannenberg, "God of History," 36. Its original German text is "Der Gott der Geschichte: Der trinitarische Gott und die Wahrheit der Geschichte," *Kerygma and Dogma*, 23, 76–92.

104. Pannenberg, *Systematic Theology*, I, 5, 310.

as well "in the handing over of lordship from the Father to the Son and its handing back from the Son to the Father."[105] Likewise, genuine mutual dependence is true among the Father, the Son, and the Holy Spirit, for the Holy Spirit is always involved in God's presence in the work of Jesus and in the fellowship of the Son with the Father. Thus there comes first the mutual relationship of dependence on one another among the Father, the Son, and the Holy Spirit, on the ground of which Pannenberg rejects the *Filioque*, which seems to him to imply a subordination of the Spirit to the Father and the Son.[106]

In applying the notion of the mutual self-differentiation to the economic-immanent Trinity relation, Pannenberg asserts that the reciprocal self-differentiation of the three persons is foundational for the unity of the immanent and the economic Trinity.[107] The deity of the Father is dependent on the historical work of the Son and the eschatological work of the Spirit. Thus God's activity comes to completion only at *eschaton*. In other words, God's lordship, or God's rule over the creation is consummated only at *eschaton*. In this sense, Pannenberg articulates that the unity of the economic Trinity and the immanent Trinity takes place eschatologically.

In addition, according to Pannenberg, *eschaton* means both the end of this history on the one hand, and the completion or fulfillment of this history on the other. Thus the kingdom of God does not take place just at the end of history, but it influences and even constitutes the present. The kingdom of God is the entering of eternity into time.[108] In this aspect, Pannenberg's eschatology holds an intimate relationship between the present and the future, and further between time and eternity: the present is to be seen as a form of manifestation and a process of becoming, and the future does not meet the present reality as a totally different reality.[109] This point is affirmed by Ted Peters who explains that, for Pannenberg, eternity is not simply a timeless realm that gener-

---

105. Pannenberg, *Systematic Theology*, I, 5, 313.

106. Ibid., I, 5, 317.

107. Pannenberg, "Problems," 252.

108. Pannenberg, *Systematic*, III, 15, 595.

109. Ibid., III, 15, 605.

ates its own reality, but rather it takes the temporal creation up into itself at the point of eschatological transition.[110]

Furthermore, for Pannenberg, his discussion on the relation between the economic Trinity and the immanent Trinity is always involved with that on the relation between God and creation. Thus the eschatological unity between the economic and the immanent Trinity is inescapably connected to the core of God's love towards the world. Pannenberg concludes his *Systematic Theology* in the following impressive passage:

> On the whole path from the beginning of creation by way of reconciliation to the eschatological future of salvation, the march of the divine economy of salvation is an expression of the incursion of the eternal future of God to the salvation of creatures and thus a manifestation of the divine love. Here is the eternal basis of God's coming forth from *the immanence of the divine life* as *the economic Trinity* and of the incorporation of creatures, mediated thereby, into the unity of the trinitarian life. The distinction and unity of *the immanent Trinity* and *the economic Trinity* constitute the heartbeat of the divine love, and with a single such heartbeat this love encompasses the whole world of creatures.[111]

Jenson: Eschatological Unity in Temporal Narrative

In his 1969 article,[112] Jenson reveals some characteristics of his conception of the immanent and the economic Trinity and of their relation. Here he makes a distinction between God in Godself and God for us, but in his own creative way: "The doctrine of the trinity was born ... as insistence that in 'God himself' we will find no other temporality than *he lives for us in his 'economy,'* i.e., in his occurrence in time. God occurs for us. ... The doctrine of the trinity says that *as he occurs for us, so he is: he is in himself...*"[113] God in Godself is related to the immanent Trinity, while God for us in economy is linked to the economic Trinity. The immanent-economic Trinity distinction accords with the distinction

110. Peters, "Wolfhart Pannenberg," 373.

111. Pannenberg, *Systematic Theology*, III, 15, 646.

112. Jenson, "Futurist Option," 17–25. See also Braaten and Jenson, *Futurist Option.*

113. Jenson, "Futurist Option," 23–24.

between God in Godself and God for us. Despite such distinction, however, Jenson emphatically insists that there are not two separate levels of beings: the eternal Trinity and the temporal Trinity. Instead, as the passage cited above indicates, Jenson suggests that we should consider the immanent and the economic Trinity as "two ways of describing the *same* reality." For God in Godself is no other than God for us, and thus the immanent Trinity is no other than the economic Trinity. In order to clarify this point, Jenson coins his own terms: "the immanent doctrine of the Trinity" and "the economic doctrine of the Trinity."[114]

Then, in his 1982 book *The Triune Identity: God According to the Gospel*, Jenson claims to espouse two rules regarding the immanent-economic Trinity relation.[115] The first is Rahner's rule of identity which says that the economic Trinity is the immanent Trinity and *vice versa*. The second is the rule of divine freedom, by which he means that the immanent Trinity could have been the economic Trinity, even if there had been no creation.[116] Jenson takes the second rule as a legitimate theological reason for the economic-immanent Trinity distinction. Despite his affirmation of the two rules, however, Jenson recognizes a possibility of constant difficulty in reconciling them to each other. To overcome it, Jenson proposes his eschatological thesis in order that the two rules might be compatible with each other: "The two rules are compatible, I propose, only if the identity of the *'economic'* and *'immanent' Trinity is eschatological*, and only if *the immanent Trinity* is simply the eschatological reality of *the economic Trinity*."[117] According to the eschatological thesis, the immanent Trinity is the eschatological reality of the economic Trinity, or, in Pannenberg's interpretation, "the escha-

114. Jenson, "Futurist Option," 25.

115. Jenson, *Triune Identity*, 139–40. This book was first published by Fortress Press in 1982. This book is much influenced by Jenson's 1975 article, "Three Identities of One Action," 1. This article is further developed and incorporated into *The Triune Identity* in 1982 and also into "Second Locus: The Triune God" in Braaten and Jenson, eds. *Christian Dogmatics*, I, 79–191.

116. Jenson, *Triune Identity*, 139. In Jenson's own words: "God 'in himself' could have been the same God he is, and so triune, had there been no creation, or no saving of fallen creation, and so also not the trinitarian history there has in fact been."

Jenson's notion of divine freedom is already articulated in his 1969 article as follows: "God *could have been* otherwise the triune God than as Jesus, the Father of Jesus and the Future of Jesus. He could have been, but in fact he is not." Jenson, "Futurist Option," 25.

117. Jenson, *Triune Identity*, 140. Author's own italics.

tologically definitive form of the economic Trinity."[118] And the identity of the economic and the immanent Trinity takes place at *eschaton*.

Jenson's eschatological thesis can be best understood in terms of his theological method which has the identification of God as the chief theological task.[119] In Grenz's assessment, Jenson's theological method is characterized by "the narrative character of theology," "the radically temporal character of God's self-disclosure," and "the eschatological character of the story of God."[120] In the first place, drawing on George Ernest Wright[121] and Hans Frei,[122] Jenson argues that narrative is the encompassing genre of the Scripture. As the Scripture as a whole is the account of God's acts and deeds,[123] God is identified by the biblical narrative, and more specifically, through particular plotted sequence of events in it. According to Jenson, the Old Testament identifies God as the One who rescued Israel from Egypt, and the New Testament identifies God as the One who raised Jesus from the dead.[124] Both are the same God in that God is whoever raised Jesus from the dead, having before raised Israel from Egypt.[125] In addition, the New Testament identifies God as the Triune God, whose proper name is "Father, Son, and Holy Spirit." Jenson states that the phrase "Father, Son, and Holy Spirit" is a very compressed telling of the total narrative, by which the Scripture identifies God.[126]

In the second place, Jenson maintains that narrative is by nature temporal, because narrative uses "the tense-structure of ordinary language." The biblical narrative uses the temporality of God who rescued Israel from Egypt in the Old Testament and that of God who raised Jesus in the New Testament.[127] This temporal character exercises a considerable impact on his understanding of deity and eternity. Notably, Jenson makes an attempt to free Western theology from its captivity

118. Pannenberg, *Systematic Theology*, 1:5:330.

119. Jenson, "Three Identities," 1; Jenson, *Systematic Theology*, I, 42.

120. Grenz, "Divine Fugue," 211–16.

121. Wright, *God Who Acts*.

122. Frei, *Eclipse of Biblical Narrative*.

123. Jenson, *Systematic Theology*, I, 57.

124. Jenson, *Triune Identity*, 1–18; *Systematic Theology*, I, 44–45.

125. Jenson, *Systematic Theology*, I, 63.

126. Ibid., I, 46.

127. Jenson, *Triune Identity*, 21 and 34.

to Hellenistic interpretation of deity or eternity as timelessness. For example, Jenson rejects the concept of *Logos asarkos* which refers to an antecedent separate entity that always was in God and then became the one sent in flesh to us. According to Jenson, the concept of *Logos asarkos* led inexorably towards a separation between the generation of the Son as timeless and the incarnation of Jesus in time, or a separation between timeless procession and temporal mission. Thus Jenson suggests that we should interpret the deity of God not as timelessness but as a final outcome of narrative, and the eternity of God not as timelessness but as faithfulness.[128]

Likewise, regarding the economic-immanent Trinity distinction, Jenson points out that the Hellenistic interpretation of deity as timelessness also gives rise to a separation between the immanent Trinity and the economic Trinity, as if they are two distinct sets of Trinitarian relations.[129] Therefore Jenson makes an attempt to temporalize traditional Trinitarian terms. Jenson regards the so-called intra-divine words, such as begetting, being begotten and proceeding, to be simply the words, which are mainly used to summarize the plot of the biblical narrative. On this point, Jenson insists that there is no other ontologically separable Trinity apart from the economic Trinity of the biblical narrative.

In the last place, the narrative and temporal characters of Jenson's theological method converge on its eschatological character. As a story is constituted by the outcome of the narrated events, God is identified by the outcome of divine events. The self-identification of God takes places not in the beginning but in the end. In addition, as an opening future with sequence of events in narrative liberates each successive present stage from what has been told before, God is ever fresh at each moment of events. He explicates it as follows: "Since the Lord's self-identity is constituted in dramatic coherence, it is established not from the beginning but from the end, not at birth but at death, not in *persistence* but in *anticipation*. The biblical God is not eternally himself in that he persistently instantiates a beginning in which he already is all he ever will be; he is eternally himself in that he unrestrictedly anticipates an end in which he will be all he ever could be."[130] And then he continues to state

---

128. Ibid., 140.

129. Ibid., 125.

130. Jenson, *Systematic Theology*, I, 66. Jenson's own italics.

as follows: "Truly, the Trinity is simply the Father and the man Jesus and their Spirit as the Spirit of the believing community. This 'economic' Trinity is *eschatologically* God 'himself,' and 'immanent' Trinity. And that assertion is no problem, for God is himself only eschatologically, since he is Spirit."[131] The economic Trinity is eschatologically God in Godself and the immanent Trinity. Jenson insists that his eschatological thesis authentically understands the freedom of God, for it considers the genuine freedom of God as the reality of possibility which is openness to the future.[132]

---

131. Jenson, *Triune Identity*, 141. Jenson's own emphasis.

132. Ibid., 141.

4

Contemporary Discussions on the Immanent-Economic Trinity Relation II

Boff and Pittenger: The Immanent Trinity "Much More Than" the Economic Trinity

DESPITE A REMARKABLE DIFFERENCE IN THEIR THEOLOGICAL METHOD, Leonardo Boff and William Norman Pittenger are common in their position on the immanent-economic Trinity relation. Boff asserts that the economic Trinity is the immanent Trinity, *but not the whole of the immanent Trinity.* And Pittenger contends that the immanent Trinity is not confined to the Palestinian Trinity experienced by the early Christians. In this regard, they maintain with one voice that the immanent Trinity is much more than the economic Trinity, though they are different in their own standpoint.

Boff: Not the Whole of the Immanent Trinity

BOFF'S BASIC THESIS OF PERICHORESIS

In his 1986 book *A Trindade, a Sociedade e a Libertação,* the third edition of which was titled *A Trindade e a Sociedade* and was translated into *Trinity and Society* in 1988,[1] Leonardo Boff makes an attempt to understand the Trinity as the perfect communion of three divine per-

1. Boff, *Trinity and Society*; The Portuguese original edition, titled *A Trindade, a Sociedade e a Libertação,* was published in 1986. *Trinity and Society* was translated in 1988 from its Portuguese third edition which was published in 1987 with the title *A Trindade e a Sociedade.* The Portuguese book was abridged and published for laity with the title *Santíssima Trindade é a melhor comunidade* in 1988, which was also translated into English in 2000. Leonardo Boff, *Holy Trinity.*

sons, in order to provide the ideal model of society in the context of oppression and desire for liberation. His understanding of the Trinity is remarkably characterized by his emphasis on the *perichoresis* of the Father, the Son, and the Holy Spirit, which could be translated into circuminsession, circumincession, co-inherence, or interpenetration.[2] By the term *perichoresis* Boff means that the three divine persons dwell in one another and interpenetrate one another. From the outset in the book, Boff declares that the term *perichoresis* is central to his explication of the Trinity.[3] In addition, he formulates "the basic thesis,"[4] which can be named as "Boff's basic thesis" in this book, that complete *perichoresis* obtains between the three divine persons. Furthermore, he goes so far as to use the basic thesis as "the structuring principle"[5] of his whole investigation of the Trinity, especially with regard to the original experience of faith, the unity of the three divine persons, and the alternatives of the term "person."

In the first place, Boff begins with the original experience of faith, with which the first disciples of Jesus of Nazareth proclaimed the Father, the Son, and the Holy Spirit in their prayer and preaching. They confessed that God is the Father, the Son, and the Holy Spirit. Boff points out that the original confession of faith is neither monotheism which asserts the solitude of one divinity, nor polytheism which admits a plurality of divinities. On the contrary, Boff maintains that the original confession of faith perceived diversity in unity and simultaneously unity in diversity, and thus it gave rise to the classical formulation of the doctrine of the Trinity, as "one God in three Persons," "one nature and three hypostases," or "three Uniques and one communion" which is preferable for him.[6]

In the second place, Boff locates the unity of the Trinity in the communion among the three divine persons who are in complete *perichoretic* relationship. On this point, Boff neither follows the Greek Fathers nor the Latin Fathers. The former finds the unity in the person of the Father who is the unoriginate origin and source of the Son and the Holy

2. Boff, *Trinity and Society*, 123.

3. Ibid., 5.

4. Ibid., 142, 191.

5. Ibid., 5.

6. Ibid., 2–3.

Spirit. The latter identifies the unity in the divine essence which makes each of three persons divine. However, Boff is opposed to both, because he is concerned that the former risks introducing subordinationism and the latter risks indicating modalism. In order to avoid these kinds of risk, Boff adheres to the notion of *perichoresis*, through which the three divine persons attain to union and unity. In addition, in order to avoid another risk evoking tritheism, Boff extends the notion of the economic *perichoresis* into the eternal *perichoresis* and emphasizes that their communion has existed from all eternity and that the three divine persons have always been co-existent and co-eternal in communion.[7]

In the last place, Boff judges that alternative concepts of person proposed by Barth and Rahner are insufficient. Barth's "mode of being" and Rahner's "distinct mode of subsistence" have an advantage of maintaining the unity of three persons. Nevertheless, in Boff's judgment, both have their serious inherent limitation in considering seriously the diversity of three persons and in dealing effectively with their interrelationships. Thus Boff adheres to the traditional concept of person, but simultaneously intends to eliminate a risk of tritheism by placing *perichoresis* in the foreground. Thus Boff states: "Our starting point is always the divine Three in communion and eternal love among themselves."[8]

Boff's Use of the Immanent Trinity and the Economic Trinity

Overwhelmed by the complete *perichoresis* among the divine three persons, Boff provides his definition of the terms "the immanent Trinity" and "the economic Trinity" as follows: "By '*economic Trinity*' we mean *the manifestation* (the self-communication in the case of the Son and the Holy Spirit) *of the divine Three in human history*, whether together or separately, for the purposes of our salvation. By '*immanent Trinity*' we mean *Father, Son and Holy Spirit in their inner, eternal life, considered in itself.*"[9] According to the definition, the economic Trinity designates the Father, the Son, and the Holy Spirit in their manifestation in history, and the immanent Trinity refers to the Father, the Son, and the Holy

7. Ibid., 4–6.

8. Boff, *Holy Trinity*, 52.

9. Boff, *Trinity and Society*, 232–33.

Spirit in their inner life in eternity. The economic-immanent distinction accords with a distinction between history and eternity, and with a distinction between the outward life of the Trinity and the inner life of the Trinity. Notably, whether in the economic Trinity or in the immanent Trinity, Boff draws our attention to the co-existence of the Father, the Son and the Holy Spirit.

With regard to the economic Trinity, though some divine works are appropriated to one person, the three divine persons fundamentally work together. For example, though creation is attributed to the Father, nonetheless the Father creates though the Son in the inspiration of the Holy Spirit. Though incarnation is appropriated to the Son, nonetheless the Son is sent by the Father and becomes flesh by virtue of the life-giving Holy Spirit. And though sanctification is appropriated to the Holy Spirit, nonetheless the Holy Spirit is sent and comes upon Mary by the Father at the request of the Son. The Father, the Son, and the Holy Spirit exist together and work together in any divine works in history.

In addition, with regard to the immanent Trinity, as Boff describes it, the Father begets the Son in the bosom of the Holy Spirit. The Father and the Son breathe out the Holy Spirit. The Son loves the Father in the Holy Spirit. And the Holy Spirit reveals the Father through the Son. Notably, by this description, Boff means not only that three divine persons have a close inner relationship with one another, but also that each person actively participates in the origin of the other persons. For Boff, "in" and "through" does not mean any secondary role in the origin of a person. On the contrary, Boff intends that every person actively participates in it with a primary role. Thus he affirms not only the *Filioque* but also the *Spirituque* and the *Patreque*. The *Filioque* literally means that the Holy Spirit is breathed out by the Father and by the Son, and it implies that the Son participates in the origin of the Holy Spirit together with the Father. By the *Spirituque*,[10] the literal meaning of which is "and by the Holy Spirit," Boff means that the Holy Spirit participates in the begetting of the Son together with the Father, and in the recognition of the Father together with the Son. And likewise, by the *Patreque*,[11] the literal meaning of which is "and by the Father," Boff implies that the Father participates in the origin of the Holy Spirit together with the Son

10. Ibid., 204.
11. Ibid., 241.

and in the love of the Son together with the Holy Spirit. In this sense, Boff proposes "a trinitarian equilibrium"[12] in the relationship among the three divine persons, because they are co-eternal in existence and even simultaneous in origin.

As has been mentioned, for Boff, the economic Trinity refers to three divine persons in their manifestations in history, such as creation, incarnation and sanctification. And the immanent Trinity denotes the three divine persons in their inner relationships in eternity, such as *Filioque*, *Spirituque*, and *Patreque*. By using traditional terms mission and procession, Boff regards the manifestations in history as mission, and the inner relationships as procession. Thus the economic Trinity refers to the mission of the three divine persons, and the immanent Trinity denotes the procession of the three divine persons. It is here noteworthy that Boff's notions of mission and procession are also much affected by his basic thesis of complete *perichoresis*. Unlike the traditional position which affirms only the mission of the Son and that of the Spirit, Boff admits the mission of the Father as well, because the Father appears and is manifested in creation.[13] Likewise, unlike the traditional position which affirms only the processions of the Son and of the Holy Spirit, Boff applies procession to the Father, too. But he uses procession not in a causal sense, but in an equal sense. He states his position as follows:

> . . . "procession" of Persons: the Father *without origin*, the Son *begotten* and the Breath (Spirit) *breathed out*. These expressions, seemingly naturally, allow the principle of causality (on the Father's part) and of causal dependence (on the part of the Son and the Holy Spirit) to enter into trinitarian thought. It is difficult to combine this language with the other sort also employed by the Councils, in which none in the Trinity is earlier or later, greater or lesser, superior or inferior . . . ; in which the divine Three are rather co-eternal . . . and equally immense and omnipotent. We need therefore to use expressions suggestive of "procession" with great care, conscious all the time that they are descriptive terms aimed at expressing the interrelationship of the Persons and also at safeguarding the differences between

12. Ibid., 6.
13. Ibid., 174.

them. Following tradition and the magisterium, I shall use them here, but always with this basic reservation.[14]

TWO DIMENSIONS: ECONOMIC AND IMMANENT

As has been mentioned above, Boff considers the economic Trinity as the manifestation of three divine persons in history and the immanent Trinity as the inner relationships of three divine persons in eternity. In this regard, Boff considers the economic Trinity and the immanent Trinity as two dimensions, levels, or aspects of the three divine persons.

Each of the three divine persons has both an economic dimension and an immanent dimension, or both an economic aspect and an immanent aspect. Firstly, with regard to God the Father, the Father is revealed in the history of salvation by the incarnate Son in the economic dimension. The Father is in his inner relationship with the Son and the Holy Spirit "in the bosom of the Trinity," on the immanent dimension.[15] Secondly, with regard to God the Son, the Son is shown and revealed by Jesus of Nazareth on the economic level. The Son is the only begotten Son of the Father "in the bosom of the Trinity," on the immanent level.[16] Lastly, with regard to God the Holy Spirit, the Holy Spirit is present in the history of salvation on the economic aspect. The Holy Spirit is eternally breathed out by both the Father and the Son "in the bosom of the Trinity," on the immanent aspect.[17]

THE RELATION BETWEEN THE ECONOMIC TRINITY AND THE IMMANENT TRINITY

Boff holds that, as two aspects or two dimensions of three divine persons, the economic Trinity and the immanent Trinity have a "close link"[18] to each other. The economic Trinity is the manifestation of three divine persons who are in their inner relationships of the immanent Trinity. And the immanent Trinity is the inner relationships of three divine persons who are manifested as the economic Trinity. In addition,

14. Ibid., 7. Boff's own italics.
15. Ibid., 164.
16. Ibid., 183.
17. Ibid., 191.
18. Ibid., 219.

according to Boff, the close link is further defined as the "correlation" between the economic Trinity and immanent Trinity.[19] The economic Trinity is correlated to the immanent Trinity, because the economic Trinity is the manifestation of the immanent Trinity. Conversely, the immanent Trinity is correlated to the economic Trinity, because the immanent Trinity serves as the interrelationships of the economic Trinity. Thus Boff states that there is always a correlation between intratrinitarian relationships, which refer to processions, and the historical-salvific missions.[20]

However, Boff's concepts of close link and correlation are very broad and loose, because those terms do not offer a way of connecting the economic Trinity and the immanent Trinity. In addition, they seem to support a unilateral direction of close link and correlation. They do so, insofar as the economic Trinity is regarded as the manifestation of the immanent Trinity. But this is what Boff does not want to affirm. Actually Boff claims to accept Rahner's rule of identity: "We can therefore formulate the basic axiom of trinitarian reflection: '*The economic Trinity* is *the immanent Trinity* and *the immanent Trinity* is *the economic Trinity*.'"[21] Then Boff formulates Rahner's rule in his own version as follows: ". . . the three Unique Beings in communion who reveal themselves in the economy of salvation are the immanent Tri-unity, and vice-versa."[22]

Boff's acceptance of Rahner's rule and his own alternative clearly show that he intends to affirm the identity of the economic Trinity and the immanent Trinity. However, despite his claims, Boff falls short of Rahner's own intention. At least, Boff's interpretation of Rahner's rule bears witness to the fact that Boff's position is slightly different from that of Rahner, for in Boff's interpretation, Rahner's rule means that the way God comes to meet human beings is the way in which God subsists.[23] For example, the way in which the Son could represent the Father properly through the hypostatic union is the way in which the Son is begotten from the Father as image and likeness. But Boff's notions

---

19. Ibid., 215.

20. Ibid., 207.

21. Ibid., 114. Boff's own emphasis.

22. Ibid., 214.

23. Ibid., 95.

of close link and correlation speak to the contrary, both by allowing a gap between the economic and the immanent Trinity, and by actually uttering only a one-sided direction of link and relation.

Thus, in order to avoid introducing a gap between the economic Trinity and the immanent Trinity, Boff uses another term, "correspondence," by which he means that there is the correspondence between the economic Trinity and the immanent Trinity. However, Boff faces the same problem with this term, too. A meticulous examination of his book *Trinity and Society* shows that Boff seems to affirm only one-sided correspondence, that is, the correspondence of the economic Trinity to the immanent Trinity, but not the other way around. Here is how he puts it:

> The Trinity reveals itself to us as it is, as Trinity, and saves us by what it is in itself. This means that what we see of its saving manifestation in history—the Father revealed as the mystery of the world, the Son being incarnate and the Holy Spirit poured out into our hearts and coming down on Mary—corresponds to what the triune God actually is. . . . Here indeed the self-communication of the Son and the Holy Spirit means the presence of the eternal in time, of the divine Person as "person" in human reality. What happens on earth corresponds exactly to what exists in heaven.[24]

The unilateral correspondence of the economic Trinity to the immanent Trinity is not tantamount to the identity of both.

In order to solve this conundrum, Boff finally resorts to making a differentiation between the manifestations of the Son in the incarnation and the Holy Spirit in the coming upon Mary on the one hand, and the other manifestations of three divine persons on the other. For the former case, Boff, drawing on Rahner, calls these manifestations as the self-communication of God, because the Son and the Holy Spirit within the immanent Trinity are themselves personally communicated through the incarnation of the Son and through the coming of the Holy Spirit in the economic Trinity. Here the economic Trinity is the immanent Trinity and *vice versa*. The identification takes place only in the incarnation of the Son and the coming of the Spirit, because the Son is, not figuratively or metaphorically but really, present as the Son in the human person of Jesus Christ, and because the Holy Spirit is also really

24. Ibid., 214–15.

present on Mary.[25] In this sense, Boff asserts that the correspondence is perfect in the sense that the *vice versa* works in the incarnation of the Son and the coming of the Spirit on Mary. And also in this sense, Boff, in his other book *Holy Trinity, Perfect Community*, an abridged version of *Trinity and Society*, intentionally adds the other way of correspondence, that is, the correspondence of the immanent Trinity to the economic Trinity: "The Trinity on earth corresponds to the Trinity in heaven. We can also say the reverse: the Trinity in heaven corresponds to the Trinity on earth."[26] However, for the latter case, that is, regarding the other manifestation of three divine persons than the incarnation and the descent, Boff remains content to say that there is a close link, correlation and correspondence between the economic Trinity and the immanent Trinity, though it is not the identity of both. Thus he states: "Only by referring to the incarnation of the Son and the sending of the Holy Spirit can we say that the economic Trinity is the immanent Trinity and vice-versa. Outside these historic, salvific events, the immanent Trinity remains an apophatic mystery."[27]

To put together both the former case and the latter case, Boff argues that the economic Trinity is the immanent Trinity, but not the whole of the immanent Trinity. For him, the immanent Trinity is "much more than" the economic Trinity which has been revealed and manifested in history. As a consequence of this point, Boff adds that not the whole of the immanent Trinity is the economic Trinity.[28] However, the last point, in turn, retroactively affects Boff's understanding of the manifestations of the incarnation of the Son and the sending of the Spirit. Regardless of his own intention to affirm the identification, it inexorably leads the identity of both Trinities to loosen up. What is worse, in comparison with Rahner's rule, Boff's identification does not reveal any further knowledge regarding how the way in which the economic Trinity exists is related to the way in which the immanent Trinity stands. At least, Boff's alleged identification shows only a sort of close relation between the economic Trinity and the immanent Trinity.

25. Ibid., 114–15, 215.

26. Boff, *Holy Trinity*, 100.

27. Boff, *Trinity and Society*, 233.

28. Ibid., 215.

Pittenger: Much More Than the Palestinian Trinity

PROCESS THEOLOGY PERSPECTIVES ON THE TRINITY

Process theology heavily draws on philosophical works such as "Philosophy of Organism"[29] by Alfred North Whitehead (1861–1947) and "Surrelativism"[30] by Charles Hartshorne (1897–2000), which, in spite of their differences, are widely known as process philosophy for their common positions. Their concepts of God are remarkably characterized by the dipolar structure of the nature of God to overcome the classical notion of divine impassibility and to build a bridge between God and the world. Whitehead makes a distinction between the primordial nature of God and the consequent nature of God.[31] And Hartshorne differentiates between the two poles of God, the abstract essence of God and the concrete actuality of God.[32]

Strongly influenced by the dipolar structure of the nature of God, process theologians are predominantly concerned with the relation between the transcendence of God to the world and the immanence of God in the world, to the neglect of the inner distinctions within God. Thus, as John B. Cobb Jr. admits, "process theology is not interested in formulating distinctions within God for the sake of conforming with traditional Trinitarian notions."[33] Cobb himself, being heavily influ-

---

29. Whitehead, *Process and Reality*, v. This book is based on his Gifford Lectures delivered in the University of Edinburgh in 1927–1928.

30. Hartshorne, *Divine Relativity*, vii. With regard to the Trinity, while mentioning in passing that the doctrine of the Trinity could offer a social relation between perfect persons, nonetheless Hartshorne himself argues for no use for the Trinity. For he remarks: "The Trinity is supposed to meet the requirements of giving God an object of love which yet agrees with his absolute self-sufficiency, and also an object of love "worthy" to be loved with so perfect a love as the divine. This is done by making the lover and the beloved identical – yet not identical. But whatever be the truth of this idea—whose meaning seems to me just as problematic as its truth, for once more, nonsense is only nonsense, however you put a halo around it—it leaves the essential problem of divine love unsolved." Hartshorne, *Man's Vision of God*, 26, 164.

31. Whitehead, *Process and Reality*, 521–24.

32. Cobb and Griffin, *Process Theology*, 47; Boyd, *Trinity and Process*, 205. Here Boyd remarks, "This, in a nutshell, is the neoclassical understanding of God's di-polarity. What is abstract is what must necessarily characterize God's actuality whatever actual divine state is being exemplified. What is concrete is the particular way this abstract character is being contingently exemplified at a given moment."

33. Cobb and Griffin, *Process Theology*, 110.

enced by Whitehead's dipolar structure, draws a distinction between the creative love of God and the responsive love of God. In addition, Cobb contends that this distinction should be the first and foremost distinction. Furthermore, Cobb goes so far as to relativize the notion of the Trinity by suggesting the Binity, the Quaternity, or the Quintity.[34] With regard to the Binity, for example, he remarks that a distinction between the God of divine transcendence to the world and the God of divine immanence in the world provides us with the Binity, and that the Binity is real both ontologically in terms of the nature of God and experientially in terms of how God is known by human beings.[35]

On the contrary, there have been some process theologians who make an attempt to explicate the doctrine of the Trinity within the framework of process theology, though they are very different to each other.[36] William Norman Pittenger deals with the Trinity in his 1967 book *God in Process*,[37] and then in his 1977 book *The Divine Triunity*,[38] he provides a fully historical and systematic understanding of the Trinity in relation to process theology.[39] In addition, Joseph A. Bracken,[40] Lewis

34. Cobb, "Relativization of the Trinity," 21. Here Cobb says, "We can analyze our doctrine of God into three elements as has been traditionally done, or into two. We could also use a fourfold distinction as one text in Whitehead suggests: The Primordial Nature, the Superject of the Primordial Nature, the Consequent Nature, and the Superject of the Consequent Nature. This could be translated easily into theological language. We could then, if we wished, add a fifth name for what unites all these."

35. Cobb, "Relativization of the Trinity," 12.

36. A pivotal book *Trinity in Process* consists of nine essays written by nine different process theologians. However, Marjorie Hewitt Suchocki who is one of the co-editors, admits that, to her amused surprise, the book has nine very different notions of the Trinity. Suchocki, "God, Trinity, Process," 173.

37. Pittenger, *God in Process*.

38. Pittenger, *Divine Triunity*. Pittenger uses the "triunity," rather than the "trinity," because he judges that the latter seems to suggest a tritheistic view of God: God the Father, God the Son or Word, and God the Spirit. On the other hand, he claims that the former speaks of both oneness and threeness and it points toward a rich complexity and fullness in the divine nature.

39. In Demarest's view, not until Pittenger's *The Divine Triunity* have process theologians produced any systematic explication of the Trinity. Demarest, "Process Trinitarianism," 22.

40. Bracken, "Holy Trinity, I" 166–82; "Holy Trinity II"; *What Are They Saying about the Trinity?*; *Triune Symbol*; "Process Perspectives"; *Society and Spirit*; "Panentheism from a Trinitarian Perspective"; "Panentheism from a Process Perspective"; "Trinity: Economic *And* Immanent."

Ford,[41] Marjorie Hewitt Suchocki,[42] William L. Power[43] and Gregory A. Boyd[44] have made various attempts to explore the Trinity by trying to grasp the triadic structure of divine reality within the framework of process theology.[45] For instance, Ford grasps the threefold structure of Whiteheadian concept of God: the divine creative act, the primordial nature, and the consequent nature.[46] Suchocki contends that process theology speaks of God in a threefold way, namely, the primordial nature, the consequent nature, and the superjective nature.[47] And Power suggests that the Father designates the primordial nature of God, the Son the eternal objects, and the Holy Spirit the consequent nature of God.[48] A focus will be put on Pittenger in Section Four, Bracken in Section Five, and Suchocki in Section Six, who are fully engaged with the relation between the immanent Trinity and the economic Trinity. However, as this chapter shows, each own position is different from each other, though all of them work in the framework of process theology.

PITTENGER: MUCH MORE THAN THE PALESTINIAN TRINITY

Pittenger makes an attempt to understand the doctrine of the Trinity within the framework of process theology, seminally in chapter 3 "The Spirit and the Divine Triunity" in his 1967 book *God in Process*,[49] and

41. Ford, "Process Trinitarianism," 199–213. This article is included in his book, *Lure of God*; "Naturalistic Trinity" 23–40; "Contingent Trinitarianism," 41–68.

42. Suchocki, *God-Christ-Church*. The new revised edition in 1989 with the title: *God, Christ, Church*; "John Cobb's Trinity"; "Sunyata, Trinity, and Community"; "Spirit in and through the World." This paper was expanded from her 1991 article on John Cobb's Trinity; "God, Trinity, Process."

43. Power, "Doctrine of the Trinity," 287–302.

44. Boyd, *Trinity and Process*. This book is based on his PhD dissertation, "*A Priori* Construction"; "Self-Sufficient Sociality," in *Trinity in Process*, 73–94.

45. Emmet (1904–2000), a philosopher at the University of Manchester, called attention to the triadic structure of divine reality in Whitehead's metaphysics in her 1932 book, and suggested that creativity, the primordial nature of God and the consequent nature of God are analogous to the creative power of the Father, the Logos and the Holy Spirit respectively. The second edition was published in 1966 by the same press and with the same title. Emmet, *Whitehead's Philosophy of Organism*, 253–55.

46. Ford, "Process Trinitarianism," 200, 205.

47. Suchocki, *God, Christ, Church*, 215.

48. Power, "Doctrine of the Trinity," 296.

49. Pittenger, *God in Process*, 40–51.

more comprehensively in his 1977 book *The Divine Triunity*. Unlike other Trinitarian process theologians, however, Pittenger does not derive the triadic structure of God from the primordial nature of God and the consequent nature of God. He asserts that it would be silly to call the primordial aspect of God as Father and to regard the consequent aspect of God as the Word or the Spirit, because such terms as the Father, the Word, and the Spirit are applied to the whole concrete actuality of God. He states: ". . . it does not readily make sense to assign specifically to these two "aspects" of deity, in Process ways of thinking, any of the three modes of divine existence and activity about which triunitarian thought would speak."[50] Instead, Pittenger appeals to human experience of the divine reality for the triadic structure of God. He contends that human experience of the divine reality is necessarily threefold, because it has "three, not just two, aspects or modes or ways": "divine transcendence," "divine immanence," and "divine concomitance" which is regarded by him as a practical equivalent of incarnation. To put them in other words, Pittenger refers the three aspects of the divine reality respectively as "God as he is in himself," "God as he acts in or reveals himself to the world," and "God as he evokes and enables the world to make its due response or answer to his working and revelation."[51] Then Pittenger attributes the first aspect to God the Father, the second mode to God the Holy Spirit, and the third way to God the Logos or Word.[52] In this way, he argues that this threefold experience becomes the material for the formulation of the doctrine of the Trinity.[53]

Despite his conspicuous treatment of the doctrine of the Trinity, however, Pittenger does not deal explicitly with the issue of the relation between the immanent Trinity and the economic Trinity. Only implicitly does he expose his position that there is a corresponding relation between the economic Trinity and the immanent Trinity, but the immanent Trinity is much more than the economic Trinity.

50. Pittenger, *Divine Triunity*, 113–14.

51. Ibid., 69–70. On this point Pittenger criticizes Cyril C. Richardson's conclusion that there is no necessary threeeness in the Godhead and thus the doctrine of the Trinity is an artificial construct, because the Godhead primarily has a twofold distinction: God's absolute transcendence and God's intimate immanence. Richardson, *Doctrine of the Trinity*, 146–48.

52. Pittenger, *Divine Triunity*, 76.

53. Ibid., 101.

His position is mentioned in the following passage: "Thus the Eternal Father, the Eternal Son or Word, the Eternal Spirit, were *more than* that which is experienced by men; in the depths of the Divine Life itself, in the very heart of the divine Reality, there was a three-foldness which *corresponded* with the three-foldness of the human experience of the divine working."[54] Here Pittenger hints that the immanent Trinity is the threefoldness in the depths of the divine reality, whereas the economic Trinity is the threefoldness in human experience of the divine reality. The immanent Trinity refers to the Eternal Father, the Eternal Word and the Eternal Spirit in the very heart of the divine reality, whereas the economic Trinity denotes the Father, the Word and the Spirit in our threefold experience of the divine reality. Conspicuously, for Pittenger, human experience of the divine reality demarcates the economic Trinity from the immanent Trinity.

How, then, does Pittenger connect the economic Trinity to the immanent Trinity? More specifically, how does he contend that the economic Trinity corresponds to the immanent Trinity? According to Pittenger, the early Christians held on to the one and only God as "the divine Reality."[55] And they experienced Jesus first as teacher and master. And through their experiences of the death and resurrection of Jesus, they came to call Jesus the Messiah or the supreme representative of God to establish the kingdom of God, and then they were compelled to confess that God had redeemed God's people in Jesus. Finally, drawing on Jewish and Greek thought, they called Jesus as the Word of God which meant the "Self-Expression"[56] of the divine Reality, or "the Divine Activity,"[57] or "the divine Action"[58] in whom God was focally and decisively present. And simultaneously, they experienced the Holy Spirit as "the divine Response"[59] which enabled them to respond to the divine Action of God in Jesus within the Christian community.

In Pittenger's judgment, this threefold experience could not mean tri-theism to the early Christians who were strict monotheists. Nor

54. Pittenger, *God in Process*, 48.

55. Ibid., 15.

56. Ibid., 20–21.

57. Ibid., 24.

58. Ibid., 42.

59. Ibid., 43.

does the threefold experience mean modalism, because, for them, it was impossible to think that these experiences represent only transitory aspects of the divine reality.[60] In this regard, Pittenger argues for a distinction between the economic Trinity and the immanent Trinity and simultaneously argues for a certain corresponding relation between them: "But if the way in which God acted in creation was *genuinely* revelatory of that which God was in himself, it was pointed out, then there must of necessity be *some correspondence* between Father, Word or Son, and Spirit known in the creation and the very reality of God himself. To put this in formal terms, the Triunity is not only *"economic,"* not only a matter of divine functioning or activity. It is also *"essential"* to the divine existence as such; it must have some ontological grounding."[61] Here the economic Trinity has something to do with the way of the activity of God in creation, whereas the essential Trinity, namely, the immanent Trinity, is concerned with the way of the very reality of God. The economic Trinity is the Trinity experienced and known in the world, whereas the immanent Trinity is the Trinity in the divine existence itself. And there is some correspondence between the economic and the immanent Trinity, because the way of divine activity reveals genuinely the way of divine reality. The economic Trinity discloses the immanent Trinity, and the immanent Trinity is the ontological ground of the economic Trinity. However, Pittenger does not go further to argue for the identity of the economic Trinity and the immanent Trinity. Rather, he mentions some correspondence, by which he alludes to a loose relation between the economic Trinity and the immanent Trinity.

This careful observation accords with Pittenger's position, as mentioned above, that the immanent Trinity is much more than the economic Trinity. And this point is strongly supported by his persistent claim that the immanent Trinity is not confined to "the Palestinian Trinity"[62] experienced by the early Christians. According to him, God as the divine reality is transcendent to the creation in the sense that the divine reality is inexhaustible, and also is immanent in the world in the sense that God works through all things in the creation. This divine reality works in the world through the divine action and divine

---

60. Ibid., 47.

61. Pittenger, *Divine Triunity*, 39.

62. Pittenger, *God in Process*, 48.

response.[63] Jesus Christ or the Word of God is the divine action as the self-expression of the divine reality, but the divine action is not limited to Jesus. God acted focally, supremely and decisively in Jesus Christ, but this divine action is not confined only to the historical person of Jesus Christ.[64] Likewise, the Holy Spirit is the divine response which enables the early Christians to respond to the divine action in Jesus, but the divine response is not restricted to the Spirit within the Christians community.[65]

Consequently, on the one hand, Pittenger urges us to see the pervasive and universal divine action in the world through the focal manifestation of the divine reality in Jesus Christ, and also to recognize the omnipresent and inclusive divine response in the creation through the focal occasion of the divine response in the Christian community. On the other hand, Pittenger suggests that we make no proud claims to an exhaustive knowledge of the inner working of the divine nature, but that we should be content to speak of intimations and hints of the divine nature.[66] Hence his position on the relation between the economic and the immanent Trinity is that the immanent Trinity is supremely expressed in the economic Trinity experienced by the Christians, but not exclusively.

Bracken: "Immersing" the Economic Trinity into the Immanent Trinity

In his 1974 articles "The Holy Trinity as a Community of Divine Persons I and II,"[67] Joseph A. Bracken makes an attempt to understand the Trinity

63. Ibid., 17.

64. Ibid., 19–20; Pittenger, *Divine Triunity*, 43–44 and 112. Here Pittenger mentions two kinds of theological mistakes to be avoided. The one is to confine the working of God as Word to Jesus Christ as known to the Christian community and to it alone. And the other is to think that the love of God for the world is exclusively recognized in this or that particular occasions, rather than to see that love in all divine operations. The first mistake is called by him "Christological error" which simply identifies the Word of God or the divine action exclusively with the Son of God. Thus he suggests a careful distinction between the Word of God and the Son of God, the latter of which is more appropriately applied to the incarnate Word of God.

65. Pittenger, *God in Process*, 47.

66. Pittenger, *Divine Triunity*, 18.

67. Bracken, "Holy Trinity I," 166–82; "Holy Trinity II," 257–70.

as a society of persons, and proposes that the three divine persons are one God in virtue of their unity in community. Next, in his 1979 and 1985 books on the Trinity, he explores several recent approaches to the Trinity and presents a processive and communitarian understanding of the Trinity through his neo-Whiteheadian framework of the God-world relationship.[68] And in his 1991 book on the Trinitarian cosmology, he goes further to suggest a field-oriented understanding of the God-world relationship.[69] In several subsequent articles, he has sought to understand the Trinity in relation to his process panentheism.[70] Finally, Bracken fully deals with the issue of the relation between the immanent Trinity and the economic Trinity in his 1998 article "Trinity: Economic *and* Immanent."

In his article on the immanent-economic Trinity relation, Bracken reaches the following conclusion: "in trying to reconceive *the Trinity as 'God for us'* one should not lose sight of the methodological importance of the notion of *the immanent Trinity*. However imperfectly and provisionally understood, the concept of *the immanent Trinity* is, . . . indispensable to guarantee an objective referent for one's understanding of *the economic Trinity or 'God for us.'"*[71] Here the economic Trinity refers to God for us, whereas the immanent Trinity is God in Godself. The economic Trinity is the Trinity as related to creation in the economy of salvation, whereas the immanent Trinity is the inner life of God within Godself. In this way the economic Trinity and the immanent Trinity are distinguished from each other. However, for Bracken, they are not unrelated to each other, because the notion of the immanent Trinity serves as the indispensable guarantee of an objective referent for an understanding of the economic Trinity. In other words, both are correlated to each other in the sense that the notion of the immanent Trinity is the necessary ontological basis for the concept of the economic Trinity.

---

68. Bracken, *What Are They Saying about the Trinity?*; *The Triune Symbol: Persons, Process and Community*. Chapter 2 of this book was revised into the following article, "Process Perspectives and Trinitarian Theology," 51–64. In his 1979 book, Bracken explored Jürgen Moltmann, Daniel Day Williams, Heribert Mühlen, Eberhart Jüngel, Juan Luis Segundo, Josiah Royce, Carl Jung, and Joan Schaupp.

69. Bracken, *Society and Spirit: A Trinitarian Cosmology.*

70. Bracken, "Panentheism from a Trinitarian Perspective," 7–28, and "Panentheism from a Process Perspective," 95–113.

71. Bracken, "Trinity: Economic *And* Immanent," 21–22.

Thus Bracken seems to claim a position of correlation between the immanent and the economic Trinity.

Bracken's position of correlation is inserted into his evaluation of the Cappadocian Fathers and Aquinas. According to Bracken, they are seriously interested in the correlation between the immanent Trinity and the economic Trinity, because the Cappadocian Fathers intimately link the processions of the Son and the Spirit to the missions of the Son and the Spirit, and Aquinas quite consciously grounds the missions of the Son and the Spirit in the processions of the Son and the Spirit. Thus, for Bracken, they all do not look upon the immanent Trinity as a reality unto itself alone apart from the economic Trinity. Instead, they correlate the immanent Trinity to the economic Trinity. However, Bracken points out that they limit the correlation exclusively to the link between the processions and the missions and thereby they do not make effectively an intimate connection between the Triune God and creation.[72] This point indicates that Bracken thinks of the correlation of the immanent and the economic Trinity inextricably in terms of God-creation relation.

Bracken's own picture of correlation between the immanent Trinity and the economic Trinity is described in more detail in his earlier book and article, where he states regarding the immanent Trinity and the economic Trinity respectively as follows: "The Father as the source of life and being within the Godhead communicates himself totally to the Son. The Son, in turn, responds perfectly to the initiative of the Father. The mediator between the Father and the Son, he who facilitates the exchange of life and love between them, is the Spirit. As such, the Spirit brings the process of self-giving love which is their common nature to its inevitable climax or perfection."[73]

> The Father transmits to each potential finite entity a vital impulse which is in effect both its radical power of self-determination and a given directionality for the exercise of that power. ... the divine Son ... incorporates that entity's response to the Father's "initial aim" for it into his own all-encompassing response to the Father's offer of life and love to him. All this is accomplished in and through the power of the Holy Spirit who as the mediating person-principle between the Father and the Son

72. Bracken, "Trinity: Economic *And* Immanent," 12–13.
73. Bracken, *Triune Symbol*, 37–38; "Process Perspectives," 53.

within the divine community likewise serves as the mediating person-principle between the Father, the Son and the world of finite occasions at any given moment.[74]

Here Bracken seems to claim that the immanent Trinity and the economic Trinity are correlated in such a way that each of three divine persons works "in the same way"[75] both within Godself and towards creation. The Father communicates his being to the Son and, in the same way, that is, through the offer of his being to the Son, the Father offers to all finite entities both the power of internal self-constitution and the directionality for the use of the power. The Son responds to the Father, and the all finite entities respond to the Father in the same way, that is, through the Son's incorporation of their response to the Father into his own response to the Father. The Spirit facilitates the relationship between the Father and the Son, and, in the same way, the Spirit facilitates the relationship of every finite being, first, to the Son in the Son's response to the Father, and, then, to the Father through the Son.

However, a careful examination of his statements makes it clear that Bracken's position of correlation does not work as perfectly as he would expect. The main reason is that the way of the workings of the immanent Trinity is qualitatively different from that of the workings of the economic Trinity. The Father gives himself totally to the Son, whereas the Father gives an initial aim to all finite entities, indirectly, that is, through his offer of being to the Son. The Son responds to the Father directly and perfectly, whereas all finite entities respond to the Father indirectly, that is, through the Son's incorporation of their response into his own perfect response to the Father. The Spirit mediates between the Father and the Son, whereas the Spirit mediates between the Father and the world, indirectly again, that is, by way of the Son. Here the workings of the economic Trinity in the world are indirectly exerted by the immanent Trinity. As a consequence, the world becomes part of the ongoing flow of life between the Father and the Son in the power of the Spirit, and simultaneously the workings of the economic

74. Bracken, *Triune Symbol*, 46; "Process Perspectives," 57–58.

75. Bracken, "Process Perspectives and Trinitarian Theology," 57. The phrase "in the same way" is used by Bracken himself in the following passage: "But insofar as in my scheme all finite beings participate in the communitarian life of the three divine persons, I can further specify that this power of self-creativity comes from God the Father *in the same way* that the latter communicates being and life to the divine Son."

Trinity in the world are being immersed into those of the immanent Trinity.

In addition to his position of overall immersion of the economic Trinity into the immanent Trinity, Bracken seems to affirm as well that the economic Trinity could affect the immanent Trinity. According to him, all finite entities respond to an initial aim which the Father provides, and then the response is incorporated into the Son's response to the Father. As a result, some response of all finite entities possibly has an effect on the Son's response to the Father. Bracken himself offers an illustration as follows: "At every instant, for example, human beings come into existence and die; other changes take place in the world of nature. Consequently, the relationship of the divine Son to the world of nature and the members of the human race is continuously changing, and this affects the relationship of the Son to the Father and the Spirit within the divine communitarian life."[76] For Bracken, it is possible that the economic Trinity affects the immanent Trinity in such a way that the world, through its relationship to the Son, may affect the relationship among the Father, the Son, and the Spirit within divine community. However, such a possibility is so much restricted that it could not change the major point that the world is a part of the divine communitarian life and thus the economic Trinity is being immersed into the immanent Trinity. Even though such possibility takes place, it is actually incorporated in the immanent Trinity. He mentions this point while he vindicates panentheism according to process theology. He states as follows: "In brief, then, the doctrine of panentheism is vindicated, because the three divine persons and all their creatures share a common life. That is, all the myriad subsocieites of actual occasions within this world together help to structure the field of activity proper to the cosmos as a whole. However, this enormous but still finite field of activity is itself incorporated into a still more comprehensive field of activity proper to the three divine persons in their dynamic interrelations."[77] Therefore Bracken's position could be better defined to be a position of "immersing" the economic into the immanent Trinity, not simply that of correlation between the immanent and the economic Trinity. This position enables him to criticize some theologians who consider the notion of

76. Bracken, "Process Perspectives," 57.
77. Bracken, "Panentheism," 102.

the immanent Trinity as a pure speculation and who focus exclusively on the economic Trinity.[78] For example, Roger Haight, in his 1988 article "The Point of Trinitarian Theology," proposes that God really is as God is encountered to be in Jesus and the Spirit. By this Haight means that, for Augustine, Aquinas and Rahner, the immanent Trinity which deals with the real distinctions within God is purely speculative, and that God is the One who is encountered only through Jesus and the Spirit in the economic Trinity.[79] And LaCugna, in her 1991 book *God for Us: The Trinity and Christian Life*, partly agrees with Maurice Wiles and Gordon Kaufmann that there is no need of the distinction between the economic Trinity, namely the Trinity *ad extra*, and the immanent Trinity, that is, the Trinity *in se*, and thus there is no need of the immanent Trinity.[80]

Suchocki and LaCugna: "Absorbing" the Immanent Trinity into the Economic Trinity

Despite a difference in their theological method, Marjorie Hewitt Suchocki and Catherine Mowry LaCugna (1952–1997) are common in proposing versions of relational ontology and thus they converge on the same position regarding the immanent-economic Trinity relation. Though each has her own distinct standpoint and different ramification, they lead inexorably towards "absorbing" the immanent Trinity into the economic Trinity, or *Oikonomia*, because Suchocki regards the immanent Trinity as the immanent-in-the-world economic Trinity, and LaCugna, being firmly opposed to the postulation of two ontologically different levels of the Trinity, proposes one ecstatic movement of God outward.

Suchocki: The Immanent-in-the-World Economic Trinity

In her book *God, Christ, Church: A Practical Guide to Process Theology*, which was originally published in 1982 and then revised in 1989,

78. Bracken, "Trinity: Economic *and* Immanent," 7 n. 1.

79. Haight, "Point of Trinitarian Theology," 201–2. Here Haight summarizes the point of the doctrine of the Trinity as follows: ". . . that God is absolutely and uniquely one, that God's saving action in Jesus and the Spirit is real, and that therefore God as such is a saving God."

80. LaCugna, *God for Us*, 225–27, 234 n. 6.

Suchocki, drawing on Whitehead, proposes "A Relational Theology" which advocates "God for Us." According to Suchocki, all existence, which refers to every occasion, is essentially relational, because to exist is to have an effect in the sense that each element of existence draws from the transmitted energies of its past and combines them in a creative movement toward its own actuality. Like all other existence, God is related to the world not merely externally but also internally. This implies that God not only affects the world but also is affected by the world. God has an effect on the world by providing it with an initial aim, and God receives the effect of the world by integrating it into Godself.[81]

Suchocki goes further to state that such a relational God is the God of revelation in that an initial aim which God provides to the world becomes the vehicle for knowledge of the nature of God. Though such knowledge is indirect and ambiguous, God's works in the world through providing an initial aim to the world are revelatory of something of God's nature. Then she insists that the relational and revelatory God leads us in the world to experience God as Presence, Wisdom and Power.[82] Here God is the Trinity as Presence, Wisdom and Power in the dimensions of our human experience. Simultaneously, the threefold experience of God leads us back to understand God's inner threefoldness. Suchocki claims that, as the outward actions of God bespeak the inward nature of God, we can speak of God's inner nature in a threefold way. That is, God has the primordial nature, the superjective nature and the consequent nature. This account of the threefold nature of God parallels the traditional terminology of Father, Son, and Spirit respectively, and economically corresponds to God as Presence, God as Wisdom, and God as Power respectively.

Here the economic Trinity refers to the Triune God as experienced by us as Presence, Wisdom, and Power. The immanent Trinity is the Triune God who has innerly the primordial nature, the superjective nature and the consequent nature. The economic Trinity is the manifestation of the immanent Trinity, and the immanent Trinity is the ground of the economic Trinity. The triadic structure of the economic Trinity is grounded in the inner threefoldness of the immanent Trinity, and the

81. Suchocki, *God, Christ, Church*, 12, 33–34.

82. Ibid., 49–84. According to her, God as presence is experienced by us as an answer to a predicament of loneliness, God as Wisdom to that of temporality, and God as Power to that of injustice.

inner threefoldness of the immanent Trinity is the presupposition of our experience of God for us as Presence, Wisdom, and Power. In this way, for Suchocki, the economic Trinity and the immanent Trinity have correlation and correspondence to each other.

However, a more careful examination of this distinction indicates that, for Suchocki, the immanent Trinity is the Trinity already intrinsically in relation to the world. According to Suchocki, the primordial nature of God is the ground of all possibilities of the world. The consequent nature of God receives all responses of the world. The superjective nature of God integrates what the consequent nature of God receives into what the primordial nature of God envisions.[83] Thus the immanent Trinity is not the Trinity as distinct from the economic Trinity, but rather the Trinity intrinsically immanent in the world. Suchocki herself admits that she appropriates the double meaning of the term "immanence." As she puts it: ". . . the double meaning of 'immanent' within the Christian tradition to mean the inner structure of God on the one hand, and the sense in which God is in the world on the other. The 'immanent' trinity yields an immanent-in-the-world economic work of God, and this work is taken into the divine life."[84] Here, for Suchocki, the immanent Trinity is the immanent-in-the-world economic Trinity. By this she means that the immanent Trinity is the economic Trinity working immanently in the world.

Considering these observations, for Suchocki, despite her intentional statements about making a distinction between the immanent and the economic Trinity, the immanent Trinity is inescapably being absorbed into the economic Trinity so that there are only two kinds of economic Trinity: the economic Trinity experienced by us as the Triune God as Presence, Wisdom, and Power, and the immanent-in-the world economic Trinity. The experienced economic Trinity is the manifestation of the economic Trinity working immanently in the world, and the immanent-in-the-world economic Trinity is the presupposition of the economic Trinity of our experience. Both economic Trinities are correlative and correspondent to each other. Hence Suchocki's position could be better defined as that of "absorbing" the immanent Trinity into the economic Trinity.

83. Suchocki, "God, Trinity, Process," 171–72.
84. Suchocki, "Spirit in and through," 186.

LaCunga: Oikonomia

LACUGNA'S TRAJECTORY ON THE TRINITY

After she completed her PhD dissertation on Hans Küng in 1979,[85] Catherine Mowry LaCugna focused on the restoration of the doctrine of the Trinity. In her 1984 paper, "Re-conceiving the Trinity as the Mystery of Salvation,"[86] LaCugna asks a fundamental question: how is the contemporary reformulated doctrine of the Trinity related to the economic Trinity, which is to say to the salvation history? In other words, how does it convey God as God for us?[87] Then she concludes that the Trinitarian model of God-in-relation is the appropriate framework for explicating the Christian's experience of salvation by God through Jesus Christ in the Holy Spirit.[88]

Then, in her 1985 paper, "The Relational God: Aquinas and Beyond,"[89] after examining carefully the category of relation in the *Summa Theologiae*, LaCugna argues that, for Aquinas, being-related is the very heart of what it means for God to be God.[90] She pushes Aquinas further to rethink God as having a "real" relation to creation and proposes the doctrine of the Trinity in the light of a relational metaphysics.[91] Likewise, in her 1986 paper, "Philosophers and Theologians on the Trinity,"[92] LaCugna avers that the Trinitarian theology fundamentally affirms that it is the very nature of God to be related and, by implication, there is no way of looking into God independent of our experience of God.[93]

---

85. LaCugna, "Theological Methodology." This dissertation was published by the American Academy of Religion in 1982. LaCugna, *Theological Methodology of Hans Küng*.

86. This paper was originally presented at the College Theology Society in 1984 and was published by *Scottish Journal of Theology* in 1985 and also by the College Theology Society in 1987. "Re-conceiving the Trinity."

87. LaCugna, "Re-conceiving the Trinity," 2.

88. Ibid., 14.

89. LaCugna, "The Relational God," 647–63.

90. Ibid., 649.

91. Ibid., 661–62.

92. LaCugna, "Philosophers and Theologians," 169–81.

93. Ibid., 177.

Through these successive papers,[94] LaCugna has made an attempt to restore the doctrine of the Trinity in our faith and our life, by focusing on God for us in salvation history. In order to do so, she emphasizes the relational character of God. Then she suggests an ontology of relations or a relational metaphysics, which would be more appropriate framework for her theological project.

REJECTION OF THE ECONOMIC-IMMANENT TRINITY DISTINCTION

LaCugna, in her 1991 book *God for Us: The Trinity and Christian Life*, admits that contemporary Trinitarian theology usually revolves around a distinction between the economic Trinity and the immanent Trinity. Here LaCugna summarizes the current uses of the terms "the economic Trinity" and "the immanent Trinity" in the following passages:

> The terms "economic Trinity" and "immanent Trinity" are ways of speaking about the life and work of God. The phrase "*economic Trinity*" refers to the three "faces" or manifestations of God's activity in the world, correlated with the names, Father, Son, and Spirit. In particular, *economic Trinity* denotes the missions, the being sent by God, of Son and Spirit in the work of redemption and deification. These missions bring about communion between God and humankind.
>
> The phrase "*immanent Trinity*," also called the "*essential*" *Trinity*, points to the life and work of God in the economy, but from an "immanent" point of view. . . . immanent means interior or inherent, as in, "the immanent activities of knowing and loving." . . . Thus "*immanent Trinity*" refers to the reciprocal relationships of Father, Son, and Spirit *to each other*, considered apart from God's activity in the world.[95]

According to LaCugna's summary, the economic Trinity denotes the manifestations of God in history through the Son and the Holy Spirit, whereas the immanent Trinity refers to the inner relationships among the Father, the Son, and the Holy Spirit. In particular, the economic Trinity is the missions of the Son and the Holy Spirit by the Father into the world, whereas the immanent Trinity is the processions

94. In addition to these papers, LaCugan deals with the doctrine of the Trinity in the following essays: "Trinitarian Mystery of God"; "God in Communion with Us"; "Doctrine of the Trinity."

95. LaCugna, *God for Us*, 211–12.

of the Son and the Holy Spirit within Godself. The economic Trinity is the life and work of the Trinity *ad extra*, whereas the immanent Trinity is the life and work of the Trinity *ad intra*. The economic Trinity refers to the Trinity for us, whereas the immanent Trinity refers to the Trinity *in se*. The economic Trinity is concerned with God *pro nobis*, whereas the immanent Trinity is related to God *in se*.

However, LaCugna points out that the current uses of the terms are misleading. In the first place, with regard to the economic Trinity, there are not three but only two missions in the economy of salvation, that is, the sendings of the Son and of the Holy Spirit. God the Father is never sent, but only sends the Son and the Holy Spirit. Thus she asserts that, strictly speaking, there is not an economic Trinity but an economic Binity. In this sense, she proposes that we should avoid use the term "economic Trinity."[96]

In the second place, with regard to the immanent Trinity, LaCugna asserts that the term "immanent Trinity" which deals with intratrinitarian relations is often imprecisely used to mean the interior life of God or God's inner state, which gives an impression that God first has an inner life and then that we can have access to this inner life. And such an imprecise use of the term, in turn, implies an ontological distinction between God *in se* and God *pro nobis*. LaCugna criticizes such an ontological distinction, because it is inconsistent with biblical revelation, with early Christian creeds, and with Christian prayer and worship.[97] And she insists that an immanent Trinitarian theology is not about the interior life of God, but about the structure or pattern of God's self-expression in salvation history.[98] Lastly, she holds that the life of God is not something that belongs to God alone, but that God's Trinitarian life includes our life.[99]

These two considerations lead LaCugna, first, to perceive that a distinction between the immanent Trinity and the economic Trinity has nothing to do with ontology. For her, the distinction is not ontological but epistemological: "There are not two ontologically distinct trinities but only one trinitarian mystery of God that may be considered under

96. Ibid., 234.
97. Ibid., 6.
98. Ibid., 225.
99. Ibid., 228.

two aspects. The economic-immanent distinction is epistemological, not ontological, since an "immanent" theology of God is nothing other than a theology of the economy, albeit considered from a non-economic point of view. By implication, the immanent Trinity is not the same as the divine essence."[100]

Second, these considerations obviate, for LaCugna, the need to adhere to the terms "economic Trinity" and "immanent Trinity." On this point, she agrees with Cyril R. Richardson, Gordon Kaufmann, Geoffrey William Hugo Lampe, and Maurice Wiles, who reject the distinction between the economic Trinity and the immanent Trinity.[101] For example, Wiles points out that the doctrine of the immanent Trinity is not necessary, both because ante-Nicene theology was as much Binitarian as Trinitarain and because Augustine's rule that God's actions *ad extra* are one does not allow us to have any knowledge of distinctions within God's being. In addition, Kaufman regards the economic-immanent distinction as a pseudo-distinction, because we can speak only about God's being-in-revelation and have no epistemological access to the inner life of God's being. Though LaCugna does not agree with them on all aspects, nevertheless what all these theologians share is their great anxiety about the point that an epistemological distinction may turn into an ontological distinction to the detriment of losing its basis in salvation history.

OIKONOMIA AND THEOLOGIA

Instead of using the imprecise and misleading terms "the economic Trinity" and "the immanent Trinity," LaCugna suggests to reinvigorate the terms "*oikonomia*" and "*theologia*." She provides her own definition of them in the following passage: "*Oikonomia* is not the Trinity *ad extra* but the comprehensive plan of God reaching from creation to consummation, in which God and all creatures are destined to exist together in the mystery of love and communion. Similarly, *theologia* is not the Trinity *in se*, but, much more modestly and simply, the mystery of God."[102]

---

100. LaCugna, "Trinitarian Mystery," 174–75.
101. LaCugna, *God for Us*, 225–27, 234 n. 6.
102. Ibid., 223.

As the quotation cited above indicates, for LaCugna, *oikonomia* is not the Trinity *ad extra* and *theologia* is not the Trinity *ad intra*. *Oikonomia* is not the Trinity *pro nobis* and *theologia* is not the Trinity *in se*. What LaCugna intends to emphasize by these negations is the point that there are not two separate Trinities and that there are not two different levels of the Trinity, with one *ad extra* and the other *ad intra*, or with one *pro nobis* and the other *in se*. What she really means is that the distinction between *oikonomia* and *theologia* is not ontological but only conceptual. For LaCunga, *oikonomia* is the comprehensive plan of God for the world and *theologia* is the mystery of God.

With regard to this point, LaCugna disagrees with Rahner.[103] Though she claims to start with Rahner's rule of identity as a point of departure and affirms several implications derived from it, LaCugna considers that Rahner's rule presupposes two different levels of the Trinity or two separate Trinities, that is, God's self-communication *in se* and God's self-communication *ad extra*. And Rahner's rule seems to mean that distinctions in God's self-communication *ad extra* are ontologically grounded in distinctions in God's self-communication *in se*. Thus LaCugna judges that Rahner's rule finally comes to be caught in the stranglehold of the post-Nicene problematic, that is, the preoccupation with God's self-communication *in se* apart from God's self-communication *ad extra*. Therefore, in her estimation, Rahner's rule, despite its claim for the axiomatic unity of both, confounds the connection between the economic and the immanent Trinity.

Instead of postulating two ontologically different levels of the Trinity, LaCugna proposes one ecstatic movement of God outward, which is *a Patre ad Patrem*. God's outwardly dynamic movement chiastically consists of emanation and return, or *exitus* and *reditus*, which shape a parabolic movement from God the Father to God the Father. According to LaCugna, all things originate from God the Father through Jesus Christ in the power of the Holy Spirit, and all things return in the Holy Spirit through Jesus Christ to God the Father. There is no distinction between the economic Trinity and the immanent Trinity in the divine dynamic movement. But there is only *oikonomia*, that is, the concrete realization of the mystery of *theologia* in time, space, history and personality. *Oikonomia* is not a mirror reflecting a hidden

103. Ibid., 221.

realm of intradivine relations, and *theologia* is not a static ahistorical and transeconomic realm.

For LaCugna, *oikonomia* is the comprehensive plan of God for the world and *theologia* is the mystery of God. *Oikonomia* and *theologia* are not two ontologically different levels. There is only one self-communication of God and only one mystery of God. And *oikonomia* and *theologia* are two aspects of the one reality, or two modalities of the one self-communication of God. In this regard, *oikonomia* and *theologia* are inseparable from each other. Thus LaCunga formulates her own principle which says that *theologia* is fully revealed and bestowed in *oikonomia*, and *oikonomia* truly expresses the ineffable mystery of *theologia*.[104]

Lee: Mutual Inclusiveness. The Economic Trinity is *in* the Immanent Trinity and the Immanent Trinity is *in* the Economic Trinity

Non-Identical Distinction

In his 1996 book *The Trinity in Asian Perspective*, Jung Young Lee claims to revise Rahner's rule of identity. Lee's own revisionist formula is: "The immanent Trinity is *in* the economic Trinity and the economic Trinity is *in* the immanent Trinity."[105] Unlike Rahner's reciprocal identity, Lee maintains that the economic Trinity and the immanent Trinity are not identical. Lee's intention is to make a proper distinction between the economic Trinity and the immanent Trinity. Lee is concerned that Rahner's reciprocal identity lacks an appropriate distinction between the economic Trinity and the immanent Trinity and that one may be easily merged into the other.

Lee appeals to an analogy of family for his insistence on a necessity of making a proper distinction between the economic and the immanent Trinity.[106] According to Lee's explanation, as my life with my family is not the same as my life without my family, so the economic Trinity is not the same as the immanent Trinity. Both my life with my family and my life without my family are my life, but my life with my family involves a new dimension of relationship. Likewise, both the economic

---

104. Ibid., 221.
105. Lee, *Asian Perspective*, 68. Lee's own italics.
106. Ibid., 67.

Trinity and the immanent Trinity are the divine Trinity, but the economic Trinity has a new dimension of relationship. In this sense, the economic Trinity is not identical with the immanent Trinity.

A careful analysis of Lee's analogy of family shows that the reason why Lee does not fully accept Rahner's rule is that Lee intends to secure a new dimension of relationship for the economic Trinity, which the immanent Trinity may not have. Such a new dimension of relationship is the relationship which the economic Trinity has with the world. In other words, while the immanent Trinity is the Trinity within Godself, the economic Trinity is the Trinity in relation to the world. In this way, Lee attempts to make it clear that God is the Triune God who is in relation to the world.

Lee goes further to argue that the Triune God, who is in relation to the world, is the God who is affected by the world. He thinks that, if the Triune God is unaffected by the world, it would be possible to hold that the immanent Trinity is identical with the economic Trinity, and thus to insist on Rahner's rule. In Lee's view, the Triune God, then, would be the God who is immutable and impassible to the world. However, Lee firmly rejects the idea of an unaffected God. For Lee, the Triune God, who is in relation to the world, is the God who is mutable, passible, and changeable. Therefore it is notable that Lee's revisionist formula is grounded in his understanding of the Triune God as the mutable, passible, and changeable God.

God's Passibiliy

As mentioned above, Lee argues that, if the Triune God is affected by the world, the economic Trinity is not identical with the immanent Trinity. Here two questions come to mind: firstly, whether God is passible or not; and secondly, whether God's passibility, which is directly related to the economic Trinity, is also related to the immanent Trinity.

With respect to the first question on divine *pathos* [πάθος], it is noteworthy that the question is the first and foremost significant theological issue with which Lee struggled from the outset of his theological journey. In 1968 he wrote his ThD thesis regarding God's suffering.[107] In 1973 he wrote an article titled "Can God Be Change Itself?"[108] And then

---

107. Lee, "Suffering of God."

108. Lee, "Can God Be Change Itself?" 752–70.

in 1974, being based on his ThD thesis, he extensively and deeply dealt with the theme of God's passibility in his book *God Suffers for Us: A Systematic Inquiry into a Concept of Divine Passibility.*[109]

According to Lee, the nature of God as the ultimate reality is *agape* [αγάπη].[110] The *agape* of God is not merely one of divine attributes but the very nature of God.[111] And it is expressed through the empathy of God, which is the way of *agape*. With such empathy, God fully participates in the world, without losing the divine essential nature, so that the world can also participate in God's participation, without losing the world's essential nature. The genuine personal relationship between God and the world or the I-Thou relationship of participation is possible because of divine empathy.[112] And God as *agape* suffers in the empathy of God due to the sin of the world.[113] In this way, Lee argues that God is the God who is passible. As a consequence, for Lee, God is not the God who stays alone far away from the world, but the God who makes a new relationship with the world, participates in the world, and suffers in the empathy of God. In this regard, Lee argues that the economic Trinity is not identical with the immanent Trinity.

God's Passibility and the Immanent Trinity

However, when Lee argues that the economic Trinity and the immanent Trinity are not identical, Lee faces another severe problem, that is, how both the economic and the immanent Trinity make a unity. To put it differently in terms of God's passibility, how is God's passibility which is directly linked to the economic Trinity, related to the immanent Trinity as well? Though Lee maintains that the *agape* of God is the very nature of God, nevertheless the *agape* of God, the empathy of God, and God's participation in the world seem to take place primarily through the economic Trinity. What about the immanent Trinity? Does God's participation in the world mean that only the economic Trinity participates in the world, without the participation of the immanent Trinity in the world? Does God's empathy mean that only the economic Trinity

109. Lee, *God Suffers for Us.*
110. Ibid., 6.
111. Ibid., 7.
112. Ibid., 13.
113. Ibid., 19.

has the empathy for the world, without the empathy of the immanent Trinity for the world? Does God's love, though it is claimed by Lee to be the very nature of God, mean that only the economic Trinity loves the world, without the immanent Trinity's loving of the world? If so, there would be two completely different and totally separated Trinities. But this consequence is not what Lee wants to affirm.

In order to solve this problem, Lee appeals, first, to Barth's theory of correspondence.[114] According to Barth, the economic Trinity is the Trinity in God's revelation attested by Scripture, whereas the immanent Trinity is the Trinity which is antecedently in Godself. And the economic Trinity corresponds to the immanent Trinity, and the immanent Trinity is the indispensable premises of the economic Trinity. With respect to the *agape* of God, it consists of both God's love within Godself and God's love for the world. God's love within Godself refers to the Father's love of the Son through the Holy Spirit. On the other hand, God's love for the world denotes the Son's love of the world by the Father through the Holy Spirit. God's love within Godself is the prototype of God's love for the world, and God's love for the world corresponds to God's love within Godself.[115]

Lee goes further to explicate the implications of Barth's position, especially in relation to the incarnation of God in Christ, the life and death of Jesus Christ, and the coming of the Paraclete at Pentecost. God's movements in history are correspondingly the re-enactment of the inner-Trinitarian movements within Godself. The incarnation of God in Christ is the re-enactment of the inner-Trinitarian receiving of the Spirit from the Father to the Son. The life and death of Jesus Christ is the re-enactment of the inner-Trinitarian remaining of the Spirit in the Son. And the coming of the Paraclete at Pentecost is the re-enactment of the inner-Trinitarian sending of the Holy Spirit from the Son to the Father.[116] Likewise, God's suffering for the world is correspondingly the re-enactment of the inner-Trinitarian suffering within Godself. That is, the suffering of Jesus Christ is correspondingly the suffering of God within Godself.[117] In this way, with the help of Barth's correspondence

114. Lee, *God Suffers for Us*, 71.

115. Ibid., 71.

116. Ibid., 72–73.

117. Ibid., 75.

theory, Lee makes an intimate connection between God's passibility and the immanent Trinity, and, by implication, between the economic Trinity and the immanent Trinity. Such an intimate connection enables Lee to maintain a proper unity between the economic Trinity and the immanent Trinity. In this way, Lee seems to successfully secure the unity as well as the distinction between the economic and the immanent Trinity.

Unity as Correspondence?

Despite Lee's seemingly successful efforts to maintain both unity and distinction, however, Lee still has to face one further problem, whether unity in correspondence is an authentic unity. This problem arises, mainly because there is no guarantee that the economic Trinity perfectly corresponds to the immanent Trinity. This is not only Lee's conundrum but also Barth's conundrum, one which is ultimately related to Barth's own theological method.

Barth starts from the reality of revelation attested by the scriptures. Through an analysis of biblical revelation which centers around Jesus Christ, Barth leads to several concepts which point to the doctrine of the Trinity: the concepts of the unimpaired unity and unimpaired distinction of Father, Son, and Holy Spirit, and the concept of the one essence of God and of the three modes of being [*Seinsweisen*] which are distinguished in one essence. On this ground, Barth claims to establish that the biblical revelation implicitly or explicitly points to the doctrine of the Trinity. In this way, Barth regards revelation as the root or the ground of the doctrine of the Trinity.

However, for Barth, the concepts resulting from an analysis of revelation are still epistemologically vulnerable on human beings' part, mainly due to divine lordship or divine freedom with respect to the world as well as human limited inner capacity with respect to God. Barth admits that the freedom of God does not wholly exclude human epistemological possibility, for there is an encounter and fellowship between God's nature and human beings in divine revelation. And he admits that human beings can be a recipient of God's Word through the act of God's free love. Nevertheless, Barth persists in asserting that God constantly tells us afresh that there is no human knowing that corresponds to the divine telling and that there is no assuming of God's nature into human knowing.[118]

For Barth, therefore, there is no warranty for the perfect correspondence. Instead, there is always a tension and gap between the economic Trinity and the immanent Trinity. In order to solve this problem, Barth makes another distinction between God's primary objectivity and God's secondary objectivity. God's primary objectivity refers to God's own knowledge of Godself, whereas God's secondary objectivity refers to the human being's knowledge of God. Barth contends that there is no difference of degree between the two. As God gives Godself to be known by us as God knows Godself, the secondary objectivity of God is not distinguished from the primary objectivity of God by a lesser degree of truth. God's secondary objectivity is fully true, too, because it has its correspondence to God's primary objectivity and its basis in God's primary objectivity.[119] God's secondary objectivity corresponds to God's primary objectivity, and God's primary objectivity is the basis of God's secondary objectivity. However, this kind of distinction only defers the same theological conundrum, without resolving it completely.[120]

Unity as Mutual Inclusiveness

Unlike Barth, Lee's final solution to the conundrum lies in his rediscovery of logical framework "in . . . and . . . in," which signifies a principle of mutual inclusiveness. By appropriating the principle, Lee provides his own revisionist formula: the economic Trinity is *in* the immanent Trinity and the immanent Trinity is *in* the economic Trinity. Lee's own formula claims to admit not only the distinction, but also the unity between the economic and the immanent Trinity. According to Lee, "in . . . and . . . in" means mutual inclusiveness. In this mutually inclusive relationship, the immanent Trinity is not free of the world, because the

118. Barth, *CD* I/1, 132.

119. Barth, *CD* II/1, 16.

120. Jüngel, much influenced by Barth, mentions that the self-relatedness of God takes place in an unsurpassable way in the very incarnation of God which is God's relatedness to us. Jüngel, *God as the Mystery*, 372; Jüngel's affirmation of the point is grounded in his notion of *analogia relationis*, by which he means that God's relation to us reiterates and corresponds to God's self-relatedness. The former derives its ontological power from the latter, and the latter constitutes the former. Jüngel, *God's Being*, 119–21.

immanent Trinity is in the economic Trinity. Neither does the economic Trinity exclude its involvement in the inner life of God, because the economic Trinity is in the immanent Trinity.[121]

Lee arrives at the rediscovery of logical structure "in . . . and . . . in" through his study of *the Book of Changes* which is known as *Yeokkyung* [역경, 易經(*YiJing*)], or as *Jooyeok* [주역, 周易(*ZhouYi*)].[122] Lee's logical structure of the formula is "A in B and B in A," and Lee derives it from an inclusive relationship between *Eum* [음, 陰(*Yin*)] and *Yang* [양, 陽(*Yang*)]. *Yang* [陽] literally means the sunny side of a hill, whereas *Eum* [陰] literally means the shady side of a hill [구(*Koo*), 丘(*Fu*)]. *Yang* [陽] signifies the sun, the south, light, day, fire, red, dryness, heat, spring-summer, and so forth, while *Eum* [陰] signifies the moon, the north, darkness, night, water, black, cold, moistness, autumn-winter, and so on. *Yang* symbolizes moving upward, being positive, being masculine, being active, being in motion, and so forth, whereas *Eum* symbolizes moving downward, being negative, being feminine, being quiescent, being in rest, and so forth. *Eum* and *Yang* are the bipolar principles of all changes in the cosmos.[123]

These bipolar principles are distinct from each other and even opposite to each other in character. However, they are not exclusive of each other. In *the Book of Changes*, according to Lee's explanation, the ideogram of change [역(*Yeok*), 易(*Yi*)] consists of the sun [일(*Il*), 日(*Ri*)] and the older form of the moon [물(*Mool*), 勿(*Wu*) = 월(*Weol*), 月(*Yue*)]. What is important is that change [역(*Yeok*), 易(*Yi*)] takes place, as the sun goes down and simultaneously the moon comes up, and as the moon goes down and simultaneously the sun comes up. First, as the sun is always related to the moon, *Yang* is always related to *Eum*. *Yang* and *Eum* are always relative to each other and united to each other. *Eum* and *Yang* are always relational. Second, the sun does not exist without the moon, and the moon does not exist without the sun. As the sun and the moon always coexist, *Eum* and *Yang* always coexist.

---

121. Lee, *Asian Perspective*, 68.

122. Lee's study of *the Book of Change* started as early as 1971, when he wrote a book *The I*. Some years later Lee provided a comprehensive introduction to *the Book of Change* in his book *The I Ching and Modern Man*. And the next year Lee wrote an article which discuss the authorship of *the Book of Change* in "Some Reflection on the Authorship of the *I Ching*."

123. Lee, *Asian Perspective*, 25.

Eum and *Yang* are distinct and opposite, but they are not exclusive. They are united, relational, coexistent, and inclusive. *Yang* is symbolized by an undivided line (—), and *Eum* is symbolized by a divided line (– –). Originally, *Yang* is represented by the light dot (◦), and *Eum* is represented by the dark dot (•). And their inclusiveness is expressed by the picture of the Great Ultimate (☯) in which the dark dot (•), referring to *Eum*, is included in the bright half area of *Yang*, and in which the light dot (◦), referring to *Yang*, is included in the dark half area of *Eum*. That is, *Yang* is in *Eum* and *Eum* is in *Yang*. "In" is the inner connecting principle of *Eum* and *Yang*, while "and" is the external connecting principle.[124] Here *Yang* and *Eum* are reciprocally inclusive.[125] The mutual inclusiveness is the most remarkable characteristic of the *Eum-Yang* relationship. And this kind of relationship embraces not only distinctiveness but also relational unity. In this way, Lee finds the answer to his theological conundrum in the *Eum-Yang* way of thinking. Thus he states as follows: "In this inclusive rather than identical relationship, we can revise Rahner's rule: The immanent Trinity is *in* the economic Trinity and the economic Trinity is *in* the immanent Trinity. This rule will help us retain their distinctiveness as well as their unity."[126]

Summary

As has been expounded in chapters 3 and 4, this book has examined the salient eleven contemporary theologians and identified the seven different positions regarding the relationship between the immanent and the economic Trinity. Each of these positions can be summarized as below, which becomes the basis for a critical analysis in chapter 5.

First, Barth's position of mutual correspondence means that the economic Trinity is the epistemological gateway to the immanent Trinity and the immanent Trinity is the ontological prototype of the economic Trinity. The economic Trinity leads us back to see the eternal

---

124. Lee finds this *Eum-Yang* way of inclusive relation in Jesus' saying, "I am in the Father and the Father is in me" (John 14:11), and "The Father and I are one" (John 10:30). Lee goes further to state that "in" represents the Holy Spirit. He says, "The Father and Son are one in their "inness," but also at the same time, they are three because "in" represents the Spirit, the inner connecting principle which cannot exist by itself." Lee, *Asian Perspective*, 58–59.

125. Lee, *Asian Perspective*, 26.

126. Ibid., 68.

Father, the eternal Son, and the eternal Holy Spirit, while the immanent Trinity is the ontological basis, way, and reason of God our Creator and our Father, Jesus Christ, and the Holy Spirit.

Second, Rahner's rule of identity means that the economic Logos is the immanent Logos and conversely, that the Holy Spirit which we experience in salvific history is the Spirit within the Trinity and *vice versa*, and thus that God the Father communicates Godself through the incarnation of the Son and the descent of the Spirit.

Third, among those who hold an eschatological unity, Moltmann maintains that the economic Trinity is the immanent Trinity eschatologically and the immanent Trinity is the economic Trinity doxologically. Pannenberg argues on the ground of his futurist metaphysics that God's activity comes to completion at *eschaton* and thus the unity of the economic and the immanent Trinity takes place eschatologically. Jenson asserts through his identification of God in biblical narratives that the identity of the economic and the immanent Trinity is eschatological in the sense that the immanent Trinity is the eschatological reality of the economic Trinity.

Fourth, despite a remarkable theological difference in that Pittenger is a process theologian, whereas Boff is a liberation theologian, both are one in their common position that the immanent Trinity is much more than the economic Trinity. Boff maintains that, in the case of the incarnation of the Son and the descent of the Holy Spirit, the economic Trinity is the immanent Trinity and *vice versa*, while in the other case outside the historical, salvific events, the immanent Trinity remains much more than the economic Trinity. Pittenger argues that the immanent Trinity is supremely expressed in the economic Trinity, but not exclusively, which implies that God acts focally and decisively in Jesus Christ, but this divine action is not confined only to the historical person of Jesus Christ, and that the Holy Spirit is the divine response which enables the early Christians to respond to the divine action in Jesus Christ, but this divine response is not restricted to the Spirit within the Christian community.

Fifth, Bracken, while developing a metaphysics of becoming and an ontology of society, has a strong tendency towards "immersing" the economic into the immanent Trinity, for the way of the workings of the immanent Trinity is not only qualitatively different from that of the workings of the economic Trinity, but also the former incorporates the latter into its own activities.

Sixth, Suchocki and LaCugna, due to a strong emphasis on a relational ontology, lead inexorably towards "absorbing" the immanent into the economic Trinity. For Suchocki, the immanent Trinity is the immanent-in-the world economic Trinity, which is the Trinity already intrinsically in relation to the world. On the other hand, LaCugna, while firmly opposing a postulation of two ontologically different levels of the Trinity, proposes one ecstatic movement of God outward, which is *a Patre ad Patrem*. Here there is only *oikonomia*, namely, the concrete realization of *theologia*, while *oikonomia* is not a mirror reflecting a hidden realm of intradivine relations, and *theologia* is not a static ahistorical and transeconomic realm.

Lastly, due to his theological interest in the *pathos* of God, Lee is concerned with Rahner's rule of identity, and maintains both the distinction and the unity between the economic and the immanent Trinity. Instead of Barth's model of correspondence, Lee grounds the unity in the bipolar mutual inclusiveness of *Eum* and *Yang*, which maintains that the economic Trinity is in the immanent Trinity and *vice versa*.

5

A Critical Analysis of Contemporary Discussions

Ontology, Epistemology, and Mystery

IN THIS CHAPTER EACH OF THE SEVEN DISTINCT POSITIONS VIS-À-VIS the question of the relation between the immanent and the economic Trinity which have been identified in earlier chapters is subjected to a critical analysis in terms of ontology, epistemology, and a concept of mystery. Ontology is an inquiry into the reality of being and epistemology is an inquiry into the knowledge of the reality of being. In this chapter ontology is generally concerned with ontological status of the immanent Trinity and the economic Trinity, and epistemology is broadly related to our knowledge of the economic Trinity and that of the immanent Trinity. Through a critical analysis of each of these positions, the current chapter shows that ontology and epistemology are intricately woven into the contemporary discussions on the immanent-economic Trinity relation, and goes further to show that a concept of divine mystery is also intimately involved in each of the positions, functioning to resolve certain tensions: ontological, epistemological, or both.

Barth: Mutual Correspondence

As has been shown in chapter 3, Barth's position of mutual correspondence means that the economic Trinity is the epistemological gateway to the immanent Trinity and the immanent Trinity is the ontological prototype of the economic Trinity. On the one hand, in an epistemological aspect, God our Creator and God our Father refers us back to the eternal Father of the eternal Son. Jesus Christ in revelation leads us to perceive the eternal Son of the eternal Father. The Holy Spirit takes us to the recognition of the eternal Spirit of the Father and the Son. The economic *Filioque* carries us into seeing the immanent *Filioque*. On the other hand, in an ontological aspect, the three divine modes of being antecedently in Godself are the ontological prototype of the three divine modes of being in revelation. The eternal Father is the ontological reason of our Creator and our Father. The eternal Son is the ontological way of our Reconciler. The eternal Spirit is the ontological basis of our Reedeemer. The immanent *Filioque* is the ontological prototype of the economic *Filioque*.

Barth's position that the immanent Trinity is the ontological prototype of the economic Trinity unavoidably gives an erroneous impression that there are two ontologically different Trinities. This is one of the main reasons why several theologians such as Moltmann[1] and Pannenberg[2] criticize Barth for holding a Platonic sense of distinction between the immanent and the economic Trinity. However, Barth's own immanent-economic distinction is not the same as Plato's distinction between *eidos* [εἶδος] (idea or form) and *phenomenon* [φαινόμενον]. For Plato, *phenomenon* is a copy of *eidos* and they are different in degree. On the contrary, for Barth, the economic Trinity and the immanent Trinity,

---

1. In Moltmann's own words: "In his distinction between the immanent and the economic Trinity, Barth first of all adhered to the Platonic notion of correspondence: what God revealed himself as being in Jesus Christ, he is eternity, 'beforehand in himself.'" Moltmann, *Trinity and the Kingdom*, 159.

2. In his 1977 article, Pannenberg comments on Barth somewhat positively, when he evaluates the convergence and divergence between Hegel and Barth. He states as follows: "Hegel's explanation of the Trinity as the one history of God within Himself . . . has been renewed by Karl Barth. . . . However, Barth departs from Hegel . . . While Hegel tried to conceive of God's essence and activity in the world directly with the ideal of divine history as a dialectical unity, Barth . . . corrected Hegel's dialectic with the Platonic concept of correspondence to ideal forms. Therefore, the Christ event, just as creation in the beginning, is only viewed as analogous to the innertrinitarian history of God. This correction is by no means marginal. Its purpose is understandable." Wolfhart Pannenberg, "God of History," 34.

On the contrary, in his 1983 letter to Timothy Bradshaw, Pannenberg provides some critical comments on Barth, by stating as follows: "Barth was correct in claiming that if God's revelation in Jesus Christ involves the trinitarian structure, then there must be a trinitarian structure in the eternal reality of God himself, prior to the existence of creation. On the other hand, the immanent Trinity is dependent on the process of history (hence on the economic Trinity) not only in the *ordo cognoscendi*, but also in its very being as soon a there is a world. I suspect that this interrelation has been underestimated in Barth's thought because of his indebtedness to Platonism. In Barth's case, it is only the doctrine of election, or thus it seems to me, that unites the immanent Trinity to a reality outside itself in repeating its structure." Timothy Bradshaw, *Trinity and Ontology*, 402.

although they are different in form, nevertheless have sameness or unity in content.[3] In addition, Barth's own eternal-temporal distinction is not the same as Plato's own eternity-time distinction.[4]

However, though Barth does not hold a dualistic distinction between the immanent Trinity and the economic Trinity in a Platonic sense, nevertheless Barth's position inexorably leads towards an implication that the immanent Trinity is ontologically apart from and prior to the economic Trinity. God, who reveals Godself as our Creator, is God the Father for us, because God is so antecedently in Godself as the Father of the Son. God, who reveals Godself as our Reconciler, is God the Son, because God is so antecedently in Godself as the Son or Word of God the Father. God, who reveals Godself as our Redeemer, is God the Holy Spirit, because God is so antecedently in Godself as the love of the Father and the Son. Thus the divine three persons antecedently in Godself are ontologically prior to the divine three persons in revelation.

The point that the immanent Trinity is ontologically apart from and prior to the economic Trinity is clearly shown by Barth's own statements in *Church Dogmatics*. First, God is our Father, because God is already the Father of the Son. God is the Father of the Son "even apart from the fact that He reveals Himself as such."[5] Second, Jesus Christ does not first become the Son of God or the Word of God in the event of revelation. Jesus Christ is already the Son of God, "before, even apart from this event."[6] Third, the Holy Spirit does not first become the Spirit of God in the event of revelation. The Holy Spirit is God the Spirit even "within the deepest depths of deity."[7]

In addition, the point of the ontological independence or priority of the immanent Trinity is affirmed by Barth's other documents. First, in his 1924 letter to Eduard Thurneysen, Barth mentions, referring to the immanent Trinity, that he comes through his hard struggle to the right key of theology, which is "A Trinity of *being*, not just an economic

---

3. Barth, *CD*, I/1, 479.

4. Ibid., III/2, 437.

5. Ibid., I/1, 390.

6. Ibid., I/1, 414.

7. Ibid., I/1, 466.

Trinity!"[8] Second, in his 1964 letters to Moltmann, Barth expresses his concern that Moltamnn subsumes all theology in eschatology by baptizing Bloch's principle of hope to the extent that theology becomes largely a matter of eschatological principle. Then Barth calls his attention to the immanent Trinity by stating, "Would it not be wise to accept the doctrine of the immanent Trinity of God?"[9] For Barth, Moltmann may only thereby achieve the freedom of three-dimensional thinking in which the *eschaton* retains its whole weight while the same honor can still be shown to the kingdoms of nature and grace.

However, such a point of the ontological independence or priority of the immanent Trinity is inevitably incomparable with Barth's theological method. For Barth claims to start with the reality of revelation attested in Scripture and preached by Church. But, as far as it is concerned with the doctrine of the Trinity, or, at least, with that of the immanent Trinity, Barth actually presupposes something of the immanent Trinity from the outset. Barth postulates an ontological state of the eternal Father, the eternal Son, and the eternal Spirit, even before and apart from the reality of revelation. This presupposition, in turn, wrongly implies that, for Barth, everything has already happened in eternity and, by implication, in the past. In this regard, some criticisms of Barth for his orientation to the past might not be totally irrelevant.[10]

When it comes to his theological method, it is noteworthy that Barth starts with the reality of revelation which is Jesus Christ, proceeds through an analysis of the biblical concept of revelation, and leads to his concepts of the Trinity in revelation, namely, the economic Trinity, and then finally his concepts of the Trinity in Godself, namely, the immanent Trinity.[11] In this regard, Barth's theological method accords better with the order of the epistemological aspect of Barth's position. As we can know God only in revelation and know the Trinity of God

8. Barth and Thurneysen, *Revolutionary Theology*, 176.

9. Barth, *Letters 1961–1968*, 175–76.

10. Gunton, *Becoming and Being*, 182. Here Gunton mentions that Henri Bouillard, G. C. Berkower, J. D. Bettis, and Robert W. Jenson critically deal with Barth on this point.

11. On the one hand, as far as he begins with the reality of revelation, Barth holds a kind of realism which centers around the actuality of divine revelation. On the other hand, as far as he leads to the concepts of the Trinity, not to the Trinity itself, Barth holds a kind of idealism.

only in the Word of God revealed, written, and proclaimed,[12] Barth is right in that he claims that the economic Trinity is the epistemological gateway to the immanent Trinity, but not the other way around. Thus the economic Trinity epistemologically refers us back to the immanent Trinity, but not *vice versa*.

Despite such an accord, however, the epistemological side of Barth's position does not perfectly agree with his theological method. The former means that the three divine modes of being in revelation epistemologically refer us back to the three divine modes of being in Godself. On the contrary, the latter is so much reserved in an epistemological sense that it merely maintains that biblical revelation is implicitly or explicitly "a pointer" to the doctrine of the Trinity, and that an analysis of revelation leads us merely to "our concepts" of the economic Trinity and further "our concepts" of the immanent Trinity.[13] There is a qualitative gap between the epistemological side of Barth's position and Barth's theological method. Accordingly, Barth's basic rule does not say that the immanent Trinity is the same as the economic Trinity, but that "statements" about the immanent Trinity cannot be different in content from "statements" about the economic Trinity.[14]

Due to such an epistemological gap, Barth cannot avoid making another further distinction between God's primary objectivity and God's secondary objectivity, with an implication that the latter is ultimately grounded in the former. God's primary objectivity refers to God's own knowledge of Godself and thus it is concerned with the immanent Trinity. On the other hand, God's secondary objectivity denotes our knowledge of God and thus it is related to the economic Trinity. Barth explains that they are distinguished only by the fact that God's secondary objectivity has its particular creaturely form suitable for us. God is objectively immediate to Godself, whereas God is objectively mediate to us. God's primary objectivity is direct, whereas God's secondary objectivity is indirect, in such a way that God is clothed under the sign and veil of other objects different from Godself.

Barth persistently denies that there is any difference of degree between God's own knowledge of Godself and our knowledge of God

12. Barth, *CD*, I/1, 172.
13. Ibid., I/1, 333.
14. Ibid., I/1, 479.

in revelation. As God gives Godself to be known by us as God knows Godself, the secondary objectivity of God is not distinguished from the primary objectivity of God by a lesser degree of truth. God's secondary objectivity is fully true, too. Nonetheless, Barth locates the ultimate ground of God's secondary objectivity in God's primary objectivity, by insisting that God's secondary objectivity has its correspondence and basis in God's primary objectivity.[15]

So far we have discovered that Barth's position of mutual correspondence is complicated by certain tensions: a tension between the ontological side of Barth's position and his theological method, and a tension between the epistemological side of Barth's position and his theological method. These tensions fundamentally result from his theological method which starts with the reality of revelation and proceeds through an analysis of it to several concepts of the Trinity. Such a method produces those tensions, but cannot answer them. Rather, it only defers and resolves those tensions into the locus of absolute divine freedom, lordship, and divine autonomy.[16] They are always kept in the foreground in Barth's theology, although Barth in his later period comes to put more and more focus on "the humanity of God" by which he means God's relation to us and turning to us.[17]

For Barth, "Godhead in the Bible means freedom, ontic and noetic autonomy."[18] All these concepts converge on the subjectivity of God in an ontic and noetic sense. Ontically, the God of the Bible as the Creator of the world is different from the world. Noetically, God in revelation is essentially inscrutable and hidden. God is both *Deus revelatus* and *Deus absconditus*.[19] Even in the self-revelation of God, God constantly tells us so afresh that there is no human knowing that corresponds to the divine telling and that there is no assuming of God's nature into human

15. Ibid., II/1, 16.

16. Timothy Bradshaw affirms that freedom is a central idea in Barth's vision of God. Bradshaw, *Trinity and Ontology*, 64.

17. Barth, *Humanity of God*, 37–38. The original German lecture "Die Menschlichkeit Gottes" was delivered in 1956. Here Barth admits that, in his early period, the humanity of God moved from the center to the periphery and from the emphasized principal clause to the less emphasized subordinate clause. Then he acknowledges that his problem in his early period is to derive the knowledge of the humanity of God from the knowledge of the deity of God.

18. Barth, *CD*, I/1, 307.

19. Ibid., I/1, 320–21.

knowing.[20] God in revelation refuses to be objectified.[21] Thus when he finds the theological "key" for which he has been searching, which is "A Trinity of *being*, not just an economic Trinity," he, two months later comes to understand the Trinity as "the problem of the inalienable subjectivity of God in his revelation."[22] "God's revelation has its reality and truth wholly and in every respect—both ontically and noetically—within itself."[23]

This subjectivity of God who has ontic reality and noetic truth in revelation leads Barth to have resort to "analogy,"[24] not *analogia entis* but *analogia fidei* and *analogia relationis*, for a connection between the immanent Trinity and the economic Trinity on the one hand, and to consider analogy as not abandoning but denoting "mystery"[25] on the other hand. In this regard, for Barth, analogy and mystery go together with *ignoramus*. For example, regarding something of the immanent Trinity, he states that we cannot establish the "How" of the divine processions and of the divine modes of being, and that we cannot define the Father, the Son, and the Holy Spirit. Instead, we can state the fact of the divine processions and modes of being. He continues as follows: "What has to be said will obviously be said definitively and exclusively by God Himself, by the three in the one God who delimit themselves from one another in revelation. . . . The *ignoramus* which we must confess in relation to the distinction that we have to maintain between begetting and breathing is thus the *ignoramus* which we must confess in relation to the whole doctrine of the Trinity, i.e., in relation to *the mystery of revelation*, in relation to *the mystery of God in general*."[26]

Rahner: Identity

As has been discussed in chapter 3, Rahner's rule of identity means that the economic Logos is the immanent Logos and *conversely*, that the Holy Spirit which we experience in salvific history is the Holy Spirit within

20. Ibid., I/1, 132.
21. Barth, *Göttingen Dogmatics*, 1:327.
22. Barth and Thurneysen, *Revolutionary Theology*, 185.
23. Barth, *CD*, I/1, 305.
24. Ibid., I/1, 372.
25. Ibid., I/1, 373.
26. Ibid., I/1, 476–77.

the Trinity and *vice versa*, and thus that God the Father communicates Godself through the incarnation of the Son and the descent of the Holy Spirit. Like Barth's position of mutual correspondence, Rahner's rule can be critically approached both in its ontological aspect and in its epistemological aspect.

With regard to an ontological aspect, Rahner's rule asserts that the immanent Trinity is the economic Trinity, that the immanent Logos is the economic Logos, and further that the hypostatic union of the economic Logos is the constitutive way of expressing the immanent Logos. It is noteworthy that Rahner bases this ontological claim on his ontology of symbol, for which he draws on some insights from Thomist ontology, including *analogia entis*.[27] According to Rahner, an ontology of symbol has two basic principles. The first is that "all beings are by their nature symbolic, because they necessarily 'express' themselves in order to attain their own nature."[28] This is true in an epistemological sense. However, Rahner does not stop here.

Instead, he goes further to make a differentiation between merely arbitrary symbols and really genuine symbols. The former, including signs, signal and codes, are "symbolic representations," whereas the latter are "symbolic realities." Then he seeks for "the highest and most primordial manner" of symbolic reality, and calls "this supreme and primal representation, in which one reality renders another present (primarily 'for itself' and only secondarily for others), a symbol: the representation which allows the other 'to be there.'"[29] Thus comes the second basic principle: "The symbol strictly speaking (symbolic reality) is the self-realization of a being in the other, which is constitutive of its essence."[30] In this way, Rahner's notion of symbol connotes an ontological sense as well as an epistemological sense. For Rahner, "A being can be and is known, in so far as it is itself ontically (in itself) symbolic because it is ontologically (for itself) symbolic." In other words, "the essence is there . . . precisely through its appearance."[31]

---

27. Rahner, "Theology of the Symbol," 231–32.

28. Ibid., 224.

29. Ibid., 225.

30. Ibid., 234.

31. Ibid., 230–31.

In terms of such an ontology of symbol, Rahner's rule of identity focally means that the immanent Logos is the symbol of the Father and that the economic Logos in a hypostatic union with humanity is the symbol of the immanent Logos, and further that the human nature in a hypostatic union with the economic Logos is "the constitutive, real symbol [*Realsymbol*] of the Logos himself."[32] However, careful analysis reveals an ontological tension, which lurks in his ontology of the symbol. According to Rahner, as being expresses itself, it is multiple in itself and it has a plurality in unity. Its supreme mode is the Trinity. A plurality in unity indicates something negative regarding finiteness and deficiency, whereas a plurality in unity for the Trinity is something positive.[33] Within the Trinity, then, the Logos, namely, the immanent Logos, is the symbol of the Father in such a way that the Logos and the Father are multiple but in unity. On the contrary, the economic Logos goes beyond the unity in plurality. To say the least, the human nature in a hypostatic unity with Logos is the exteriorization of the Logos and thus of the Father.

In Rahner's own differentiation, the immanent Logos is "the inward symbol" which remains distinct from and within what is symbolized. On the other hand, the economic Logos is the outward symbol.[34] As mentioned in chapter 3, Rahner firmly criticizes the Augustinian position that every divine person might assume a hypostatic union, for the economic Logos would then reveal properly nothing about the Logos and thus about the Father. Considering this critique, Rahner's intent could be at least understandable, which is to establish a link and continuity between the inward symbol and the outward symbol:

> ... one needs have no difficulty in thinking that the Word's being symbol of the Father has significance for God's action *ad extra*. . . . It is because God "must" "express" himself inwardly that he can also utter himself outwardly; the finite, created utterance *ad extra* is a continuation of the immanent constitution of "image and likeness"—a free continuation, because its object is finite— and takes place in fact "through" the Logos (Jn 1:3), ... we could

32. Rahner, *Trinity*, 33.

33. Rahner, "Theology of the Symbol," 227–29.

34. Ibid., 236.

> not hardly omit this link between a symbolic reality within and
> without the divine . . .[35]

In spite of his intent, however, the ontological tension remains unanswered and even unresolved. What is worse, as will be shown below, such an ontological tension inevitably has an impact on an epistemological aspect of Rahner's rule of identity.

With regard to the epistemological aspect, Rahner's rule of identity means that the economic Trinity is the immanent Trinity, that the economic Logos is the immanent Logos, that the Holy Spirit which we experience in salvific history is the Spirit of the Father and the Son within the Trinity, and thus that we experience God the Father through the incarnation of the Son and the descent of the Holy Spirit.

For such epistemological claim, Rahner appeals to the threefold self-communication of God. According to Rahner, God's self-communication is "a *quasi-formal* causality," rather than "*efficient* causality."[36] By this he means that God bestows uncreated grace, that is, Godself, but not that God indirectly gives some parts of Godself to the creature by giving created finite realities. In this regard, God's self-communication is given not only as gift, but also as "the necessary condition which makes possible human acceptance of the gift."[37] It is a "supernatural existential" in which we have a transcendental, though unthematic, orientation toward God's offer of self-communication, and in which we have potential obedience through which we receive God's uncreated grace.[38] Therefore, for Rahner, there is not any possibility of making an epistemological gap "between God's self-communicating, gratuitous, self-bestowing activity, and the reception of grace by the justified."[39] We can experience Godself outwardly communicated through the incarnation of the Logos in the grace of the Holy Spirit, who is also inwardly expressed through the Logos in the Spirit within the Trinity.

However, for Rahner, a serious problem arises from an ontological tension inherent in his rule of identity. Epistemologically, we have a transcendental possibility of receiving Godself through the offer of

---

35. Ibid., 236–37.

36. Rahner, *Trinity*, 36.

37. Rahner, *Foundations*, 128.

38. Ibid., 126–29.

39. LaCugna, "Re-conceiving the Trinity," 7.

God's threefold self-communication. On the contrary, ontologically, as the economic Logos, or the human nature of the economic Logos goes beyond the divine unity in plurality as the exteriorization of the immanent Logos and thus of God the Father, we could not be given Godself as the same much as the immanent Logos ontologically symbolizes God the Father. Instead, we could merely receive something of Godself.

This ontological tension and its incompatibility with an epistemological possibility lead Rahner to be hesitant to fully confirm that the incarnation of the Logos and the descent of the Holy Spirit are the totally whole reality of God. Though he claims that God communicates Godself through them, Rahner regards them merely as "absolute proximity." As he puts it: "Hence when we reach the point of absolute *proximity* of the 'coming' of God, the covenant, in which God really communicates himself radically and bindingly to his partner . . . the inner, mutually related moments of the one self-communication, through which God (the Father) communicates himself to the world unto absolute proximity."[40] Moreover, this tension leads Rahner further to put the notion of the mystery of God in the foreground of his entire theology, in order to resolve the problem. However, it is notable that Rahner's concept of mystery does not merely have an epistemological sense of mystery. According to Rahner, the conventional notion of mystery, as represented by the first Vatican Council, is characterized by its inseparable orientation to reason [*ratio*]. Thus it understands mystery from the outset as the property of propositions, which is able to be multiplied with provisionally incomprehensible truths. In addition, such a notion of mystery corresponds exactly to an ordinary notion of revelation as the communication of statements and assertions.[41] Rahner maintains that such an epistemological sense of mystery would be then eliminated by grace.

Standing in opposition to such an obsolete concept of mystery, Rahner makes an attempt to identify "the primordial concept of mystery" on the ground that God remains as the incomprehensible mystery even in *visio beatifica*.[42] In this regard, Rahner's own notion of mystery is what can be ontologically encountered in the original transcendental

---

40. Rahner, *Trinity*, 41 (Rahner's own italics), 85.

41. Rahner, "Concept of Mystery," 37–39.

42. Ibid., 41, 53.

experience. This is the reason why Rahner regards mystery not only as "the incomprehensible and ineffable mystery," but also as "the holy mystery."[43] Therefore he concludes a section of his explication on the identity of the economic and the immanent Trinity, by putting his rule of identity in a balance with the incomprehensible mystery of God:

> It is only through this doctrine [the Christian doctrine of the Trinity] that we can take with radical seriousness and maintain without qualifications the simple statement which is at once so very incomprehensible and so very self-evident, namely that God himself as the abiding and holy mystery, as the incomprehensible ground of man's transcendent existence is not only the God of infinite distance, but also wants to be the God of absolute closeness in a true self-communication.... Here lies the real meaning of the doctrine of the Trinity.[44]

Moltmann, Pannenberg, and Jenson: Eschatological Unity

Moltmann: Doxological and Eschatological Unity

Moltmann position of doxological and eschatological unity means that the economic Trinity is the immanent Trinity eschatologically and the immanent Trinity is the economic Trinity doxologically. With regard to the economic-immanent Trinity relation, Moltmann begins with the cross event of three divine subjects in salvation history, from which he discovers both the economic Trinity and the immanent Trinity. But it is considerably remarkable that Moltmann insists that the economic Trinity is not merely a kind of manifestation of the immanent Trinity antecedently in itself. He is firmly opposed to an understanding of the economic-immanent Trinity relation "as a one-way relationship—

---

43. Ibid., 53; Rahner, *Foundations of Christian Faith*, 136.

44. Rahner, *Foundations of Christian Faith*, 137. Yves Congar accepts Rahner's rule of identity but likes to limit its absolute character and to clarify its second half. Congar has two reasons which are related to his distinction between free mystery and necessary mystery. The first reason is that "the free mystery of the economy" is not the same as "the necessary mystery of the Trinity. The other is that God's self-communication will not be full until the beatific vision at the end of time. Yves Congar, *I Believe in the Holy Spirit*, III, 13–15.

the relation of image to reflection, idea to appearance, essence to manifestation."[45]

Moltmann instead claims that the economic Trinity has a retroactive effect on the immanent Trinity. For example, the surrender of the Son for us on the cross has a retroactive effect on the Father and causes infinite pain to the Father. On the cross God creates salvation outwardly for us. Simultaneously God also suffers this disaster of the world inwardly within Godself. In this sense God's relationship to the world has a retroactive effect on God's relationship to Godself. The pain of the cross determines the inner life of the Triune God from eternity to eternity. The economic Trinity is determinative of the immanent Trinity.[46]

Such notion of a retroactive effect of the economic Trinity on the immanent Trinity is intended by Moltmann as a corrective to the traditional one-way relationship from the immanent to the economic Trinity. Moltmann, however, does not go so far as to insist that the retroactive effect of the economic Trinity on the immanent Trinity is all. Rather, Moltmann supports a mutual relationship between them. Actually he admits a correspondence of the economic Trinity to the immanent Trinity as well. For example, when he understands salvation history as the Trinitarian history of God in the concurrent and joint workings of the Father, the Son and the Holy Spirit, Moltmann considers that the Trinitarian history of God corresponds to the eternal *perichoresis* of the Trinity.[47] In addition, Moltmann states: "From the foundation of the world, the *opera trinitatis ad extra* [the economic Trinity] correspond to the *passiones trinitatis ad intra* [the immanent Trinity]."[48] Besides, Moltmann states: "the divine relationship to the world [the economic Trinity] is primarily determined by that inner relationship [the immanent Trinity]."[49]

Such being the case, Moltmann's notion of a retroactive effect of the economic on the immanent Trinity seems to be in an incompatible tension with that of the correspondence of the economic to the immanent Trinity. How does Moltmann resolve such an incompatible tension? One

45. Moltmann, *Trinity*, 160–61.

46. Ibid., 160.

47. Ibid., 156–57.

48. Ibid., 160.

49. Ibid., 161.

possible answer lies in his highly delicate distinction between an epistemological sense of the Trinity and an ontological sense of the Trinity,
which may pass unnoticed. In fact, he makes a distinction between the
economic Trinity *itself* and our *knowledge* of the economic Trinity, and,
likewise, between the immanent Trinity *itself* and our *knowledge* of the
immanent Trinity: "If the immanent Trinity is the counterpart of praise,
then knowledge of the economic Trinity (as the embodiment of the history and experience of salvation) precedes knowledge of the immanent
Trinity. In the order of being it [the economic Trinity] succeeds it [the
immanent Trinity]."[50] In an epistemological aspect, our knowledge of
the economic Trinity goes ahead of our knowledge of the immanent
Trinity and has a retroactive effect on our knowledge of the immanent
Trinity. The economic Trinity is our knowledge of the object of kerygmatic and practical theology, and the immanent Trinity is the content
of doxological theology. On the other hand, in an ontological aspect,
the immanent Trinity is prior to the economic Trinity. The economic
Trinity is primarily determined by the immanent Trinity, and the economic Trinity corresponds to the immanent Trinity.

Here we can notice that Moltmann makes a distinction between
the economic Trinity and the immanent Trinity in terms of epistemology as well as ontology. Notably, the distinction is mainly due to his
theological method. As he begins with our experienced salvation on
the cross on Golgotha, from which he discovers three different divine
subjects in *perichoresis*, what remains for him to do is to formulate our
right knowledge of the Trinity, and especially that of the immanent
Trinity. For the purpose, he criticizes some erroneous knowledge of the
immanent Trinity. For instance, he firmly rejects a notion of the immanent Trinity in which God is simply by Godself without the love which
communicates salvation to us. For, as Moltmann maintains, such a notion would then bring an arbitrary element into the concept of God.[51]
Besides, he rebuffs a notion of the immanent Trinity within which the
cross in the economy of salvation does not stand.[52] For these reasons,
Moltmann affirms Rahner's rule of identity which seems to him to admit of an interaction between the economic and the immanent Trinity,

50. Ibid., 152–53.

51. Ibid., 151.

52. Ibid., 160.

though he does not hide his concern that Rahner's rule may leave the door open for the dissolution of the one in the other.

So far we have noted that Moltmann attempts to resolve an incompatible tension between his notion of a retroactive effect of the economic Trinity on the immanent Trinity and that of the correspondence of the economic Trinity to the immanent Trinity. However, such an attempt does not completely resolve the tension, because of a manifest fact that there are some passages which clearly indicate an ontologically retroactive effect of the economic Trinity on the immanent Trinity. For a representative example, the surrender of the Son for us on the cross has a retroactive effect on the Father and causes infinite pain to the Father.

Thus, in order to resolve the tension a little further, Moltmann proposes his own doxological and eschatological understanding of the Trinity, which allows us to be transformed to see an ontologically retroactive effect of the economic Trinity on the immanent Trinity. This doxological and eschatological understanding still has something to do with our ideas and concepts. Nonetheless, it includes not only our knowledge of the immanent Trinity which derives from our experience of the economic Trinity, but also our possibility of seeing an ontologically retroactive effect of the economic Trinity on the immanent Trinity. In a doxological aspect, while mentioning that our knowledge of the immanent Trinity has its *Sitz im Leben* in doxology as the praise and worship of Church, simultaneously Moltmann stresses that, in the doxology of the economic Trinity, we participate in the fullness of the divine life of the immanent Trinity.[53] And the doxological aspect is linked to an eschatological aspect. For our doxological response through the Spirit to the economic Trinity determines the inner life of the immanent Trinity. Therefore, for Moltmann, the economic Trinity eschatologically completes and perfects itself in the immanent Trinity, and the economic Trinity at the *eschaton* is raised into and transcended in the immanent Trinity.[54]

Such a doxological and eschatological understanding of the Trinity finally leads to Moltmann's concept of mystery. It is not merely an epistemologically impenetrable mystery. Rather, it is a living mystery which

---

53. Ibid., 152; Moltmann, *Spirit of Life*, 302.

54. Moltmann, *Trinity*, 161.

is intimately interwoven with an epistemological knowability and an ontological encounterability. This is how he puts it: "In this eschatological sense *the Trinity is a mystery (mysterion)* which is only manifested to us there in the experience of salvation. To talk about *'the mystery of the Trinity'* does not mean pointing to some impenetrable obscurity or insoluble riddle. It means with unveiled face already recognizing here and now, in the obscurity of history, the glory of the triune God and praising him in the hope of one day seeing him face to face."[55] The mystery of the Trinity is manifested to us in the experience of salvation. But also the mystery of the Trinity is in our hope for us to see face to face at the *eschaton*. In the meantime, our knowledge, ideas, terms, and concepts of the Trinity suffer "a transformation of meaning"[56] so as to encounter the Trinity face to face.

Pannenberg: Futurist and Eschatological Unity

Pannenberg's position regarding the relation between the economic and the immanent Trinity says that God's activity comes to completion at *eschaton* and thus the unity of the economic Trinity and the immanent Trinity takes places eschatologically. For the position, Pannenberg appeals to the biblical statement of the reciprocal self-differentiation of three divine persons: the Father, the Son and the Holy Spirit. That is, the deity of the Father is dependent on the historical work of the Son and the eschatological work of the Holy Spirit.

On the one hand, Pannenberg's position implies that, as the deity of the Father is dependent on the Son's self-differentiation, so the immanent Trinity is dependent on the economic Trinity. There is no presupposed immanent Trinity without the economic Trinity in the history of economy.[57] The immanent Trinity cannot be considered independent of the economic Trinity. In Grenz's expression, "the immanent Trinity

---

55. Ibid., 161.

56. Ibid., 162.

57. Pannenberg, *Systematic Theology*, III, 13, 193. Here Pannenberg explicates the relation between love of neighbor and love of God by analogy with the relation between the economic Trinity and the immanent Trinity: "As the works of the economic Trinity proceed from the life of the immanent Trinity, so love of neighbor issues from love of God, and thus also from faith, which precedes the works of neighborly love.... As there can be no immanent Trinity without the economic Trinity, so there can be no faith without works of neighborly love."

flows from the economic Trinity."[58] On the other hand, Pannenberg's position implies as well that, as the Father's eschatological deity is the ground of the Son's self-differentiation, so the immanent Trinity as the eschatological reality of completion has priority over the economic Trinity, with the implication that the former executes an influence on the latter.[59]

It is worth noting that Pannenberg's position is inextricably grounded in his earlier metaphysical thoughts, especially with regard to *ordo essendi* and *ordo cognoscendi*, ontology and epistemology, reality and truth, or being and knowing. Since Pannenberg insists upon an inseparable relation between theological discourse and metaphysical reflection,[60] his position regarding the relation between the economic and the immanent Trinity cannot be considered apart from his methodological positions.

First of all, as has been indicated in chapter 3, Pannenberg from the outset puts a great methodological emphasis on history: "History is the most comprehensive horizon of Christian Theology. All theological questions and answers are meaningful only within the framework of the history which God has with humanity and through humanity with his whole creation—the history moving toward a future still hidden from the world but already revealed in Jesus Christ."[61]

This methodological focus on history leads him to articulate an indirect character to revelation as the historical acts of God, and further to maintain that revelation is only to be completely comprehended at the end of history, not at the beginning.[62]

In the second place, this methodological concentration on history enables Pannenberg to adhere to an inseparable relation between *eidos* (idea or form) and *phenomenon* (appearance), or, between essence and

---

58. Grenz, *Rediscovering*, 95.

59. Olson, "Pannenberg's Doctrine," 200.

60. Pannenberg, *Metaphysics and the Idea of God*, 6. The original German text *Metaphysik und Gottesgedanke* was published by Vandenhoeck & Ruprecht in Göttingen in 1988; On the same page Pannenberg points out that a theological doctrine of God which lacks metaphysics runs the danger of either a kerygmatic subjectivism or a thoroughgoing demythologization, and frequently of both.

61. Pannenberg, "Redemptive Event and History," I, 15. The original lecture was delivered in 1959.

62. Pannenberg, *Revelation as History*, 125.

existence. Criticizing a Platonic dualism between being and appearance, Pannenberg agrees with Hegel that appearance not only points back to essence, but also that essence is not behind or beyond appearance. However, unlike Hegel who holds an ontological precedence of essence over appearance, Pannenberg agrees with Heinrich Barth that appearance as existence have priority over essence.[63] As a consequence, Pannenberg suggests that we should conceive the essence of God in terms of God's existence in the world, namely, God's rule over the world, but not the other way around.[64]

In the third place, Pannenberg advances an ontological priority of appearance to essence especially in terms of his exegesis of the kingdom of God in the message and life of Jesus Christ. According to him, the kingdom of God does not lie in the distant future, but it is so imminent that the future of the coming kingdom of God executes a considerable impact on our present existence. The future has an imperative claim upon the present, and even creates the past and the present. The future is active in the present through anticipation and is the necessary condition for meaning and truth.[65] It is here noteworthy that Pannenberg derives two remarkable insights from his interpretation of the kingdom of God. The first one is his creative formulation that appearance is the arrival of the future. The second insight is his provocative proposal of an ontological priority of eschatological future, which is named an ontology of future or futurist ontology.[66]

In the last place, Pannenberg's notion of futurity has significant ramifications for the concept of eternity. He firmly denies that his notion of the futurity of the kingdom of God merely projects the essence of God into the future, as if the substantial notion of God's essence would trace back to the past. He explains this point as follows: "It [the notion of the futurity] does not mean that God is only in the future and was not in the past or is not in the present. Quite to the contrary, as the power of the future he dominates the remotest past."[67] For Pannenberg, the God of the futurity is eternal, because God is not only the future of

---

63. Pannenberg, "Appearance," 104–6.

64. Pannenberg, "Problems," 254.

65. Pannenberg, *Metaphysics and the Idea of God*, x.

66. Pannenberg, "Theology and the Kingdom of God," 5.

67. Ibid., 11.

our present but has also been the future of every past age. He criticizes Plato's concept of eternity which implies an everlasting present without change; instead, for Pannenberg, as God is the power of the ultimate future, the very essence of God's eternity implies time as well.[68]

Taking these points into consideration, Pannenberg's doctrine of the Trinity is intimately interwoven with ontology and epistemology. Bradshaw speaks very highly of him on this point as follows: "Pannenberg's trinitarian doctrine is therefore the foundation for his ontology and epistemology. It is the very condition for thinking of God in relationship to the world in an integrated way and orientated to the future. The doctrine of the Trinity unites, for Pannenberg, ontology and epistemology, as well as divine transcendence and immanence in creation."[69]

It is remarkable that, thanks to such an intimate relation between *ordo essendi* and *ordo cognoscendi*, Pannenberg hardly relies on the divine concept of mystery with regard to the doctrine of the Trinity. In comparison to Barth, Rahner, and even Moltmann, his discussion of mystery is quite rare except one prominent fact that, for Pannenberg, mystery predominantly refers to Jesus Christ or the divine plan of salvation revealed in Jesus Christ. Pannenberg insistently argues that Jesus Christ in the New Testament is himself "the mystery,"[70] and "the quintessence of the mystery of God."[71] Jesus Christ is "God's mystery of salvation in person,"[72] "the embodiment of the mystery of salvation that puts the divine plan of salvation into effect,"[73] and "the one divine mystery of salvation."[74] All the other things which are called mysteries such as baptism and the Lord's Supper are mystery only in a secondary and derivative sense.

More remarkably, Pannenberg understands the mystery of Jesus Christ or the historical plan for salvation already proleptically revealed in Jesus Christ is eschatological in such a way that it is manifest "through

---

68. Pannenberg, "Theology and the Kingdom of God," 11.

69. Bradshaw, *Trinity and Ontology*, 332.

70. Pannenberg, *Systematic Theology*, III, 13, 40.

71. Ibid., III, 13, 238, and 364.

72. Ibid., III, 13, 43.

73. Ibid., III, 13, 44.

74. Ibid., III, 13, 345; Also refer to I, 4, 211; I, 4, 216; I, 6, 440; II, 9, 312.

the Spirit whom Christ gives" and thus manifest "in anticipation of the outcome of history."[75] In this aspect, all events in the history of Jesus Christ such as his birth, crucifixion and resurrection bear reference to the future eschatological consummation of human history, which is the main reason that they are called mysteries in the post-apostolic period. In addition, baptism and the Lord's Supper are called mysteries or sacraments, in that through them we have access to the eschatological salvation of Jesus Christ.[76]

Jenson: Eschatological Unity in Temporal Narrative

Jenson's eschatological thesis with regard to the relation between the economic and the immanent Trinity is that the identity of the economic Trinity and the immanent Trinity is eschatological, and the immanent Trinity is the eschatological reality of the economic Trinity. As chapter 3 has shown, his eschatological thesis is grounded in his theological method which has as its task to identify God through biblical narrative which is both temporal and eschatological. However, Jenson's eschatological thesis has two tensions inherent in his the theological method. The first is an ontological one, for it is concerned with a move from God's self-identification by events in time to God's identification with those events. And the other is an epistemological one, which is related to a move from God's self-identity to human identification of *dramatis dei personae*[77] through biblical narrative.

In the first place, with regard to the first move, Jenson mentions: "a conceptual move has been made from the biblical God's self-identification *by* events in time to his identification *with* those events."[78] Without expounding the move in more detail, Jenson asserts that this move is theologically justifiable. For, if there is no identification of God with events themselves, then the identification of God reveals merely something of God, but that is what would be ontologically other than Godself. And the revealing events would be just some "clues to God," or "a pointer to deity," but not Godself.[79] Therefore, for Jenson, the

75. Ibid., I, 6, 440.

76. Ibid., III, 13, 347.

77. Jenson, *Systematic Theology*, I, 89.

78. Ibid., I, 59. Jenson's own italics.

79. Ibid., I, 59–60.

events by which God is identified should be the same as Godself in an ontological sense. This move may be understandable, if we consider Jenson's intent, namely, to be firmly opposed to the Hellenistic eternal-izing tendency which makes a dualistic separation between essence and existence, between being and appearance, between eternity and time, with the inevitable implication that the events by which God is identi-fied have merely something of God, but not Godself.

However, this identification of God with events inescapably en-counters an ontological tension, that is, whether revealing events them-selves are ontologically the same as Godself, or not. First, as Jenson maintains that the Old Testament identifies God as the One who res-cued Israel from Egypt and the New Testament identifies God as the One who raised Jesus from the dead,[80] the identification means that God is the One who are engaged in the rescue of Israel from Egypt and in the resurrection of Jesus from the dead. But it goes further to mean that the God of Israel and Jesus is the same as the event of rescue of Israel and also the same as the event of resurrection. If God is first and foremost an event itself,[81] it may efface an ontological distinction be-tween agent and event, and finally lead towards the absorption of God as actor into acts.

Second, the identification of God with events risks blurring an-other ontological distinction among the three divine persons, or, in Jenson's own terms, "three identities," which are Jesus the Son, the God of Israel whom Jesus called "Father," and the Spirit of their future.[82] The three are ontologically distinct, in that the Father is the past whence of divine life, the Spirit as the future whither of divine life, and the Son as the present in which divine past and divine future hold together in one life.[83] However, this identification of God with events has a tendency to reduce three identities, or three divine persons into mere impersonal structural relations. In fact, Jenson states that God is an event which is constituted in relations and is personal in structure.[84] Accordingly, he regards some intra-divine words, such as begetting, being begotten

80. Jenson, *Triune Identity*, 1–18; *Systematic Theology*, I, 44–45.

81. Jenson lists four characteristics of the one God as "an event," "a person," "a deci-sion," and "a conversation." Jenson, *Systematic Theology*, I, 221–23.

82. Ibid., I, 108.

83. Ibid., I, 218.

84. Jenson, *Triune Identity*, 161.

and proceeding, to be merely the words which summarize the plot of biblical narrative.[85] Besides, Jenson goes further to attribute personal consciousness only to the Triune event itself, but not to the Father, the Son, or the Spirit: "God is indeed describable as personal in the modern sense, but it is the triune event of which this is true, not the Father merely as Father. *The person that is consciousness is the Trinity.* The Trinity is constituted as a centered and possibly faithful self-consciousness by his object-reality as Jesus, the Son."[86] In this sense, Jenson goes so far as to regard Jesus, who is the Son, simply as "an individual personal *thing*."[87] Likewise, "what ontologically precedes the birth ... of Jesus who is God the Son, ... is the narrative pattern of being going to be born. What in eternity precedes the Son's birth ... is ... a pattern of movement within the event of the Incarnation."[88]

In the second place, a move from God's self-identity to our identification of *dramatis dei personae* through biblical narrative carries with it an epistemological tension. The self-identification of God by events, strictly speaking, does not accord perfectly with our identification of God through biblical narrative. For, as Jenson acknowledges, we as creatures lack faithfulness of each of our own acts and, as fallen creatures, even betray our own coherence with ourselves to the extent that we are threatened by absurdity.[89] Thus, in order to resolve the epistemological tension, on the one hand, Jenson merely contends that God is knowable because and only because God is in fact known. He explicates this point as follows: "God is first known by himself, for the Father is freed by the Spirit to find himself in the Son; in the Spirit, the Son knows himself loved by the Father and just so knows the Father; the Spirit knows the love he brings to the Father and the Son."[90]

By this statement Jenson seems to locate the ground of human epistemological knowledge of God in God's self-knowledge in the mutual life of Father, Son, and Spirit.[91] However, this is not different in

---

85. Jenson, *Systematic Theology*, I, 108.

86. Jenson, *Triune Idenity*, 175.

87. Ibid., 175.

88. Jenson, *Systematic Theology*, I, 141.

89. Ibid., I, 222.

90. Ibid., I, 227.

91. Ibid., I, 228.

its basic structure from the Hellenistic eternalizing tendency, which he himself rigidly criticizes. This is, therefore, an epistemological impasse for Jenson's position.

In order to resolve the epistemological tension, on the other hand, Jenson appeals to the point that the Triune life in which God actually knows Godself is "in its actuality a life with us."[92] For him, God is what happens between God and us, and God's story is our story. However, this effort does not resolve the tension at all. On this point, David B. Hart is rightly concerned that Jenson may collapse an analogical interval between the event of our salvation in Christ and the event of God's life as Trinity.[93]

What is worse, such an epistemological impasse is actually grounded in his epistemic ontology. At the end of his book *The Triune Identity*, Jenson answers the ontological question, "What is it to be?" by saying that to be is epistemologically interpretive relatedness across time. Here Jenson reveals a qualitative difference between God and creature in terms of epistemic ontology: "To be God is to anticipate a future self by an inexhaustible interpretive relation to an other that God himself is; to be a creature is to anticipate a future self, by a finite interpretive relation to an other that the creature is not."[94] Such a qualitative difference between God and creature rather makes a gap wider between God and creatures, with an implication that there is no warrant for conceiving that God's self-identity would ever accord epistemologically with our identification of *dramatis dei personae* through biblical narrative.

So far we have noted two tensions: ontological and epistemological, which are inherent in Jenson's own theological method, and which are not resolved within his own framework. There is only one possible seed of solution, which Jenson does not fully discuss, and which he calls the "final mystery," or "the deepest mystery of his [God's] identity." It is surprising that Jenson rarely discusses a concept of mystery except in two places in the *Systematic Theology*. Even when he explicates divine hiddenness, he does not appeal to a concept of mystery at all.[95]

92. Ibid., I, 228.

93. Hart, "Lively God," 31.

94. Jenson, *Triune Identity*, 182.

95. For Jenson, God's proper hiddenness is not any metaphysical distance, but both cognitive and moral. He explains: "God is not hidden because he holds back some part of the selfknowing he shares with us, but because that self-knowing is alive and moving and we cannot keep up with its moral intentions." Jenson, *Systematic Theology*, I, 233.

For Jenson, the deepest mystery refers to a transition of the identity of God of Israel into the Father of the Son and the Spirit: "Therewith we have introduced a final mystery. . . . Not only the Son and the Spirit appear as *dramatis dei personae*; also the God whose Son and Spirit these are is identified as himself one *persona* of God, as the Father of the Son and sender of the Spirit. The God of Israel appears as himself one of the *personae dramatis* of the very God he is. That is the deepest mystery of his identity and the final necessity of the doctrine of the Trinity."[96] The core of the deepest mystery of God's identity is the biblical fact that Jesus determines the Father's personhood by calling God the Father and conversing with the Father to the extent that the being of God is conversation and communion. In this sense, Jenson expresses it as "the first and foundational mystery of communion," or "the primal mystery of communion," in which the conversation of the Triune God opens to us to be the conversation of God within a historically actual human community.[97] In this regard, it is unfortunate that Jenson did not choose to advance his concept of mystery as an answer to his ontological and epistemological tensions.

Boff and Pittenger: "Much More Than"

Boff: Not the Whole of the Immanent Trinity

Despite his intention of accepting Rahner's Rule, though in his own version,[98] Boff's actual position with regard to the relation between the economic and the immanent Trinity is that the immanent Trinity is much more than the economic Trinity. The most prominent reason for the disparity between this intention and his actual position lies in his strong focus on the mystery of the Trinity, which connotes both an ontological sense of mystery and an epistemological sense of mystery. In this regard, Boff's doctrine of the Trinity is remarkably characterized by its conspicuous concentration on mystery.

From the outset, Boff's starts with the original faith experience of mystery by the first disciples. They met and lived together with Jesus

96. Ibid., I, 89.

97. Ibid., II, 250 and 270–71.

98. Boff's version of Rahner's Rule is: "the Three Unique Beings in communion who reveals themselves in the economy of salvation are the immanent Tri-unity, and vice versa." Boff, *Trinity and Society*, 214.

Christ and proclaimed the Father, the Son, and the Holy Spirit in prayer and preaching. They perceived both unity and diversity "in the experience of the Mystery,"[99] which later explications of the original faith experience led subsequent Christians to formulate as the economic Trinity, namely, the Trinity manifested and revealed in human history. Boff explains that their experience of mystery led them to proceed immediately from the economic Trinity to the immanent Trinity. As they were faced with "the ineffable Mystery,"[100] they acknowledged that concepts and expressions are inadequate and only analogical and indicative in their meaning. Thus they thought that there is something else behind or beyond what is manifested and revealed. In this way, they were led to seek a corresponding reality, that is, the immanent Trinity which is the Trinity in its eternal inner relationship. To put it in terms of Boff's basic thesis of *perichoresis*, they thought that there is the immanent *perichoresis* to which the economic *perichoresis* corresponds. Throughout these developments of the doctrine of the Trinity, the concept of mystery executes a considerable influence both ontologically and epistemologically.

Boff's outstanding concentration on mystery is well shown in his contention that the Trinity is a mystery not only for us, but also in itself: "What the Trinity is in itself is beyond our reach, hidden in unfathomable mystery, mystery that will be partially revealed to us in the bliss of eternal life, but will always escape us in full, since the Trinity is a mystery in itself and not only for human beings."[101] This notion of the Trinity as a mystery includes both an ontological sense and an epistemological sense. As the Trinity is a mystery ontologically and epistemologically, the Trinity is beyond our reach, and is also hidden and unfathomable. Though it is manifested to us, it is only partially revealed to us. The Trinity always escapes our full comprehension. As the Trinity is the unfathomable and hidden Trinity, the economic Trinity is not the whole of the immanent Trinity, and the whole of the immanent Trinity does not manifest itself in the economic Trinity alone.

Therefore, for Boff, the mystery of the Trinity is "*mysterium stricte dictum*" both in its ontological aspect and in its epistemological aspects.

---

99. Ibid., 3.

100. Ibid., 7.

101. Ibid., 215.

However, Boff, like Rahner, rejects a one-sidedly epistemological sense of mystery, such as that proposed by the first Vatican Council. Boff maintains that it rightly understands that the mystery of the Trinity surpasses human epistemological possibility and cannot be apprehended positively. However, he contends that such a lopsidedly epistemological notion of mystery is only posited as an argument to counter a rationalism which attempts to turn revealed truth into mere products of human reason and language. And he continues to point out that such an unbalanced notion of mystery is hardly conducive to our adoration and veneration in the face of the Trinity. Hence he formulates a more balanced concept of mystery which includes both aspects, ontological and epistemological. On the one hand, he considers the mystery of the Trinity as the "revealed mystery" and the "sacramental mystery,"[102] as it has been revealed and communicated in the actions of Jesus Christ and in the manifestations of the Spirit. On the other hand, he stresses that the mystery of God is more than a revealed truth. God is an intrinsic mystery and will remain so even in the eternity to come.[103]

However, Boff's strong focus on mystery makes inevitable impacts on his understanding of the relation between the economic and the immanent Trinity. In the first place, this focus has an unavoidable tendency to trace back to the ultimate ground of mystery on and on even beyond the mystery of the Trinity, though not *ad infinitum*. Original faith experience of mystery through Jesus Christ proceeds to the mystery of the economic Trinity which, in turn, leads to the mystery of the immanent Trinity. In terms of life inside the Trinity, as Boff explains, the Father is the deepest and darkest mystery, the Son is the shining mystery, and the Spirit is the mystery which unites the Father and the Son.[104] The mystery is "the Father himself, the Son himself and the Spirit itself."[105] And Boff does not stop at this point. Rather, he goes further to maintain that the mystery of the Trinity is the ultimate mystery, but it is the mystery indwelt by "the Infinite." The mystery of the Trinity is "a doorway through which we go to the infinity of God."[106]

102. Ibid., 159.
103. Ibid., 160.
104. Ibid., 160.
105. Ibid., 237.
106. Ibid., 159.

Where is, then, the Infinite, or the infinity of God? Boff seems to answer by locating it in God the Father. When he discusses God the Father, God the Son and God the Spirit respectively in chapters 9-11 in *Trinity and Society*, Boff considers God the Father alone as the "unfathomable mystery,"[107] but without remarking that the other persons are the mystery. However, this seeming answer is contradictory to his basic thesis of the complete *perichoresis*, both economic and immanent, among the three divine persons, whereby he proposes not only *Filioque*, but also *Spirituque* and *Patreque*.

In the second place, Boff's strong focus on mystery runs the risk of loosening the close link, correlation, or even correspondence between the economic and the immanent Trinity. We may understand Boff's loose link between them a little bit sympathetically, if we consider that he actually means by it that the mystery of the Trinity is present not only in the incarnation of the Son and the descent of the Spirit, but also that the mystery of the Trinity is "present in creation and history in a thousand different ways" to such an extent that "the universe is pregnant with this unutterable mystery."[108]

However, this loose link inescapably makes a negative impact even on his narrow claim that the economic Trinity is the immanent Trinity and *vice versa*. For Boff states that the mystery of the Trinity is partially, not fully, revealed and manifested to us,[109] and that the economic Trinity, though regarded to be the gateway to the immanent Trinity, provides merely "glimpses" of the immanent Trinity.[110] On this point, Ted Peters is rightly critical of Boff's emphasis on the eternity of the immanent Trinity which causes him to shrink from the implications of Rahner's rule, and to retreat to an affirmation of the sublime Trinity unreachable by us because it is shrouded in eternal mystery.[111] That is one of reasons why Boff is not able to claim to perceive the mystery of God exclusively through the incarnation. Instead, Boff steps back to take into consideration not only the incarnation but also as much as various expressions of Jesus' human life such as "his prayers of thanks-

---

107. Ibid., 165.
108. Ibid., 226.
109. Ibid., 215.
110. Ibid., 163.
111. Ted Peters, *GOD as Trinity*, 113.

giving, his proclamation of the good news, his dealings with the poor, his encounters with the Pharisees, his acts of healing and exorcism, his sharing with the Apostles."[112]

In the last place, moreover, since the link between the economic and the immanent Trinity which Boff claims is not as close as he intends, it severely weakens his well-known "social project" or "liberation program," by which to "seek transformations in social relations."[113] Boff's prominent concentration on mystery finally betrays his theological prospect that faith in the Holy Trinity is able to unleash its liberating potential amidst the present economic inequality and political oppression.[114] Ted Peters continues to remark a further contradictory element lurking in his focus on the eternal mystery of the Trinity: "Although Boff wants to work with a correlation between a divine society and a human society on a nonhierarchical basis, the divine society of which he speaks is in fact a monarchy; and because this monarchy is shrouded in eternal mystery apart from the time in which we live, no genuine correlation with human society can be made."[115]

Pittenger: Much More Than the Palestinian Trinity

With regard to the relation between the economic and the immanent Trinity, Pittenger argues that there is some correspondence between them, but that the immanent Trinity is not confined to the Palestinian Trinity. More specifically, his position on the one hand means that Jesus Christ as the Word of God is the divine action as the self-expression of the divine reality, but that the divine action is not confined to Jesus Christ, and on the other hand that the Holy Spirit is the divine response which enables the early Christians to respond to the divine action in Jesus Christ, but the divine response is not restricted to the Spirit within the Christian community.

Pittenger approaches the doctrine of the Trinity primarily through an analysis of human experience which leads us to acknowledge the mystery of divine reality. He explains it as follows: "it is my belief that there is an approach to trinitarian thought through an analysis of what

---

112. Boff, *Trinity and Society*, 162.

113. Boff, *Holy Trinity*, xiii–xvii.

114. Boff, *Trinity and Society*, 11–13.

115. Peters, *GOD as Trinity*, 114.

might be called man's *wider experiential awareness . . . in human experience generally there is a sense of mystery,* in which meaning is believed to be discovered as humankind makes a response to what is given in the happenings of nature and history and the concrete existence that we know so well."[116]

For his approach, Pittenger draws on Thomas Aquinas and on Gabriel Marcel.[117] According to him, Aquinas, who says that all lead to mystery [*omnia abeunt in mysterium*], provides a profound insight into human experience, that is, that there remains an element of the given in it which is not explicable by human reason. Thus, agreeing with Aquinas, he maintains that we live in the midst of mystery. In addition, Marcel understands mystery as presenting us with ultimate questions which cannot be solved, with an implication that there always remains more in our experience than can be solved, which is mystery. As Marcel regards family bond such as fatherhood and sonship as bringing in mystery,[118] so Pittenger takes human relationships as an excellent example of mystery.[119]

With regards to the doctrine of the Trinity, while acknowledging that religion in all its forms is a response to the mystery of divine reality, Pittenger sets out to analyze Palestinian religious experience: "There is the circumambient mystery and there is the meaning of that mystery disclosed to us in the love which makes its urgent appeal to human beings everywhere, supremely and decisively (so Christians dare to say) in the Man of Nazareth."[120] For him, the Palestinian religious experience grasps a threefold structure of the mystery of divine reality: God, the divine Action in Jesus Christ and the divine Response through the Holy Spirit.[121] Pittenger maintains that the threefold pattern becomes the basic material for the formulation of the doctrine of the Trinity which is what he calls "the Palestinian Trinity."[122]

---

116. Pittenger, *Divine Triunity*, 50–51.

117. Ibid., 51–52.

118. Marcel, *Mystery of Being*, I, 204. The first volume concentrates on the notion of mystery, on which the second volume develops. This book was published from Gifford Lectures which Marcel delivered in 1949 and 1950.

119. Pittenger, *Divine Triunity*, 53–54.

120. Ibid., 59.

121. Pittenger, *God in Process*, 42–43.

122. Ibid., 48.

However, it is noteworthy that Pittenger does not identify the Palestinian Trinity with the mystery of divine reality itself. Though there is some correspondence between them, there still remains a slight gap between them. This is because he starts from human experience and proceeds through an analysis of it to the recognition of mystery. Such an experiential and epistemological approach to mystery always leaves room for non-identification between them. However, the non-identification relation, in turn, may widen an ontological gap between them.

Instead of identifying the Palestinian Trinity with the mystery of divine reality, Pittenger proceeds to extrapolate the triadic structure from the Palestinian Trinity and then transplants the triadic pattern into the mystery of divine reality. In this way, he differentiates between the threefold structure of the economic Trinity and that of the immanent Trinity. On this point, Bruce A. Demarest points out that Pittenger makes a logical leap to contend that "what is true of God's relationships with the creation is true of God himself."[123] For Pittenger, the former refers to God, Jesus Christ and the Holy Spirit, while the latter refers to God, the divine Action and the divine Response; divine transcendence, divine concomitance and divine immanence,[124] or the Eternal Father, the Eternal Son, and the Eternal Spirit.[125]

As a consequence of the extrapolative differentiation, Pittenger leads inexorably towards a distinction and even separation between Jesus Christ and the Eternal Son or the Eternal Word on the one hand, and between the Holy Spirit and the Eternal Spirit on the other hand. Here he considers Jesus Christ as the incarnate Word, but not as the Eternal Word itself. In this aspect, Pittenger denies that God is exhaustively present in Jesus, a view which he names a "christological error."[126] Instead, he asserts that God is focally and decisively manifested in Jesus Christ, and he repeats that the incarnation of the Eternal Word is not confined to the man Jesus. This kind of logic is true of the Spirit, too. God is not exhaustively active through the Holy Spirit which the

123. Demarest, "Process Trinitarianism," 26–27.

124. Pittenger, *Divine Triunity*, 102.

125. Pittenger, *God in Process*, 48.

126. Pittenger, *Divine Triunity*, 43.

Christian community experiences, and the work of the Eternal Spirit is not limited to the Holy Spirit of Church.

Until now, we have noted that an experiential and epistemological notion of mystery is so overwhelming that, in spite of maintaining some correspondence between the economic Trinity and the immanent Trinity, Pittenger actually argues that the immanent Trinity is much more than the economic Trinity, that is, what we experience in the Palestinian Trinity. Therefore he asserts that we should make no proud claims to an exhaustive knowledge of the inner workings of the divine nature. Instead, he is content to say that we can only speak of intimations and hints of the mystery of divine reality.[127] In this sense, the Christian doctrine of the Trinity is "a symbol"[128] for the divine reality, which offers a hint or intimation into the mystery of divine reality.

Bracken: "Immersing" the Economic into the Immanent Trinity

Bracken's position with regards to the relation between the economic and the immanent Trinity leads inexorably towards "immersing" the economic into the immanent Trinity. The Father gives himself directly and totally to the Son, and the Father, through the offer of his being to the Son, gives an initial aim to all finite entities. The Son responds to the Father directly and perfectly, and the Son incorporates the response of all finite entities into his own perfect response to the Father. The Spirit mediates completely between the Father and the Son, and the Spirit, as the mediation between the Father and the Son in the divine community, includes the mediation between the Father and the world of finite occasions at every moment. The economic Trinity is incorporated into the immanent Trinity

In order to propose his position on the economic-immanent Trinity relation, Bracken has made an attempt to shift from a metaphysics of being to a metaphysics of becoming.[129] For the latter, he develops "social ontology," or "an ontology of society," by appropriating creatively the Cappadocians' notion of *perichoresis* and Thomas Aquinas' concept of subsistent relations together with Whiteheadian principle of cre-

127. Ibid., 18.
128. Pittenger, *God in Process*, 50.
129. Bracken, "Trinity: Economic *and* Immanent," 8.

ativity.[130] For such a social ontology, relation has an ontological priority over person. Relations are neither accidental nor external to reality, but internal to reality to the extent that relations are constitutive of reality. And being is neither individually personal nor merely interpersonal, but rather intrinsically intersubjective.[131] Drawing on Whitehead's notion of actual entities as the final real things of which the world is made up,[132] he means by intersubjectivity "a common field of activity for two or more subjects of experience."[133]

Thus, for Braken, the ultimate reality within this social ontology is what he calls "the Cosmic Society"[134] which consists of all existents, both finite and infinite, in which God, not as the external ground but as the internal ground of existence, is intersubjectively in ongoing relationship with some totality of finite actual entities. Rather, God is the name for the complex society of all actual occasions of the world. In this sense, there is no ontologically clear-cut distinction between God and the world, which conventional substantial notions of God presupposes. Most of all, for this ontology of society, even God is understood as a society, namely, a society of three divine persons, whose relations make a *perichoretic* unity of the Trinity. The ontological unity of persons-in-community represents a higher level of being and intelligibility than that of individual substance. Thus the Triune God has a dynamic interaction with one another and with the world, and in this sense God is always in process in the sense that a community of three divine persons is constantly growing in knowledge and love of one another and of the world.

130. Bracken, "Trinity: Economic *and* Immanent," 14–16. Despite his positive grasp of Greek notion of *perichoresis*, Bracken is critical of Zizioulas, who has introduced the Cappadocians to the Western Church. Bracken claims that Zizioulas' implicit repristination of dualism between nature and person would lead inexorably towards separation between God and the world.

131. A field-oriented interpretation of Whiteheadian societies of actual occasions enables Bracken in his later period to develop "a metaphysics of inter-subjectivity" in his book *The One in the Many*, an, further to deal with it more extensively in relation to other topics. For example, "Intersubjectivity and the Coming of God"; "Hiddenness of God"; "Intentionality Analysis"; "Dependent Co-Origination and Universal Intersubjectivity."

132. Whitehead, *Process and Reality*, 27.

133. Bracken, "Hiddenness of God," 174.

134. Bracken, "Panentheism from a Trinitarian Perspective," 7, 19.

Such being the case, for Bracken, there is no much room left for an ontological distance between God and the world. Though he insists upon a distinction between God and the world, it is not separation at all, because he considers the former as the internal ground of the latter, not external at all. On the other hand, Braken seems to admit of some slight epistemological gap between God and us. However, this is never a constant impossibility, but merely a temporary *incognitio*. Braken maintains that, though we normally do not recognize an initial aim offered to us, nonetheless we can recognize ongoing directions from the Triune God and can incorporate it into an actuality of our life. Bracken expounds this point as follows:

> the "Father's" presence is felt in the *"lure"* toward the achievement of higher ethical and religious values in our lives at any given moment. Similarly, the "Son" is, indeed, the principle of provisional actuality for ourselves and for the world process as a whole, in that all finite occasions are, *sometimes consciously but more often unconsciously*, united with the "Son" in the latter's ongoing response to the "Father." But [this is] ... only instrumental to the achievement of further goals and values in the light of the "Spirit," the principle of ultimate actuality for the world process and, thereby, the long-term goal of the "Father's" initial aims for each occasion at every moment.[135]

Considering these observations, Braken's position does not leave any room for a notion of mystery in his doctrine of the Trinity, either in an ontological or an epistemological sense. If there is any mystery, it is something already expected to take place. In applying this point to the notion of divine hiddenness, Braken states: "the hiddenness of God in the person of Jesus and as manifest in the workings of divine providence in salvation history is *not a total mystery* but something to be expected in a world constituted by subjects of experience in dynamic interrelation."[136] Furthermore, Bracken's concluding remarks in his article "Trinity: Economic *And* Immanent," as quoted as below, implies that the mystery of the immanent Trinity is rather what can be proved. "[E]ven if the apophatic tradition within Christian theology is correct

---

135. Bracken, "Panentheism," 103.
136. Bracken, "Hiddenness of God," 174.

in maintaining that God is ultimately incomprehensible, human beings must never give up the attempt to prove *that divine mystery*."[137]

Suchocki and LaCugna: "Absorbing" the Immanent into the Economic Trinity

Suchocki: The Immanent-in-the-World Economic Trinity

Suchocki's position with regard to the relation between the economic and the immanent Trinity leads inexorably towards "absorbing" the immanent Trinity into the economic Trinity, because the immanent Trinity is the immanent-in-the-world economic Trinity which enables us to experience the economic Trinity, namely, the Triune God as Presence, Wisdom and Power. With regard to an ontological aspect, Suchocki, drawing on Whitehead,[138] proposes an ontology of internal relation. Suchocki's ontology of internal, rather than external relation specifically means that even God is in an intrinsic relation to the world to the extent that God, who is immanent in the world, is affected by it. To be is to have an effect in the sense that every actuality transmits its energy to all its successors.[139] This point leads her to consider the immanent Trinity not as closed in itself, but as immanent in the world.

With regard to an epistemological aspect, Suchocki appeals for a possibility of knowing the Triune God to two kinds of revelation: general and special. However, unlike the traditional notion of revelation from above down, her notion of revelation is the opposite, that is, up from below. And it is dependent on her presupposition that God's work in the world is revelatory of something of God's nature. By general revelation she means an initial aim which God provides to us, through which we can know something of God. The works of God in the world

137. Bracken, "Trinity: Economic *and* Immanent," 16. Conspicuously, quite a few of the process theologians have discussed a notion of mystery: Norman Pittenger who is discussed in the above section of the current chapter; Owen Sharkey, "Mystery of God in Process Theology"; and Catherine Keller who approaches mystery in terms of process thought: *On the Mystery*.

Instead, a panentheistic relation between God and the world enables some process scholars to explore mysticism in terms of process thought. For example, Culbertson, "Western Mysticism"; Epperly, "Mysticism of Becoming"; Reynolds, "Christian Mysticism"; Stiernotte, "Process Philosophies."

138. Suchocki, *God, Christ, Church*, 4, 12.

139. Ibid., 33.

can indicate something of the nature of God so as to lift some veil of divine hiddenness. Though she admits that such knowledge through general revelation is indirect and even ambiguous, nonetheless she insists that our knowledge of God is possible anyway.

In addition, she goes further to insist that general revelation possibly allows us to move to "an understanding of God as the one who is pervasively present to the world, the one who is ultimate in wisdom, and the one who is the power of justice."[140] However, for the movement, she does not rely on special revelation. While acknowledging that special revelation accords with and affirms what general revelation leads us to know of God, Sochocki mostly resorts to our experience of God in our life. According to her, as we are in a predicament of loneliness, we experience God as Presence. As we are in a predicament of temporality, we experience God as Wisdom. And as we are in a predicament of injustice, we experience God as Power. Such an experiential approach leads her to maintain that our comprehension of God as Presence, Wisdom, and Power is not dependent upon special revelation in the Bible. Though acknowledging Christian special revelation which is God's intensifying presence in Jesus of Nazareth, she holds that special revelation takes place through intensifying the image of God in human consciousness and thus special revelation and incarnation are not a once-for-all actual occasion, but a continuous process and a series of many occasions.

In spite of some logical leaps inherent in her ontology and epistemology, Sochock's relational ontology and experiential epistemology lead her to affirm that God is the Trinity as Presence, Wisdom, and Power in the dimensions of human experience. In conclusion, she maintains that the deepest way to express it is to say: "God is for us." For Suchocki, "God for us" conveys the Trinity and also the gospel. To put it differently, the Trinity and the gospel are finally just this mystery: that God is for us.[141] However, she does not deal with the character of mystery in detail. The main reason for it is that the Triune God as Presence, Wisdom, and Power is the given in our internally relational ontology, which is recognized ambiguously now but will be explicitly and fully known through our experience anyway.

140. Ibid., 47–48.
141. Ibid., 235.

LaCugna: Oikonomia

Instead of using the imprecise and misleading terms "the economic Trinity" and "the immanent Trinity," LaCugna suggests the terms "*oikonomia*" and "*theologia*." She means by *oikonomia* the comprehensive plan of God for the world and by *theologia* the mystery of God. For LaCungna, *oikonomia* is not the Trinity *ad extra* and *theologia* is not the Trinity *ad intra*. *Oikonomia* is not the Trinity *pro nobis* and *theologia* is not the Trinity *in se*. Through these negations LaCugna stresses that there are not two separate Trinities and that there are no two different levels of the Trinity. Thus she elucidates the essential concerns of both the economic-immanent distinction and the essence-energies distinction into her own principle: "*theologia* is fully revealed and bestowed in *oikonomia*, and *oikonomia* truly expresses the ineffable mystery of *theologia*."[142] The point of LaCugna's principle is that *oikonomia* and *theologia* are inseparable from each other, and that a distinction between *oikonomia* and *theologia* is not ontological, but conceptual or epistemological. In this way, LaCugna claims to establish "a methodological principle" which maintains "a basic correlation between the economy of salvation and the eternal being of God."[143]

In order to develop her theological project to maintain the relationship between *oikonomia* and *theologia* as a structuring principle, LaCugna proposes an ontology which seems to her to be more appropriate to it, that is, "an ontology of relation or communion," or "a relational ontology."[144] For the purpose, she is rigidly opposed to two previous ontologies; the one which posits two different ontological levels, represented by a theology of revelation which inexorably leads towards an ontological distinction between the economic and the immanent Trinity, with a result of fastening on the latter; and the other which, easily combined with functionalism and nominalism, denies any basis for the economy beyond itself. She judges both to be inadequate.

Instead, she proposes an ontology of relations which is intended to preserve the unity of *oikonomia* and *theologia*, and also to keep theological speculation rooted in the economy of salvation: "A relational ontology understands both God and the creature to exist and meet as

142. LaCugna, *God for Us*, 221.
143. Ibid., 249.
144. Ibid., 249–50.

persons in communion. The economy of creation, salvation, and consummation is the place of encounter in which God and the creature exist together in one mystery of communion and interdependence. The meaning of to-be is to-be-a-person-in-communion.... God's To-Be is To-Be-in-relationship, and God's being-in-relationship-to-us *is* what God is."[145] As the quotation cited above indicates, LaCugna's relational ontology holds that God is essentially relational with us. God's being is to be in relation to us, and God's being in relation to us is God's being. LaCugna intends that such relational ontology maintains an inseparable correlation between *oikonomia* and *theologia* so as to enable us to focus on God for us, neither on God *in se* nor on God's intra-divinity.

Remarkably, LaCugna's ontology of relation is grounded in an ontology of personhood which understands person as communion and relation. For the ontology of personhood, LaCugna heavily draws on the insights of the Cappadocians who make a distinction between *ousia* and *hypostasis*, but identify *ousia*, not in essence apart from three divine persons, but in the *hypostasis*, namely, the person of God the Father.[146] On this point, she agrees with John D. Zizioulas that no *ousia* exists without *hypostasis*, that is, without person, and thus being is traced back to person not to *ousia*.[147]

Despite some advantages, however, LaCunga's ontology of relation has a tendency to collapse God into a set of relations with us, because God's being in relationship to us is God's being and God's essence, and conversely. Such a tendency is confirmed, when LaCugna elucidates an essential difference between God and us, by stating that "God's self-expression is always perfect and full," and "God alone can perfectly express Godself in act, *even* under the conditions of the world."[148] It seems that God would, then, be reduced to a set of relations in act. For this reason, she evokes critical responses from several scholars. For example, Thomas Weinandy argues that LaCugna's Trinity is merged and fused into economy.[149] Paul D. Molnar also maintains that LaCugna

---

145. Ibid., 250. LaCugna's own italics.

146. LaCugna, *God for Us*, 243.

147. Zizioulas, *Being as Communion*, 41–42.

148. LaCugna, *God for Us*, 304.

149. Weinandy, "Immanent Trinity and the Economic Trinity," 661.

reduces God's existence to God's existence in the economy.[150] In addition, Colin E. Gunton claims that LaCugna's theology ultimately leads towards pantheism.[151]

If these criticisms are right, then LaCugna's *theologia* would be merged finally and completely into *oikonomia*. But this consequence is not what LaCugna wants to affirm. For LaCugna from the outset actually intends to preserve a distinction between *oikonomia* and *theologia*, while, at the same time, she does not want to exhaust *theologia* into *oikonomia* even amidst the inseparable relation between them. In this regard, LaCugna is faced with an ontological tension in holding the non-reducible preservation of the distinction between *oikonomia* and *theologia*.

How, then, does she resolve, or, at least, lessen the ontological tension which lurks in her ontology of relation? LaCugna's possible answer lies in another notion of person as "an ineffable and inexhaustible mystery,"[152] which has itself an epistemological aspect as well as an ontological aspect. A person is inexhaustible in an ontological sense, because it is not fully communicated to another. And a person is ineffable in an epistemological sense, because it could not completely be expressed and named. Such a notion of person as mystery leaves the room for the non-reducible preservation of the distinction between *oikonomia* and *theologia*. Though a person is essentially relational, interpersonal, interdependent, and intersubjective, nonetheless a person is not totally exhausted into relations ontologically and also epistemologically. What is here the most remarkable point is that LaCugna, through the notion of person as mystery, subtly converts an ontological tension into an epistemological tension.

Actually, such a notion of person as an ineffable and inexhaustible mystery is ultimately grounded in "the Absolute Mystery of God"[153] which has, for LaCugna, more of an epistemological character than ontological one. She is heavily influenced by the Greek notion of God as the incomprehensible and ineffable mystery, but in her own dialectical way. That is, as LaCugna explicates, while God reveals Godself to the

150. Molnar, *Divine Freedom*, 4.

151. Gunton, *Promise of Trinitarian Theology*, xviii–xix.

152. LaCugna, *God for Us*, 289.

153. Ibid., 322.

extent that there is no *deus absconditus* behind the revelation of God in history, God always and forever remains the incomprehensible and inexpressible mystery. Here an ontological tension is delicately converted into an epistemological tension. While there is no other ontological *theologia* than *oikonomia*, nonethelss *theologia* revelaed in *oikonomia* still exceeds our epistemological comprehension and formulation. Though God is revealed in Jesus Christ and the Holy Spirit, God the Father stills remains the "Unoriginate Origin"[154] which is beyond our comprehension.

How, then, does LaCugna deal with this epistemological tension? At this juncture, she appeals to a doxological concept of icon in order to resolve the epistemological tension. According to LaCugna, as God is the absolute mystery, the only appropriate path to *theologia* as the mystery of God in *oikonomia* is adoration. In doxology, we can never exactly articulate the whole character of *theologia*, but we need to be only content to acknowledge that it is the mystery of God which goes beyond comprehension. For this reason, LaCugna compares the doctrine of the Trinity as an icon, which "is not a photographic likeness but an image to contemplate, to look through and beyond, toward a reality that ultimately eludes all discursive knowledge and evokes praise."[155] In this sense, LaCugna maintains that the doctrine of the Trinity is iconic of the mystery of God, in which *oikonomia* and *theologia* are kept together in practice.

Considering all these observations, LaCugna is firmly opposed to the postulate of two different ontological levels such as the economic Trinity and the immanent Trinity. Instead, she insists upon the one and same ontological level having tow aspects or two modalities of the one reality: *theologia* as the mystery of God and *oikonomia* as the comprehensive plan of God for us. Accordingly, she goes so far as to maintain that the eternal begetting of the Son and the breathing forth of the Spirit, which are considered by her to be merely "rich metaphors,"[156] take place in God's *oikonomia*. However, LaCugna is obliged to encounter an ontological tension between her intent to preserve a distinction between *theologia* and *oikonomia* and her proposed ontology of rela-

154. Ibid., 321.
155. Ibid., 321–22.
156. Ibid., 354.

tion which seems to her to fit better with her intent. Without resolving it, LaCugna coverts it into an epistemological tension, by appealing to another notion of an ineffable and inexhaustible mystery, but which is ultimately grounded in her more epistemological character of the absolute mystery of God.

In conclusion, LaCugna leads inexorably towards "absorbing" the immanent Trinity into the economic Trinity in an ontological sense. At the same time, due to her focus on the absolute mystery of God, she still has some epistemological tensions which lead her to regard the doctrine of the Trinity as an icon of the mystery of God.

Lee: Mutual Inclusiveness

As we have discussed in chapter 4, Lee finally arrives at the answer to his theological conundrum through the *Eum-Yang* way of thinking by studying *the Book of Changes*. With the help of the *Eum-Yang* inclusive relationship, Lee provides his own creative formula. This fact, however, does not mean that Lee selectively takes only the logical structure of inclusive relationship from *the Book of Changes*. Rather, it means that Lee is firmly grounded in the worldview of *the Book of Changes*. In fact, Lee proposed his own constructive theology named *A Theology of Change* in 1979,[157] and then applied it to the contemporary issue of the relation between the economic Trinity and the immanent Trinity in 1996. Thus it is appropriate to identify some characteristics of Lee's *Theology of Change*.

From the earlier period of his theological journey, Lee sought to understand the biblical understanding of God, that is, the God of the Judeo-Christian faith, especially on the ground of his exegesis of Exodus 3:1-15 in the Old Testament. The biblical passage reveals God as "I AM WHAT I AM (I WILL BE WHAT I WLL BE)." As this God is incomprehensible, unknowable, and indescribable in human terms, Lee suggests that the God of YHWH is described only by "*is*-ness."[158] And by enlisting *the Book of Changes*, Lee is able to claim that the concept of God as change itself is more in keeping with the Judeo-Christian tradition than the more dominant views derived from Geek philosophy.

---

157. Lee, *Theology of Change*.

158. Lee, "Can God Be Change Itself?," 756.

Lee asserts that, in *the Book of Changes*,[159] the ultimate reality is change itself.[160] For Lee, the ultimate reality is comparable with God, the Way [도(*Do*), 道(*Dao*)], or the Great Ultimate [태극(*TaeGeuk*), 太極 (*TaiChi*)]. Change is regarded as the absolute. And change itself as the ultimate reality always manifests itself in a dipolar process of *Eum* and *Yang*. That is, change itself operates through the interaction between *Eum* and *Yang*, which generates all the other kinds of changes. As the ultimate reality is change itself, all beings in the cosmos are in change and all beings change through the interaction between *Eum* and *Yang*. More specifically, change itself produces two primary forms, the prime *Yang*, which is symbolized by heaven [건(*Geon*), 乾(*Chien*)] and the prime *Eum*, which is symbolized by earth [곤(*Gon*), 坤(*Kun*)]. And *Eum* and *Yang*, by being doubled, makes four duograms. The four duograms then evolve into eight trigrams, which, by being squared, become sixty-four hexagrams. Lee claims that *the Book of Changes* understands all changes in the world through these several levels.[161]

Ontology is an inquiry into the reality of being. Notably, Lee's *Theology of Change* does not consider being but change as the ultimate reality. Change consists of creativity (signified by *Yang*) and receptivity (signified by *Eum*). Thus, Lee points out that it is a mistake to think of change in terms of action alone. Change includes both action and inaction, for change, which changes all, is also changeless. And change

159. For an explanation of the Book of Changes, see Yu-Lan Fung, *A History of Chinese Philosophy*, 1:379–99; According to Lee, the main texts of *the Book of Change* deals with 64 different hexagrams, each of which is made up of six divided (--) or undivided (—) lines. In addition, there are Commentaries, as appendixes, to the main texts, which are known as *Ten Wings* [십익(*ShipIk*), 十翼(*ShiYi*)]. The first and second wings are the Commentary on the Judgments [상전(*SangJeon*), 傳(*TuanZhuan*)]. The third and fourth wings are the Commentary on the symbols of hexagrams [상전(*SangJeon*), 象傳 (*XiangZhuan*)]. The fifth and sixth wings are the Great Commentary [대전(*DaeJun*), 大傳(*DaZhuan*)]. The seventh wing is the Commentary on Words of the Texts [문언 전(*MoonEonJun*), 文言傳(*WenYanZhuan*)]. The eighth wing is the Explanation of the 8 different trigrams [설괘전(*SeolKoaeJun*), 說卦傳(*ShuoGuaZhuan*)]. The ninth wing is the Commentary on the sequence of the hexagrams [서괘전(*SeoKoaeJun*), 序卦傳 (*XuGuaZhuan*)]. And the tenth wing is the Commentary on the Miscellaneous Notes on hexagrams [잡괘전(*JabKoaeJun*), 雜卦傳(*ZaGuaZhuan*)].

160. Lee, "Can God Be Change Itself?," 767; Lee, *Theology of Change*, 38 and 42; Lee, *Trinity*, 26.

161. Lee, *Theoloy of Change*, 3–9.

presupposes a cyclic view of time,[162] because the ontology of change supports a cyclic movement of change, which is commonly expressed in terms of growth and decay, expansion and contraction, coming and going, movement and rest, active and passive, and so on. However, Lee asserts that it is not a repetitious cycle of movement, because of the infinite varieties of minimum and maximum intensities. For example, the four seasons are repetitious because one season follows another, but they are not repetitious, because each season is different.

For an ontology of change, change is *a priori* to being. Being is not absolute, but only relative to change. In this aspect, Lee claims that the ontology of change is very different from the ontology of being or the ontology of substance, which has dominated western ways of thinking. Ontology of substance assumes that being is a static being which is called substance. And it considers change and relation merely as a function of being. Thus ontology of substance does not properly understand change.

In addition, Lee claims that the ontology of change is not the same as the ontology of becoming or the ontology of process which process philosophy affirms. In Lee's view, the idea of becoming in process philosophy, though sharing the Eastern worldview in many respects, presupposes being rather than change, because it is based on a linear concept of time. And Lee points out that, when process is understood as creativity which is the creative advance into novelty, the ontology of process presupposes only a one-sided direction of advance. Lee asserts that creativity presupposes change itself, and that change itself consists of creativity and receptivity, and that creativity is only one function of change process.

Now let us proceed to an epistemology of change. As Lee's *Theology of Change* understands that all beings in the cosmos are in change, the epistemology of change is more cosmocentric than anthropocentric. The epistemology of change considers anthropology as a part of cosmology and affirms cosmocentric anthropology, whereas the epistemology of being tries to understand cosmology through anthropology, and supports an anthropocentric cosmology.

In addition, as everything in the cosmos is in change, and as change takes place through the interaction between *Eum* and *Yang*, the episte-

---

162. Lee, *Theology of Change*, 13–15.

mology of change does not fully accept substantial epistemology which seeks to penetrate into the substance of being. Instead, the epistemology of change tries to look at changes through the relational principles of *Eum* and *Yang*. In this aspect, the epistemology of change gives a priority to relations rather than to ontic entities, and affirms that everything in the cosmos is related with one another.

What is more notable in the epistemology of change is its logical structure of thinking. The epistemology of change is fundamentally grounded in its own characteristic epistemological logic, that is, the both-and way of thinking. As everything in the cosmos is in change through the interaction of *Eum* and *Yang*, the epistemology of change does not affirm the either-or way of thinking alone. In Lee's view, the root problem of Greek philosophy and of its effects on Western theology is the Aristotelian either-or logic, which is present in the philosophy of substance and visible in process philosophy. As this either-or logic is ultimately based on the ontology of substance, it is always required to choose either A or B within the framework of the logic. However, this either-or way of thinking does not explain any change from A to B, or from B to A.

Finally, what about the concept of divine mystery? As mentioned above, the God of YHWH is, for Lee, incomprehensible, unknowable, and indescribable in human terms. Thus Lee suggests that the God of YHWH is described only by "*is*-ness." For Lee, the God of YHWH as "*is*-ness" is the God as change itself. In this sense, God is mystery in both the ontological sense, and the epistemological sense, and the concept of divine mystery is the ultimate ground of his *Theology of Change*.

Lee identifies some basic assumptions of his theology.[163] The first is that God is an unknown mystery. God transcends human knowing and perceiving, and God is not categorized in human finite expressions. In the Bible, God's name of YHWH cannot be described and named. This God is comparable with the Way [도(*Do*), 道(*Dao*)] in the *DoDeokKyeong* [도덕경, 道德經(*DaoDeJing*)], the first chapter of which says, "The way that can be spoken of is not the constant way; the name that can be named is not the constant name."[164] And this God is comparable with the Great Ultimate [태극(*TaeGeuk*), 太極(*TaiChi*)],

---

163. Lee, *Trinity*, 12–14.

164. "道可道, 非常道; 名可名, 非常名." Lau, *Tao Te Ching*, 2–3.

because this Great Ultimate is also the Great Void [무극(*MooGeuk*), 無極(*WuChi*)].

The second basic assumption is that, as God is mystery to us, we must not speak of the reality of God, but of a limited human symbolic understanding of God. It is notable that Lee's own theological methodology has changed from an analogical understanding of God to a symbolic understanding of God. This change resulted from Lee's change of focus from the revelation of God to the mystery of God. In 1969 Lee wrote a comprehensive treatise on Barth's use of analogy titled "Karl Barth's Use of Analogy in his *Church Dogmatics*." Here he rejected analogy of being [*analogia entis*] and affirmed Barth's analogy of faith [*analogia fidei*] and analogy of relation [*analogia relationis*]. However, in this later period of his theological journey, Lee came to concentrate on the symbols of God, which are not the same as the reality of God, but which are considered to point to, or to participate in the reality of God. This change of his theological methodology goes together with his increased focus on the mystery of God.

Summary

Chapter 5 has critically analyzed each of the seven different positions in terms of ontology, epistemology, and a concept of mystery. As has been shown, ontology and epistemology are indispensable elements in each position, but nonetheless each position exposes certain tensions: ontological or epistemological. At the same time, this chapter has shown that a concept of mystery, though not in the same meaning , has been used to resolve these tensions. A matrix of ontology, epistemology, and a concept of mystery in each of these positions can be summarized as follows.

1. Barth's position of mutual correspondence, despite its determination to hold fast to the sameness and unity in content between the economic and the immanent Trinity, unavoidably implies the ontological independence or priority of the immanent Trinity, which, in turn, inevitably evokes an epistemological tension. Thus, in order to resolve the tension, Barth makes a further distinction between God's primary objectivity and God's secondary objectivity, and then finally resorts to a concept of mystery as *ignoramus*.

2. Rahner's rule of identity strongly affirms that the God whom we meet in our transcendental experience is Godself, because the economic Logos is the immanent Logos and the Holy Spirit in history is the Spirit within God. Nonetheless, due to its inherent ontological tension, he makes a further distinction between the immanent Logos as "the inward symbol" and the economic Logos as "the outward symbol" in an ontological sense, and regards divine self-communication as "absolute *proximity*." This ontological tension is finally resolved in his location of the incomprehensible mystery of God in the foreground of his entire theology.

3. First, for Moltamnn, despite an inseparable link between the cross of Jesus Christ and the doctrine of the Trinity, his notion of the retroactive effect of the economic on the immanent Trinity seems to be incompatible with his acknowledgement of the correspondence of the economic to the immanent Trinity. For a solution, on the one hand, he makes an epistemological distinction between the economic Trinity itself and our knowledge of the economic Trinity, and that between the immanent Trinity and our knowledge of the immanent Trinity. On the other hand, he resolves an ontological tension with his doxological and eschatological understanding of the Trinity, which enables us to encounter a living mystery of the Trinity.

   Second, Pannenberg's futurist ontology, which maintains an intimate relation between *ordo essendi* and *ordo cognoscendi*, enables him to formulate his doctrine of the Trinity as inseparably interwoven with ontology and epistemology, thus without any serious tensions. Thus he rarely discusses mystery and hardly relies on a divine concept of mystery with regard to the immanent-economic Trinity relation. While he is clear in understanding mystery in the New Testament as Jesus Christ or the divine plan of salvation in Jesus Christ, he does not explore an intimate link between mystery and the Trinity.

   Third, Jenson's eschatological thesis through the identification of God in biblical narratives exposes both an ontological tension and an epistemological tension, which are not resolved within his own framework. He seems to appeal for the resolution to the final mystery or the deepest mystery of God's identity, but without a full discussion of it.

4. Boff and Pittenger's strong focus on the mystery of the Trinity makes an impact on their position which opens a wide gap between the immanent and the economic Trinity. Thus Boff states that the mystery of the Trinity is partially, not fully, manifested to us, and that the economic Trinity provides merely glimpses of the immanent Trinity. Likewise, Pittenger considers the immanent Trinity as much more than the Palestinian Trinity.

5. Bracken does not leave any room for a notion of mystery in his doctrine of the Trinity. For him, there is no constant mystery, but merely a temporary *incognitio*, which is already expected to take place. It is something to be proved in the end.

6. Suchocki maintains that God is experienced as the Trinity of Presence, Wisdom, and Power. Thus God for us is the mystery, but it is something to be experienced, and the given in our internally relational ontology. In this sense, it is what can be explicitly and fully known through our experience of it, though it is now recognized ambiguously. On the other hand, LaCugna's ontology of relation has an inherent ontological tension, which is resolved in her notion of person as an ineffable and inexhaustible mystery, which is also ultimately grounded in the absolute mystery of God.

7. Lee's position of mutual inclusiveness is based on his ontology and epistemology of change, which regards the ultimate reality as change itself, and thus as the mystery which is unknowable and unnameable.

6

Conclusion

A Constructive Proposal for Future Discussions

CHAPTERS 3 AND 4 CONSIDERED THE WORK OF ELEVEN CONTEMPOR-
ary theologians and identified seven different positions with regard to
the relationship between the immanent and the economic Trinity: Barth's
mutual correspondence; Rahner's identity; Moltmann, Pannenberg, and
Jenson's eschatological unity; Boff and Pittenger's "much more than";
Bracken's "immersing"; Suchocki and LaCugna's "absorbing"; and Lee's
mutual inclusiveness. And chapter 5 analyzed each of these positions
and showed that ontology and epistemology are indispensably woven
into these discussions, while each position exposes certain tensions: ontological, epistemological, or both, and that a concept of divine mystery
is used to resolve these tensions in each case.

Considering these expositions and analyses, therefore, in this final
part of the book I shall be concerned to suggest some fruitful directions
for future discussions of the issue. I propose that it is necessary to put
in the foreground a biblical concept of mystery which refers to Jesus
Christ, not merely as a device for resolving epistemological or ontological tensions, but rather that a concept of divine mystery needs to
determinative of ontology and epistemology.

It is certainly remarkable that all these theologians should have
attempted to maintain both the distinction and unity between the
immanent and the economic Trinity, even though they differ in their
motives, directions, and ways of achieving this. In this regard, all these
theologians form a distinctive theological current of thought, which is
in sharp contrast to some other streams which criticize this distinction

between the immanent and the economic Trinity and, further, attempt to eliminate the need for a concept of the immanent Trinity.

Actually there has been a strong theological stream which argues that a concept of the immanent Trinity is inadequate and that the immanent-economic Trinity distinction is unnecessary. Maurice F. Wiles, for instance, in his 1957 article maintains that the immanent-economic Trinity distinction is a product of both Greek thought and post-exilic Jewish thought,[1] and that the doctrine of the Trinity is "an arbitrary analysis of the activity of God, which, though of value in Christian thought and devotion, is not of essential significance."[2] Thus he argues that it is absurd to claim that we know the immanent Trinity through the threefold character of revelation in the economic Trinity.[3] Accordingly, he proposes that theology must make no attempt to speak of the immanent Trinity, while focusing on speaking of the effects of God as experienced.[4] Similarly, Cyril C. Richardson, in his 1958 book *The Doctrine of the Trinity*, considers the doctrine of the Trinity as "an artificial construct,"[5] and the traditional statements about the immanent Trinity as "dark and mysterious statements, which are ultimately meaningless."[6] He concludes that "there is no necessary threeness in the Godhead."[7] Along similar lines, Gordon D. Kaufmann, in his 1968 book *Systematic Theology*, considers the immanent-economic Trinity distinction as "a pseudo-distinction"[8] which he maintains results from a failure to grasp the relational character of our knowledge of God. He restricts our knowledge of God only to the external relationship of God to us. As he puts it: "[T]here is no reason whatsoever to maintain that the structure of that external relationship which we perceive in our

1. Wiles, "Some Reflections," 92. This article becomes chapter 1 in his 1976 book *Working Papers in Doctrine*, 1–17.

2. Wiles, "Some Reflections," 104.

3. Ibid., 94.

4. Wiles, *Remaking of Christian Doctrine*, 25.

5. Richardson, *Doctrine of the Trinity*, 148.

6. Ibid., 148.

7. Ibid., 149.

8. Kaufman, *Systematic Theology*, 251 n. 6. It was reprinted by the same publisher in 1978. The other books by Kaufman which touch an issue of the Trinity explicitly or implicitly are: *God the Problem*; *The Theological Imagination*; *In Face of Mystery*; *God-Mystery-Diversity*; *In the beginning . . . Creativity*.

experience somehow directly mirrors a similar but more primordial threefold structure in the innermost recesses of the divine being. To the internal structure of this innermost essence we have no access in history or revelation; and anything said about it is pure speculation."[9] Thus he proposes that we should reject any attempt to speak of the inner-Trinitarian relations, namely, of the immanent Trinity.[10]

This tendency went hand in hand with those scholars who focused on Christology and approached the doctrine of the Trinity exclusively in light of their Christological concepts. Piet J. A. M. Schoonenberg, for example, in his 1969 book,[11] deals with Christology and then in his 1973 article explains its implications for the doctrine of the Trinity. While presupposing that all our thinking moves from the world to God, but not the reverse, he maintains that the immanent-economic Trinity distinction is only a distinction between aspects of the same reality, and that the immanent Trinity is accessible to us only as the economic Trinity. As a consequence, any questions about the immanent Trinity, as distinguished from the economic Trinity, must necessarily remain unanswered and even unanswerable.[12]

Roger Haight, who was heavily influenced by Schoonenberg, stresses that that the doctrine of the Trinity emerges out of the experience of salvation through Jesus and in God's Spirit. He goes further to conclude that the doctrine of the Trinity is only a derivative of

---

9. Kaufman, *Systematic Theology*, 102 n. 9.

10. Ibid., 251 n. 7; It is notable that Kaufmann's theological method starts with his focus on the ultimately profound mystery of God which utterly escapes our efforts to grasp it. This method leads him to consider theological terms and concepts merely as metaphors or symbols, which is to say, as constructs of the theological imagination (*God the Problem*, 95); Instead of reifying the traditional Trinitarian metaphors such as substance and person, Kaufmann attempts to grasp "three principles of God as absoluteness, humaneness, and presence" (*Theological Imagination*, 270–72), "three motifs or intentions of the Christian understanding of God" (*In Face of Mystery*, 420–25), or "three themes" (*God–Mystery–Diversity*, 152–56); Then in his later period Kaufmann understands the profound mystery of God as creativity which has three modalities: creativity1, creativity2, and creativity3 (*In the Beginning . . . Creativity*, 100; *Jesus and Creativity*, 52).

11. Schoonenberg, *Christ: A Study of the God-Man Relationship*. Its original edition *Hij is een God van Mensen* was published in 1969.

12. Schoonenberg, "Trinity," 111–12. This article was first published in German in the Swiss periodical *Orientierung* in 1973. It was translated by Robert C. Ware and afterwards modified by Schoonenberg himself.

Christology.[13] It is a function of Christology in the sense that the doctrine of the Trinity is completely dependent on the experience of Jesus as the bringer of divine salvation. He argues that it is a pure postulate to speak of the inner distinctions of God, namely, the immanent Trinity. In this regard, he points out that Rahner's rule involves an epistemological "jump."[14]Furthermore, Geoffrey W. H. Lampe, in his 1977 book *God as Spirit*, proposes a "Spirit Christology" which sees Jesus as God in the sense that Jesus is full of the Spirit.[15] For Lampe, as the one God as Spirit reveals Godself decisively for us in Jesus, so the one God as Spirit is here and now. In this aspect, he claims that the doctrine of the Trinity itself, not to mention the immanent Trinity, is less satisfactory for the articulation of basic Christian experience than his concept of God as Spirit.[16] Rather, for him, the inner distinctions within God are "more likely to confuse our attempt to answer the question, 'In what sense is Jesus alive today?'"[17] which is the basic motif of the book.

The positions of the eleven theologians vis-à-vis the immanent-economic Trinity relation with which this book has been primarily concerned are, of course, in conflict with those other theological streams that argue for the inadequacy of the immanent-economic Trinity distinction and attempt to eliminate the need for a concept of the immanent Trinity, with whom this book has been discussing in the first part of this chapter. The efforts of those who seek to maintain both the distinction and unity between the immanent and the economic Trinity are more significant, in that they accord with the main theological tradition which was examined in the second section of chapter 2.

To recapitulate, first, the concept of *Logos* maintains the distinction and unity between the immanent *Logos* and the expressed *Logos*, showing not only the intimate relationship between God the Father and Jesus Christ, but also the inseparable relationship between God and the world.

Second, *dispositio* or *dispensation* (dispensation) does not merely refer to the incarnation of the Son of God in Jesus Christ, but also

13. Haight, "Point of Trinitarian Theology," 192. This article was incorporated in chapter 16 on the Trinity of his later book *Jesus: Symbol of God.*

14. Haight, "Point of Trinitarian Theology," 201; *Jesus: Symbol of God*, 487.

15. Lampe, *God as Spirit*, 33.

16. Ibid., 228.

17. Ibid., 33.

points to all the co-workings of the Father, the Son, and the Spirit, and even goes further to denote all the co-existence of the three from all eternity.

Third, *oikonomia* (economy), though focally and sometimes exclusively referring to the incarnation of the Son, does not exclude all the works of God towards the world, which are ultimately grounded in the co-existence of the three in eternity.

Fourth, *energeia* (activity, operation) always refers to all divine activities in relation to the world, but it is inseparably linked to divine *ousia*, in the sense that every *energeia* which pervades from God to creation starts from God the Father, proceeds from God the Son, and is completed by the Holy Spirit.

And lastly, despite a difference in order, Augustine and Aquinas hold an inseparable relationship between *missio* and *processio*, in that, for Augustine, *missio* reveals *processio*, and, for Aquinas, *processio* grounds *misso* and, further, creation.

This main theological tradition has been preserved in the work of subsequent theologians as well. For example, although Martin Luther (1483–1546) and John Calvin (1509–1564) predominantly focus on the economy of the Triune God in the Bible and warn against going beyond it, nonetheless they do not completely deny the necessity of the immanent Trinity.[18]

The theological stream which maintains both the distinction and unity between the immanent and the economic Trinity has two complementary subcurrents. Peters epitomizes them as follows: "the profound and thoroughgoing relatedness of God to the world" and "the protection of the freedom of God."[19] Therefore both the distinction and unity

18. Olson and Hall, *Trinity*, 67–69 and 71–73; Regarding Calvin's understanding of the Trinity, see Philip Walker Butin, *Revelation, Redemption, and Response*. In addition, for the doctrine of the Trinity approached by post-reformation reformed theologians, see Rihcard A. Muller, *Post-Reformation Reformed Dogmatics Vol. 4*.

19. Peters, *GOD (1st)*, 108–9; *GOD (2nd)*, 112–13; *God as Trinity*, 22–23. Peters considers these two motives as a dilemma: "On the one hand, to affirm the immanent-economic distinction risks subordinating the economic Trinity and hence protecting transcendent absoluteness at the cost of genuine relatedness to the world. On the other hand, to collapse the two together risks producing a God so dependent upon the world for self-definition that divine freedom and independence are lost." Thus, as a solution to the dilemma, he, like Moltmann, Pannenberg and Jenson, suggests an eschatological identity of the immanent and the economic Trinity, which is remarkably characterized by its modified concept of eternity, not as timelessness, but as everlastingness which

between the immanent and the economic Trinity need to be acknowledged simultaneously, in order to establish the equilibrium between God's relatedness to the world and God's gracious freedom.

Peters' acknowledgement of these crucial elements accords well with Grenz's analysis of contemporary discussions. As has been mentioned in the second section of chapter 1, Grenz's golden thread is the question about how to conceptualize the relationship between the immanent and the economic Trinity "in a manner that takes seriously the importance of the latter to the former and avoids collapsing the former into the latter or compromising the freedom of the eternal God."[20] A careful look indicates that the golden thread offers three criteria: the importance of the economic to the immanent Trinity; no collapsing the immanent into the economic Trinity; and no compromising the freedom of God.

In applying Peters' two crucial elements and Grenz's three categories to the seven different positions, it is observed that some positions among them do not keep an appropriate balance. As chapter 4 has analyzed, Boff and Pittenger put more emphasis on the immanent than on the economic Trinity, thereby widening the gap between them. Bracken has a strong tendency towards "immersing" the economic into the immanent Trinity, while Suchocki and LaCugna lead inexorably towards "absorbing" the immanent into the economic Trinity.

Unlike these theologians, Peters, following Moltamnn, Pannenberg and Jenson, suggests an eschatological unity of the immanent and the economic Trinity, which is one of the seven different positions. Basically agreeing with such an eschatological direction, Grenz suggests that a further task should be to answer what kind of ontology would fit with his categories. Actually, when Grenz remarks that contemporary discussions have reached a point of consensus regarding the immanent-economic Trinity relation, he contends that the point of consensus has it as a "theological objective" to maintain both an "ontological primacy" for the immanent Trinity and an "epistemological priority" to the economic Trinity.[21] The theological objective is thus pursued in his second

---

takes up into itself the course of temporal history.

20. Grenz, *Rediscovering the Triune God*, 222.

21. Ibid.

volume of *The Matrix of Christian Theology*, which attempts to develop
what he names a "Trinitarian ontology," or a "theo-ontology."[22]

In this volume Grenz points out that Christian thinkers have
tended to understand God within the framework of being, the result
of which is a Procrustean bed of an "onto-theology" which makes God
fit within a substantialist ontology, and which leads finally to the death
of onto-theology itself.[23] Much influenced by Jenson's method of identifying God through biblical narratives,[24] Grenz discovers that the self-
naming of the Triune God unfolds in the narratives of the Bible, which,
for him, starts with the revelation of the "I AM " name to Moses (Exod
3:14), through the incarnation of the "I AM " in Jesus Christ (John 6:35,
8:12, 10:9, 10:11–14, 11:25, 14:6, 15:1), to the exaltation of Jesus as the
eternal "I AM " in the Holy Spirit (Rev 1:8, 1:17, 21:6). Thus Grenz explores the implications of the event of the self-naming of the Triune
God for the questions of ontology.

However, despite his thoroughly critical analysis and constructively exegetical creativity, his so-called theo-ontology does not seem to
provide a fully integrative relationship between the immanent and the
economic Trinity. First, Grenz's theo-ontology, which finds its beginning point in the divine self-naming does not seem to be consistent
with his original theological objective which is to hold fast to both an
ontological primacy for the immanent Trinity and an epistemological
priority to the economic Trinity.[25]

Second, Grenz's theo-ontology seems to support the position of
"immersing" the economic Trinity into the immanent Trinity, which
is basically similar to Bracken's position. According to Grenz, the di-

22. Grenz, *Named God*, 292.

23. There have been a lot of critiques of classical theism which is based on a substantialist ontology of being. For example, John B. Cobb and David Ray Griffin reject
five points which are regarded to be based on it: first, God as cosmic moralist; second,
God as the unchanging and passionless absolute; third, God as controlling power;
fourth, God as sanctioner of the status quo; and lastly, God as male. Cobb and Griffin,
Process Theology, 8–9.

Another example is from Gunton. He addresses critical remarks on process theology's conception of God as becoming, while being more sympathetic with Barth's
notion of God as becoming. In so doing, Gunton summarizes three characteristics of
the classical concept of God: first, supernaturalism; second, God as timeless; and lastly,
dependence on a hierarchical ordering of reality. Gunton, *Becoming and Being*, 2–3.

24. Grenz, "Divine Fugue," 211–16.

25. Grenz, *Named God*, 342.

vine self-naming is the event in which the three divine members of the
Trinity are involved in a process of mutual naming, and the divine event
extends to the world and incorporates all creation into the dynamic of
the divine self-naming.[26]

And lastly, due to his failure to fully explore an epistemological
aspect, Grenz comes to depend too readily on the apophatic theology of the Eastern Orthodox tradition. Though he expresses a positive
expectation that "it [apophatic theology] opens the door to revelation
and . . . elevates the category of Other as the central feature of reality,"
which is extended to the world as well, his own interpretation of the
incomprehensibility of God, which he regards as the hallmark of Greek
theology, betrays his own expectation. Contrary to what this dissertation has noted in the second section of chapter 2, Grenz considers that
the Eastern distinction between *ousia* and *energeia* allowed the Greek
theologians to conclude that "the inner being of God [the immanent
Trinity] need not correspond exactly to the activities of God in the
economy of salvation [the economic Trinity]."[27] For this reason, Grenz's
own theo-ontology admits unwittingly of a wide gap between the immanent and the economic Trinity.

As a matter of fact, a serious limitation of Grenz's golden thread
lies in the point that his analysis of contemporary discussions falls
between the Scylla of ontology and the Charybdis of epistemology.
This is also the case with all the seven positions, and especially with
the remaining four positions: mutual correspondence, identity, eschatological unity, and mutual inclusiveness. As we have seen in chapter 5,
each of the positions exposes either an ontological tension or an epistemological tension, or even both. What is worse, such tensions are not
completely resolved by ontology and epistemology themselves. For this
reason, to seek an integrative relationship between the immanent and
the economic Trinity in terms of ontology and epistemology from the
outset does not get the discussion any further forward.

That being the case, this book has paid special attention to the fact
that a concept of divine mystery is used, though not univocally, to resolve the tensions in each of these positions. However, as this book has
also noted, it is used in a restricted way, in that contemporary discus-

26. Ibid., 343.
27. Ibid., 11, 319.

sions on the immanent-economic Trinity relation relegate mystery to the second rank, considering it a function of ontology and epistemology. What is required, therefore, for further fruitful discussions is to reverse the order between ontology and epistemology, on the one hand, and the concept of mystery on the other. In other words, what is required is to keep a concept of mystery in the foreground, not merely as a device for resolving epistemological or ontological tensions, but rather that a concept of divine mystery needs to be determinative of ontology and epistemology. In this regard, an important further question to be answered is which concept of mystery to start with, rather than what kind of ontology and epistemology to presuppose.

In the New Testament, the word mystery [μυστήριον], which is translated into *Sacramentum* in Latin, occurs twenty-eight times.[28] Most of these occurrences clearly refer to Jesus Christ.[29] For example, Paul in Col 1:25–27 explains that he becomes a servant to make fully known "the mystery [μυστήριον] that has been hidden throughout the ages and generations, but has now been revealed to his saints," and that "to them God chosen to make known how great among the Gentiles are the riches of glory of this mystery [μυστήριον], which is Christ in you, the hope of glory" (NRSV). In Col 2:2–3, he continues to manifest his final purpose of mission that Christians at Colosse "may have all the riches of assured understanding and have the knowledge of God's mystery [μυστήριον], that is, Christ himself, in whom are hidden all the treasures of wisdom and knowledge" (NRSV). And in Eph 3:4, Paul expresses his expectation that Ephesian Christians, by reading his writings, "will perceive my understanding of the mystery [μυστήριον] of Christ" (NRSV). In this sense, the concept of mystery [μυστήριον] is easily linked to revelation (Rom 16:25; Eph 3:3; Col 1:26) and *oikonomia* (Eph 1:9–10, 3:2, 3:9).[30]

In a striking contrast to the biblical meaning of mystery [μυστήριον] as Jesus Christ, most contemporary discussions of the immanent-economic Trinity relation locate a primary sense of mystery [μυστήριον] not in Jesus Christ but in God or God the Father. As chapter 5 has shown clearly, Boff and Pittenger start with their strong focus on the experi-

---

28. *EDT*, 803 and 1047; *TRE*, XXIII, 519–22.

29. According to Beeely, Gregory of Nazianzus comprehends clearly that mystery [μυστήριον] is Jesus Christ. Beeley, *Gregory of Nazianzus*, 125–26, 239.

30. Munitz, *Mystery of Existence*, 24.

ence of the mystery of God through Jesus Christ. Suchocki regards our threefold experience of God as Presence, Wisdom and Power itself as mystery. LaCugna depends for her proposal of relational ontology on her notion of person as "an ineffable and inexhaustible mystery," which is ultimately grounded in "the Absolute Mystery of God." Lee, drawing on his exegesis of Exod 3:1–15, stresses that God is the unknowable and unnameable mystery.

In addition, Rahner holds fast to the incomprehensible mystery of God the Father, and thereby regards the incarnation of Jesus Christ as the absolute *proximity*. Barth acknowledges both the mystery of revelation in Jesus Christ and the mystery of God in general, but the latter of them is more influential in his understanding of mystery as *ignoramus*.[31] Jenson does not start from the identity of Jesus Christ, but from the identity of God, which forces him to consider as the final mystery the transition from God in the Old Testament to one Person as the Father in the New Testament. In comparison to these theologians, Moltmann and Pannenberg may be regarded to be in relatively better positions, for both begin with the life and ministry of Jesus Christ, such as the cross and the resurrection. Nonetheless, their positions are limited, in that Moltmann puts a concept of divine mystery merely in the end of his discussion on the immanent-economic Trinity relation, while Pannenberg deals with a concept of mystery as Jesus Christ in a theological *locus* separate from that of his treatment of the Trinity.

To put together what have been discussed above, I propose three points for further discussions on the issue of the relationship between the immanent and economic Trinity.

First, in order to keep the balance between the gracious freedom of God and the profound relatedness of God to the world, it is necessary to maintain both the distinction and unity between the immanent and the economic Trinity, which accords with the main theological tradition.

Second, in order to seek a more fully integrative relationship between the immanent and the economic Trinity, it is also necessary to put a concept of divine mystery in the foreground, not merely as

31. Profoundly influenced by Kaufmann and Derrida, William Stacy Johnson makes an attempt to pay attention to the theocentrism in Barth, which he regards as the counter-stream to the christocentrism of Barth. The point of Johnson's theocentric reading of Barth is to incessantly underscore the hiddenness and mystery of God. William Stacy Johnson, *Mystery of God*, ix, 1, and 20–21.

a device for resolving epistemological or ontological tensions. And, in order to do so, it is noteworthy that the biblical meaning of mystery primarily refers to Jesus Christ, which is strikingly contrasted with some theological options which locate a concept of mystery in God or God the Father.

Third, a concept of divine mystery needs to be determinative of ontology and epistemology, not the other way around. This would provide an appropriate method to overcome a substance ontology and even its variants which presuppose two separate ontological levels. In addition, this would enable us to exclude a static kind of epistemology, but to grasp a spiritual epistemology which allows our epistemological transformation in face of the mystery of Jesus Christ.

These three points, taken together, can lead us towards realizing that the Triune God is both the mystery of salvation and the mystery of the world.

Exile unlocks this — How?

Bibliography

Karl Barth

Primary Sources

Barth, Karl. *Church Dogmatics*. Translated by Geoffrey W. Bromiley. Ediburgh: T. & T. Clark, 1975.

———. *The Epistle to the Romans*. 2nd ed. Translated by Edwyn C. Hoskyns. Oxford: Oxford University Press, 1968.

———. *The Göttingen Dogmatics: Instruction in the Christian Religion*. Edited by Hannelotte Reiffen. Translated by Geoffrey W. Bromiley. Grand Rapids: Eerdmans, 1991.

———. *The Humanity of God*. Translated by John Newton Thomas. Richmond: John Knox Press, 1960.

———. *Die Kirchliche Dogmatik*. Zollikon: Evangelischer, 1947–1970.

———. *Letters 1961–1968*. Translated by Geoffrey W. Bromiley. Grand Rapids: Eerdmans, 1980.

———. *The Theology of Schleiermacher: Lectures at Göttingen, Winter Semester of 1923/1924*, Translated by Geoffrey W. Bromiley. Grand Rapids: Eerdmans, 1982.

Barth, Karl, and Eduard Thurneysen. *Revolutionary Theology in the Making: Barth-Thurneysen Correspondence (1914–1925)*. Translated by James D. Smart. Richmond: John Knox, 1964.

The Digital Karl Barth Library. Online: http://solomon.dkbl.alexanderstreet.com/

Secondary Sources

Bradshaw, Timothy. *Trinity and Ontology: A Comparative Study of the Theologies of Karl Barth and Wolfhart Pannenberg*. Edinburgh: Rutherford, 1988.

Bromiley, Geoffrey W. *An Introduction to the Theology of Karl Barth*. Grand Rapids: Eerdmans, 1979.

Busch, Eberhard. *The Great Passion: An Introduction to Karl Barth's Theology*. Translated by Geoffrey W. Bromiley. Grand Rapids: Eerdmans, 2004.

Deddo, Gary W. *Karl Barth's Theology of Relations: Trinitarian, Christological, and Human: Towards an Ethic of the Family*. New York: Lang, 1999.

Gunton, Colin E. *Becoming and Being: The Doctrine of God in Charles Hartshorne and Karl Barth*. New edition. London: SCM, 2001.

Hunsinger, George. *Disruptive Grace: Studies in the Theology of Karl Barth*. Grand Rapids: Eerdmans, 2000.

Jenson, Robert W. *Alpha and Omega: A Study in the Theology of Karl Barth.* New York: Nelson, 1963.

Johnson, William Stacy. *The Mystery of God: Karl Barth and the Postmodern Foundations of Theology.* Louisville: Westminster John Knox, 1997.

Jüngel, Eberhard. *God's Being is in Becoming: The Trinitarian Being of God in the Theology of Karl Barth.* Translated by John Webster. Edinburgh: T. & T. Clark, 2001.

———. *Gottes Sein ist im Werdn: Verantwortliche Rede von Sein Gottes bei Karl Barth. Eine Paraphrase.* Tübingen: Mohr/Siebeck, 1965.

Kim, Kyun Chin. *Hegel and Barth.* Seoul: The Christian Literature Society of Korea, 1983.

Leslie, Benjamin C. *Trinitarian Hermeneutics: The Hermeneutical Significance of Karl Barth's Doctrine of the Trinity.* New York: Lang, 1991.

McCormack, Bruce L. *Karl Barth's Critically Realistic Dialectical Theology: Its Genesis and Development 1909-1936.* Oxford: Clarendon, 1995.

———. "The Unheard Message of Karl Barth." *Word & World* 14 (1994) 59–66.

Migliore, Daniel L. "Karl Barth's First Lectures in Dogmatics: Instruction in the Christian Religion." In *The Göttingen Dogmatics: Instruction in the Christian Religion,* edited by Hannelotte Reiffen, translated by Geoffrey W. Bromiley, 15–62. Grand Rapids: Eerdmans, 1991.

Powell, Samuel M. *The Trinity in German Thought.* Cambridge: Cambridge University Press, 2001.

Taylor, Iain. "In Defence of Karl Barth's Doctrine of the Trinity." *International Journal of Systematic Theology* 5 (2003) 33–46.

Thompson, John. "The Humanity of God in the Theology of Karl Barth." *Scottish Journal of Theology* 29 (1976) 249–69.

Webster, John, editor. *The Cambridge Companion to Karl Barth.* Cambridge: Cambridge University Press, 2000.

Yoon, Chul-Ho. "A Christocentric Theology of Karl Barth and His Christology." In *Jangshin Nondan,* 180–211. Seoul: Presbyterian College & Theological Seminary, 1992.

Karl Rahner

PRIMARY SOURCES

Rahner, Karl. "The Concept of Mystery in Catholic Theology." In *Theological Investigations IV: More Recent Writings,* translated by Kevin Smyth, 36–73. Baltimore: Helicon, 1966.

———. *Foundations of Christian Faith: An Introduction to the Idea of Christianity.* Translated by William V. Dych. New York: Crossroad, 1978.

———. "Divine Trinity" and "Trinity in Theology." In *Encyclopedia of Theology: The Concise Sacramentum Mundi,* edited by Karl Rahner, 1755–71. New York: Seabury, 1975.

———. "Divine Trinity." In *Sacramentum Mundi: An Encyclopedia of Theology VI,* edited by Karl Rahner, 295–303. New York: Herder & Herder, 1968–1970.

———. "History of the World and Salvation-History." In *Theological Investigations V: Later Writings*, translated by Karl-H. Kruger, 97–114. Baltimore: Helicon, 1966.

———. "Oneness and Threefoldness of God in Discussion with Islam." In *Theological Investigations XVIII: God and Revelation*, translated by Edward Quinn, 105–21. New York: Crossroad, 1983.

———. "On the Theology of the Incarnation." In *Theological Investigations IV: More Recent Writings*, translated by Kevin Smyth, 105–20. Baltimore: Helicon, 1969.

———. "Remarks on the Dogmatic Treatise '*De Trinitate*.'" In *Theological Investigations IV: More Recent Writings*, translated by Kevin Smyth, 77–102. Baltimore: Helicon, 1966.

———. "The Theology of the Symbol." In *Theological Investigations IV: More Recent Writings*, translated by Kevin Smyth, 221–52. Baltimore: Helicon, 1966.

———. *The Trinity*. Translated by Joseph Donceel. New York: Herder & Herder, 1970.

SECONDARY SOURCES

Carr, Ann. "Karl Rahner." In *A New Handbook of Christian Theologians*, edited by Donald W. Musser and Joseph L. Price, 375–86. Nashville: Abingdon, 1996.

Congar, Yves. *I Believe in the Holy Spirit*. 3 Vols. Translated by David Smith. New York: Seabury, 1983.

Kasper, Walter. *The God of Jesus Christ*. Translated by Matthew J. O'Connell. New York: Crossroad, 1984.

Pekarske, Daniel T. *Abstracts of Karl Rahner's Theological Investigations I–XXIII*. Milwaukee: Marquette University Press, 2002.

Jürgen Moltmann

PRIMARY SOURCES

Moltmann, Jürgen. *The Church in the Power of the Spirit: A Contribution to Messianic Ecclesiology*. Translated by Margaret Kohl. Minneapolis: Fortress, 1993.

———. *The Coming of God: Christian Eschatology*. Translated by Margaret Kohl. Minneapolis: Fortress, 1996.

———. *The Crucified God: The Cross of Christ as the Foundation and Criticism of Christian Theology*. Translated by R. A. Wilson and John Bowden. Minneapolis: Fortress, 1993.

———. *History and the Triune God: Contributions to Trinitarian Theology*. Translated by John Bowden. New York: Crossroad, 1992.

———. *The Spirit of Life: A Universal Affirmation*. Translated by Margaret Kohl. Minneapolis: Fortress, 1992.

———. *The Trinity and the Kingdom: The Doctrine of God*. Translated by Margaret Kohl. Minneapolis: Fortress, 1993.

SECONDARY SOURCES

Conyers, A. J. *God, Hope, and History: Jürgen Moltmann and the Christian Concept of History*. Macon: Mercer University Press, 1988.

Willis, W. Waite. *Theism, Atheism, and the Doctrine of the Trinity: The Trinitarian Theologies of Karl Barth and Jürgen Moltmann in Response to Protest Atheism.* American Academy of Religion Academy Series 53. Atlanta: Scholars, 1987.

Wolfhart Pannenberg

PRIMARY SOURCES

Pannenberg, Wolfhart. "Appearance as the Arrival of the Future." *Journal of the American Academy of Religion* 35 (1967) 107–18.

———. *Basic Questions in Theology: Collected Essays.* Vols. 1–2. Translated by George H. Kehm. Philadelphia: Fortress, 1971.

———. "The God of History: The Trinitarian God and the Truth of History." Translated by M. B. Jackson. *The Cumberland Seminarian* 19.2–3 (1981) 28–41.

———. "Der Gott der Geschichte: Der trinitarische Gott und die Wahrheit der Geschichte." *Kerygma and Dogma* 23 (1977) 76–92.

———. *Metaphysics and the Idea of God.* Translated by Philip Clayton. Grand Rapids: Eerdmans, 1990.

———. "Problems of a Trinitarian Doctrine of God." *Dialog* 26 (1987) 250–57.

———. *Revelation as History.* Translated by David Granskou. New York: Macmillan, 1968.

———. *Systematic Theology.* 3 Vols. Translated by Geoffrey W. Bromiley. Grand Rapids: Eerdmans, 1988–1993.

———. "Theology and the Kingdom of God." *Una Sancta* 24.2 (1967) 3–19.

———. *Theology and the Kingdom of God.* Edited by Richard John Neuhaus. Philadelphia: Westminster, 1969.

SECONDARY SOURCES

Braaten, Carl E., and Philip Clayton, editors. *The Theology of Wolfhart Pannenberg: Twelve American Critiques.* Minneapolis: Augsburg, 1988.

Bradshaw, Timothy. *Trinity and Ontology: A Comparative Study of the Theologies of Karl Barth and Wolfhart Pannenberg.* Edinburgh: Rutherford, 1988.

Grenz, Stanley J. *Reason for Hope: The Systematic Theology of Wolfhart Pannenberg.* Oxford: Oxford University Press, 1990.

Olson, Roger E. "Wolfhart Pannenberg's Doctrine of the Trinity." *Scottish Journal of Theology* 43 (1990) 175–206.

Peters, Ted, "The Systematic Theology of Wolfhart Pannenberg." *Dialog* 37 (1998) 123–33.

———. "Wolfhart Pannenberg." In *A New Handbook of Christian Theologians,* edited by Donald W. Musser and Joseph L. Price, 363–74. Nashville: Abingdon, 1996.

Polk, David Patrick. *On the Way to God: An Exploration into the Theology of Wolfhart Pannenberg.* Lanham, MD: University Press of America, 1988.

Tupper, Elgin Frank. *The Theology of Wolfhart Pannenberg.* Philadelphia: Westminster, 1973.

Robert W. Jenson

PRIMARY SOURCES

Jenson, Robert W. "Creation as a Triune Act." *Word & Word* 2 (1982) 34–42.

———. "Does God Have Time? The Doctrine of the Trinity and the Concept of Time in the Physical Sciences." *The Center for Theology and the Natural Sciences* 11 (1991) 1–6.

———. "The Futurist Option in Speaking of God." *Lutheran Quarterly* 21 (1969) 17–25.

———. *God after God: The God of the Past and the God of the Future Seen in the Work of Karl Barth.* Indianapolis: Bobbs-Merrill, 1969.

———. "The Hidden and Triune God." *International Journal of Systematic Theology* 2 (2000) 5–12.

———. "Second Locus: The Triune God." In *Christian Dogmatics, I–II,* edited by Carl E. Braaten and Robert W. Jenson, I, 79-101. Philadelphia: Fortress, 1984.

———. *Systematic Theology: The Triune God (1), The Works of God (2).* Oxford: Oxford University Press, 1997–1999.

———. "Three Identities of One Action." *Scottish Journal of Theology* 28 (1975) 1–15.

———. *The Triune Identity: God according to the Gospel.* 1982. Reprinted, Eugene, OR: Wipf & Stock, 2002.

Braaten, Carl E., and Robert W. Jenson, editors. *The Futurist Option.* New York: Newman, 1970.

SECONDARY SOURCES

Grenz, Stanley J. "The Divine Fuge: Robert Jenson's Renewed Trinitarianism: A Review Essay." *Perspectives in Religious Studies* 30.2 (2003) 211–16.

Gunton, Colin E., editor. *Trinity, Time, and Church: A Response to the Theology of Robert W. Jenson.* Grands Rapids: Eerdmans, 2000.

Hart, David B. "The Lively God of Robert Jenson." *First Things* 156 (2005) 28–34.

Russell, Robert John. "Is the Triune God the Basis for Physical Time?" *The Center for Theology and the Natural Sciences Bulletin* 11 (1991) 7–19.

Leonardo Boff

PRIMARY SOURCES

Boff, Leonard. *Ecology & Liberation: A New Paradigm.* Maryknoll, NY: Orbis, 1995.

———. *Holy Trinity, Perfect Community.* Translated by Phillip Berryman. Maryknoll, NY: Orbis, 2000.

———. *Jesus Christ Liberator: A Critical Christology for Our Time.* Maryknoll, NY: Orbis, 1978.

———. *Liberating Grace.* Translated by John Drury. Maryknoll, NY: Orbis, 1979.

———. *Trinity and Society.* Translated by Paul Burns. New York, NY: Orbis, 1988.

SECONDARY SOURCES

Conn, Marie. "The Sacramental Theology of Leonardo Boff." *Worship* 64 (1990) 523–32.

Maduro, Otto. "Leonardo Boff." In *A New Handbook of Christian Theologians*, edited by Donald W. Musser and Joseph L. Price, 74–84. Nashville: Abingdon, 1996.

Peters, Ted. *God as Trinity: Relationality and Temporality in Divine Life.* Louisville: Westminster John Knox, 1993.

William Norman Pittenger

PRIMARY SOURCES

Pittenger, William Norman. *Christ and Christian Faith: Some Presuppositions and Implications of the Incarnation.* New York: Round Table, 1941.

———. *The Divine Triunity.* Philadelphia: United Church, 1977.

———. *God in Process.* London: SCM, 1967.

———. *The Holy Spirit.* Philadelphia: United Church, 1982.

———. *Picturing God.* London: SCM, 1982.

———. *Process-Thought And Christian Faith.* New York: Macmillan, 1968.

———. *Reconceptions in Christian Thinking 1817-1967.* New York: Seabury, 1968.

———. *The Word Incarnate: A Study of the Doctrine of The Person of Christ.* New York: Harper & Brothers, 1959.

SECONDARY SOURCES

Demarest, Bruce A. "Process Trinitarianism." In *Perspectives on Evangelical Theology: Papers from the 30th Annual Meeting of the Evangelical Theological Society,* edited by Kenneth S. Kantzer and Stanley N. Gundry, 15–36. Grand Rapids: Baker, 1979.

Geisler, Norman L. "Process Theology." In *Tensions in Contemporary Theology,* edited by Stanley N. Gundry and Alan F. Johnson, 237–84. Chicago: Moody, 1976.

Russell, John M. "Pittenger on the Triune God: A Process *Apologia.*" *Encounter* 53 (1992) 55–77.

Joseph A. Bracken

PRIMARY SOURCES

Bracken, Joseph A. "Dependent Co-Origination and Universal Intersubjectivity." *Buddihist-Christian Studies* 27 (2007) 3–9.

———. "The Hiddenness of God: An Inter-Subjective Approach." *Dialog* 45 (2006) 170–75.

———. "The Holy Trinity as a Community of Divine Persons I." *The Heythrop Journal* 15 (1974) 166–82.

———. "The Holy Trinity as a Community of Divine Persons II." *The Heythrop Journal* 15 (1974) 257–70.

———. "Intentionality Analysis and Intersubjectivity." *Horizons* 33 (2006) 207–20.

————. "Intersubjectivity and the Coming of God." *Journal of Religion* 83 (2003) 381–400.

————. *The One in the Many: A Contemporary Reconstruction of the God-World Relationship.* Grand Rapids: Eerdmans, 2001.

————. "Panentheism from a Trinitarian Perspective." *Horizons* 22 (1995) 7–28.

————. "Panentheism from a Process Perspective." In *Trinity in Process: A Relational Theology of God,* edited by Joseph A. Bracken and Marjorie Hewitt Suchocki, 95–113. New York: Continuum, 1997.

————. "Process Perspectives and Trinitarian Theology." In *Word & Spirit—A Monastic Review 8: Process Theology and the Christian Doctrine of God,* edited by Santiago Sia, 51–64. Petersham: St. Bede's, 1986.

————. *Society and Spirit: A Trinitarian Cosmology.* Selingsgrove, PA: Susquehanna Uni-versity Press, 1991.

————. "Trinity: Economic *and* Immanent." *Horizons* 25 (1998) 7–22.

————. *The Triune Symbol: Persons, Process and Community.* Lanham, MD: University Press of America, 1985.

————. *What Are They Saying about the Trinity?* New York: Paulist, 1979.

Secondary Sources

Cecil, Paul Lewis. "A Response to Joseph Bracken's 'Prehending God in and through the World.'" *Process Studies* 29 (2000) 358–64.

Ryan, Robert J. "How Process and Ecumenical Experience Ground Communion: A Study of the Practical Implications of Joseph Bracken's Trinitarian Theology." *Diakonia* 30 (1997) 29–37.

Stupar, Lisa. "Implications of Bracken's Process Model of the Trinity for a Contemporary Feminist Theology." *Horizons* 27 (2000) 256–75.

Marjorie Hewitt Suchocki

Primary Sources

Suchocki, Marjorie Hewitt, *God-Christ-Church: A Practical Guide to Process Theology.* New York: Crossroad, 1982.

————. *God, Christ, Church: A Practical Guide to Process Theology.* Rev. ed. New York: Crossroad, 1989.

————. "God, Trinity, Process." *Dialog* 30 (2001) 169–74.

————. "John Cobb's Trinity: Implications for the University." In *Theology and the University: Essays in Honor of John B. Cobb, Jr.,* edited by David Ray Griffin and Joseph C. Hough Jr. Albany: State University of New York Press, 1991.

————. "Spirit in and through the World." In *Trinity in Process: A Relational Theology of God,* edited by Joseph A. Bracken and Marjorie Hewitt Suchocki, 173–90. New York: Continuum, 1997.

————. "Sunyata, Trinity, and Community." In *Divine Emptiness and Historical Fullness,* edited by Christopher Ives, 136–49. Valley Forge, PA: Trinity, 1995.

————. "The Unmale God: Reconsidering the Trinity." *Quarterly Review* 3 (1983) 34–49.

SECONDARY SOURCES

Meland, Bernard Eugene. "In Response to Suchocki." *American Journal of Theology & Philosophy* 5.2/3 (1984) 89–95.

Catherine Mowry LaCugna

PRIMARY SOURCES

LaCugna, Catherine Mowry. "The Doctrine of the Trinity." In *Commentary on the Catechism of the Catholic Church*, edited by Michael J. Walsh, 66–80. London: Chapman, 1994.

———. *God for Us: The Trinity and Christian Life*. New York: HarperCollins, 1991.

———. "God in Communion with Us: The Trinity." In *Freeing Theology: The Essentials of Theology in Feminist Perspective*, edited by Catherine Mowry LaCugna, 83–114. San Francisco: HarperSanFrancisco, 1993.

———. "Philosophers and Theologians on the Trinity." *Modern Theology* 2.3 (1986) 169–81.

———. "Re-conceiving the Trinity as the Mystery of Salvation." *Scottish Journal of Theology* 38 (1985) 1–23.

———. "Re-conceiving the Trinity as Mystery of Salvation." In *Rising from History: U.S. Catholic Theology Looks to the Future*, the Annual Publication of the College Theology Society 30, edited by Robert J. Daly, 125–37. Lanham, MD: University Press of America, 1987.

———. "The Relational God: Aquinas and Beyond." *Theological Studies* 46 (1985) 647–63.

———. "The Theological Methodology of Hans Küng." PhD Diss., Fordham University, 1979.

———. *The Theological Methodology of Hans Küng*. AAR Academy Series 39. New York: Scholars, 1982.

———. "The Trinitarian Mystery of God." In *Systematic Theology: Roman Catholic Perspectives*, vols. 1–2, edited by Francis Schüsler Fiorenza and John P. Galvin, I, 149–92. Minneapolis: Fortress, 1991.

SECONDARY SOURCES

Groppe, Elizabeth T. "Creation *Ex Nihilo* and *Ex Amore*: Ontological Freedom in the Theologies of John Zizioulas and Catherine Mowry LaCugna." *Modern Theology* 21.3 (2005) 463–95.

———. "Catherine Mowry LaCugna's Contribution to a Relational Theology." In *Theology and Conversation: Towards a Relational Theology*, edited by J. Haers and P. De Mey, 239–54. Leuven: Leuven University Press, 2003.

———. "Catherine Mowry LaCugna's Contribution to Trinitarain Theology." *Theological Studies* 63 (2002) 730–63.

Gunton, Colin E. *The Promise of Trinitarian Theology*. 2nd ed. Edinburgh: T. & T. Clark, 1997.

Hilkert, Mary Catherine. "The Mystery of Persons in Communion: The Trinitarian Theology of Catherine Mowry LaCugna." *Word & World* 18 (1998) 237–43.

Leslie, Benjamin C. "Does God Have a Life: Barth and LaCugna on the Immanent Trinity." *Perspectives in Religious Studies* 24 (1997) 377–98.

Molnar, Paul D. *Divine Freedom and the Doctrine of the Immanent Trinity: In Dialogue with Karl Barth and Contemporary Theology.* London: T. & T. Clark, 2002.

Torrance, Alan J. "The Ecumenical Implications of Catherine Mowry LaCugna's Trinitarian Theology." *Horizons* 27 (2000) 347–53.

Weinandy, Thomas G. "The Immanent Trinity and the Economic Trinity." *Thomist* 57 (1993) 655–66.

Jung Young Lee

PRIMARY SOURCES

Lee, Jung Young. "Can God Be Change Itself?" *Journal of Ecumenical Studies* 10 (1973) 752–70.

———. "Can God Be Change Itself?" In *What Asian Christians Are Thinking: A Theological Source Book*, 1st ed., edited by Douglas J. Elwood, 173–93. Quezon: New Day, 1976.

———. *God Suffers for Us: A Systematic Inquiry into a Concept of Divine Passibility*, The Hague: Nijhoff, 1974.

———. *The I: A Christian Concept of Man.* New York: Philosophical Library, 1971.

———. *The I Ching and Modern Man: Essays on Metaphysical Implications of Change*, Secaucus, NJ: University Books, 1975.

———. "Some Reflection on the Authorship of the *I Ching*." *Numen* 17 (1976) 200–10.

———. "The Suffering of God: A Systematic Inquiry into a Concept of Divine Passibility." ThD diss., Boston University, 1968.

———. *The Theology of Change: A Christian Concept of God in an Eastern Perspective.* Maryknoll: Orbis, 1979.

———. *The Trinity in Asian Perspective.* Nashville: Abingdon, 1996.

SECONDARY SOURCES

Kärkkäinen, Veli-Matti. *The Trinity: Global Perspectives.* Louisville: Westminster John Knox, 2007.

Patristic and Medieval Works on the Trinity

Augustine. *On the Trinity.* NPNF 1st Series 3.

Athanasius. *Four Discourses Against the Arians.* NPNF 2nd Series 4.

Athenagoras of Athens. *A Plea for the Christians.* ANF 2.

Gregory of Nazianzus. *The Fourth Theological Oration: On the Son (Or. 30).* NPNF 2nd Series 7.

———. *Oration on Pentecost (Or. 41).* NPNF 2nd Series 7.

———. *Oration on the Theophany, or Birthday of Christ (Or. 38).* NPNF 2nd Series 7.

———. *The Third Theological Oration: On the Son (Or. 29).* NPNF 2nd Series 7.

Gregory of Nyssa. *Against Eunomius*. NPNF 2nd Series 5.

———. *On the Difference Between Ousia and Hypostasis*. NPNF 2nd Series 5.

———. *On the Holy Trinity, and of the Godhead of the Holy Spirit: To Eustathius*. NPNF 2nd Series 5.

———. *On Not Three Gods*. NPNF 2nd Series 5. Hippolytus of Rome. *Against Heresy of One Noetus*. ANF 5.

———. *The Refutation of All Heresies*. ANF 5.

Ignatius of Antioch. *To the Ephesians*. FC 1.

———. *To the Magneisans*. FC 1.

———. *To the Philadelphians*. FC 1.

———. *To the Romans*. FC 1.

Irenaeus of Lyons. *Against Heresies*. ANF 1.

Justin Martyr. *The Dialogue with Trypho*. FC 6.

———. *The First Apology*. FC 6.

———. *The Second Apology*. FC 6.

Tatian of Assyria. *Address to the Greeks*. ANF 2.

Tertullian. *Against Praxeas*. ANF 3.

———. *Apology*. ANF 3.

Theophilus of Antioch. *To Autolycus*. ANF 2.

Thomas Aquinas. *Summa Theologica*. New York: McGraw-Hill, 1964.

Other Works on the Trinity

Altaner, Berthold. *Patrology*. Translated by Hilda C. Graef. Edinburgh: Nelson, 1960.

Augustine. *De Trinitate*. Translated by Edmund Hill. New York: New City, 1991.

Beeley, Christopher. "Gregory of Nazianzus: Trinitarian Theology, Spirituality and Pastoral Theory." PhD diss., University of Notre Dame, 2002.

———. *Gregory of Nazianzus on the Trinity and the Knowledge of God: In Your Light We Shall See Light*. Oxford: Oxford University Press, 2008.

Boyd, Gregory A. "The *A Priori* Construction of the Doctrine of God in the Philosophy of Charles Hartshorne: A Critical Examination and Reconstruction of Di-Polar Theism Towards a Trinitarian Metaphysics." PhD diss., Princeton Theological Seminary, 1988.

———. *Trinity And Process: A Critical Evaluation and Reconstruction of Hartshorne's Di-Polar Theism Towards a Trinitarian Metaphysics*. New York: Lang, 1992.

Bracken, Joseph A., and Marjorie Hewitt Suchock, editors. *Trinity in Process: A Relational Theology of God*. New York: Continuum, 1997.

British Council of Churches. *The Forgotten Trinity*, vols. 1–3: *The Report of the BCC Study Commission on Trinitarian Doctrine Today*; *A Study Guide on Issues Contained in the Report of the BCC Study Commission on Trinitarian Doctrine Today*; *A Selection of Papers Presented to the BCC Study Commission on Trinitarian Doctrine Today*. London: British Council of Churches, 1989–1991.

Butin, Philip Walker. *Revelation, Redemption, and Response: Calvin's Trinitarian Understanding of the Divine-Human Relationship*. Oxford: Oxford University Press, 1995.

Cobb, John B., Jr., and David Ray Griffin. *Process Theology: An Introductory Exposition*. Philadelphia: Westminster, 1976.

Crawford, R. G. "Is the Doctrine of the Trinity Scriptural?" *Scottish Journal of Theology* 20 (1967) 282–94.

Emmet, Dorothy Mary. *Whitehead's Philosophy of Organism*. 2nd ed. London: Macmillan, 1966.

Emery, Gilles. "The Doctrine of the Trinity in St. Thomas Aquinas." In *Aquinas on Doctrine: A Critical Introduction*, edited by Thomas G. Weinandy, Daniel A. Keating, and John P. Yocum, 45–65. London: T. & T. Clark, 2004.

Ford, Lewis S. *The Lure of God: A Biblical Background for Process Theism*. Philadelphia: Fortress, 1978.

———. "Process Trinitarianism." *Journal of the American Academy of Religion* 43 (1975) 199–213.

Fortman, Edmund J. *The Triune God: A Historical Study of the Doctrine of the Trinity*. London: Hutchinson, 1972.

Grenz, Stanley J. *The Matrix of Christian Theology 1: The Social God and the Relational Self: A Trinitarian Theology of the Imago Dei*. Louisville: Westminster John Knox, 2001.

———. *The Matrix of Christian Theology*, vol 2: *The Named God and the Question of Being: A Trinitarian Theo-Ontology*. Louisville: Westminster John Knox, 2005.

———. *Rediscovering the Triune God: The Trinity in Contemporary Theology*. Minneapolis: Fortress, 2004.

Gunton, Colin E. *The Promise of Trinitarian Theology*. 2nd ed. Edinburgh: T. & T. Clark, 1997.

Haight, Roger. *Jesus: Symbol of God*. Maryknoll, NY: Orbis, 1999.

———. "The Point of Trinitarian Theology." *Toronto Journal of Theology* 4.2 (1988) 191–204.

Hartshorne, Charles. *Man's Vision of God and the Logic of Theism*. Chicago: Willett, Clark, 1941.

Hegel, G. W. F. *Phenomenology of Spirit*. Translated by A. V. Miller. Oxford: Clarendon, 1977.

Hill, William J. *The Three-Personed God: The Trinity as a Mystery of Salvation*. Washington, DC: Catholic University Press, 1982.

Jüngel, Eberhard. *God as the Mystery of the World*. Grand Rapids: Eerdmans, 1983.

Kaufman, Gordon D. *An Essay on Theological Method*. 3rd ed. Atlanta: Scholars, 1995.

———. *God-Mystery-Diversity: Christian Theology in a Pluralistic World*. Minneapolis: Fortress, 1996.

———. *God the Problem*. Cambridge: Harvard University Press. 1972.

———. *In Face of Mystery: A Constructive Theology*. Cambridge: Harvard University Press, 1993.

———. *In the beginning . . . Creativity*. Minneapolis: Fortress, 2004.

———. *Jesus and Creativity*. Minneapolis: Fortress, 2006.

———. *Systematic Theology: A Historical Perspective*. New York: Scribner's, 1968.

———. *The Theological Imagination: Constructing the Concept of God*. Philadelphia: Westminster, 1981.

Kelly, J. N. D. *Early Christian Doctrines*. Rev. ed. San Francisco: Harper & Row, 1978.

Knight, G. A. F. *A Biblical Approach to the Doctrine of the Trinity*. Scottish Journal of Theology Occasional Papers 1. Edinburgh: Oliver & Boyd, 1953.

Lampe, Geoffrey W. H. *God as Spirit*, Oxford: Clarendon, 1977.

Lossky, Vladimir. *The Mystical Theology of the Eastern Church*. Crestwood: St. Vladimir's Seminary, 1985.

Meredith, Anthony. *The Cappadocians*. New York: St. Vladimir's Seminary, 1995.

Metzger, Paul Louis, editor. *Trinitarian Soundings in Systematic Theology*. New York: T. & T. Clark, 2005.

Min, Anselm K. *Paths to the Triune God: An Encounter between Aquinas and Recent Theologies*. Notre Dame: University of Notre Dame Press, 2005.

Muller, Richard A. *Post-Reformulation Reformed Dogmatics: The Rise and Development of Reformed Orthodoxy, ca. 1520 to ca.1725*. Vol 4: *The Triunity of God*. Grand Rapids: Baker, 2003.

Neville, Robert Cummings. *A Theology Primer*. Albany: State University of New York Press, 1991.

Olson, Roger E., and Christopher A. Hall. *The Trinity*. Grand Rapids: Eerdmans, 2002.

Park, Mann. *Study on the Contemporary Doctrine of the Trinity*. Seoul: The Christian Literature Society of Korea, 2003.

Pelikan, Jaroslav. *The Christian Tradition: A History of the Development of Doctrine*. 5 vols. Chicago: University of Chicago Press, 1971–1989.

Peters, Ted. *God as Trinity: Relationality and Temporality in Divine Life*. Louisville: Westminster John Knox, 1993.

———. *GOD—The World's Future: Systematic Theology for a New Era*. 2nd ed. Minneapolis: Fortress, 2000.

———. "Trinity Talk: Part I." *Dialog* 26.1 (1987) 44–48.

———. "Trinity Talk: Part II." *Dialog* 26.2 (1987) 133–38.

Placher, William C. *The Triune God: An Essay in Postliberal Theology*. Louisville: Westminster John Knox, 2007.

Power, William L. "The Doctrine of the Trinity and Whitehead's Metaphysics." *Encounter* 45.4 (1984) 287–302.

Rhee, Jong-Sung. *Augustine's Doctrine of the Trinity: The Influence of Plotinus on Augustine as Illustrated in his Doctrine of the Trinity*. Seoul: Korea Institute of Advanced Christian Studies, 2001.

Richardson, Cyril C. *The Doctrine of the Trinity*. Nashville: Abingdon, 1958.

Rusch, William G. *The Trinitarian Controversy*. Philadelphia: Fortress, 1980.

Sanders, Fred. "Entangled in the Trinity: Economic and Immanent Trinity in Recent Theology." *Dialog* 40.3 (2001) 175–82.

———. "The Image of the Immanent Trinity: Implications of Rahner's Rule for a Theological Interpretation of Scripture." PhD diss., Graduate Theological Union, 2001.

———. "Trinity Talk, Again." *Dialog* 44.3 (2005) 264–72.

Schoonenberg, Piet J. A. M. "Trinity—The Consummated Covenant: Theses on the Doctrine of the Trinitarian God (1973)." *Studies in Religion / Sciences Religieuses* 5.2 (1975/1976) 111–16.

Schwöbel, Christoph, editor. *Trinitarian Theology Today: Essays on Divine Being and Act*. Edinburgh: T. & T. Clark, 1995.

Studer, Basil. *Trinity and Incarnation: The Faith of the Early Church*. Translated by Matthias Westerhoff. Collegeville, MN: Liturgical, 1993.

Thomas Aquinas. *Summa Theologica*. Translated by Fathers of the English Dominican Province. Westminster: Christian Classics, 1981.

Thompson, John. *Modern Trinitarian Perspectives*. New York: Oxford University Press, 1994.

Wainwright, Arthur W. *The Trinity in the New Testament*. 1962. Reprint, Eugene, OR: Wipf & Stock, 2001.

Warfield, Benjamin Breckinridge. "The Biblical Doctrine of the Trinity." In *Biblical Doctrines*, 133–71. New York: Oxford University Press, 1929.

———. "The Biblical Doctrine of the Trinity." In *Biblical and Theological Studies*, edited by Samuel G. Craig, 22–59. Philadelphia: Presbyterian and Reformed, 1952.

———. "Trinity." In *The International Standard Bible Encyclopedia*, edited by James Orr, 3012–22. Chicago: Howard-Severance, 1915.

Welch, Claude. *In This Name: The Doctrine of the Trinity in Contemporary Theology*. New York: Scribners, 1952.

White, James R. *The Forgotten Trinity: Recovering the Heart of Christian Belief*. Minneapolis: Bethany, 1998.

Wiles, Maurice. *The Remaking of Christian Doctrine*. The Hulsean Lectures 1973. London: SCM, 1974.

———. "Some Reflections on the Origins of the Doctrine of the Trinity." *Journal of Theological Studies* 8 (1957) 92–106.

Wiles, Maurice, and Mark Santer. *Documents in Early Christian Thought*. Cambridge: Cambridge University Press, 1975.

Zizioulas, John D. *Being as Communion: Studies in Personhood and the Church*. New York: St. Vladimir's Seminary Press, 1985.

The Other Works

Allen, Diogenes. *Philosophy for Understanding Theology*. Atlanta: John Knox, 1985.

Baird, Forrest E., and Walter Kaufmann, editors. *Twentieth-Century Philosophy*. 3rd ed. Upper Saddle River, NJ: Prentice Hall, 2003.

Culbertson, Diana. "Western Mysticism and Process Thought." *Listening* 14 (1979) 204–22.

Derrida, Jacques. *Of Grammatology*. Translated by Gayatri Chakravorty Spivak. Baltimore: Johns Hopkins University Press, 1997.

Elwood, Douglas J., editor. *What Asian Christians Are Thinking: A Theological Source Book*. Quezon: New Day, 1976.

Epperly, Bruce. "A Mysticism of Becoming: Process Theology and Spiritual Formation." *Encounter* 50 (1989) 326–36.

Ferguson, Everett, editor. *Encyclopedia of Early Christianity*. 2nd ed. New York: Garland, 1997.

Foucault, Michel. *Power/Knowledge: Selected Interviews and Other Writigns 1972–1977*. Edited by Colin Gordon. New York: Pantheon, 1972.

Frei, Hans. *The Eclipse of Biblical Narrative*. New Haven: Yale University Press, 1974.

Fung, Yu-Lan. *A History of Chinese Philosophy*. 2 vols. Translated by Derk Bodde. Princeton: Princeton University Press, 1983.

Harnack, Adolf von. *History of Dogma*. 7 vols. Translated by Neil Buchanan. New York: Russell & Russell, 1958.

———. *What is Christianity?* Translated by Thomas Bailey. Philadelphia: Fortress, 1986.

Hartshorn, Charles. *The Divine Relativity: A Social Concept of God*. New Haven: Yale University Press, 1948.

Hasel, Gerhard. *Old Testament Theology: Basic Issues in the Current Debate*. 4th ed. Grand Rapids: Eerdmans, 1991.

Heidegger, Martin. *Being and Time*. Translated by John Macquarrie and Edward Robinson. New York: Harper, 1962.

———. *An Introduction to Metaphysics*. Translated by Gregory Fried and Richard Polt. New Haven: Yale University Press, 2000.

Husserl, Edmund. *Ideas Pertaining to a Pure Phenomenology and to a Phenomenological Philosophy: First Book: General Introduction to a Pure Phenomenology*. Translated by F. Kersten. Dordrecht: Kluwer, 1998.

Kant, Immanuel. *Critique of Practical Reason*. Translated by Lewis White Beck. New York: Macmillan, 1993.

———. *Critique of Pure Reason*. Translated by Norman Kemp Smith. New York: St. Martin's, 1929.

———. *Der Streit der Fakultäten*. Hamburg: Meiner, 1959.

Keller, Catherine. *On the Mystery: Discerning Divinity in Process*. Minneapolis: Fortress, 2008.

Kirk, G. S., J. E. Raven, and M. Schofield. *The Presocratic Philosophers: A Critical History with a Selection of Texts*. 2nd ed. Cambridge: Cambridge University Press, 1983.

Lamprecht, Sterling P. *Our Philosophical Traditions: A Brief History of Philosophy in Western Civilization*. New York: Appleton-Century-Crofts, 1955.

Lau, D. C. *Tao Te Ching: A Bilingual Edition*. Hong Kong: The Chinese University Press, 2001.

Levinas, Immanuel. *Discovering Existence with Husserl*. Translated by Richard A. Cohen and Michael B. Smith. Evanston, IL: Northwestern University Press, 1998.

———. *Otherwise than Being or Beyond Essence*. Translated by Alphonso Lingis. Boston: Kluwer, 1978.

Marcel, Gabriel. *The Mystery of Being: 1 Reflection & Mystery, 2 Faith & Reality*. Translated by G. S. Fraser and René Hague. London: Harvill, 1950–1951.

Moser, Paul K., and Arnold Vander Nat. *Human Knowledge: Classical and Contemporary Approaches*. 3rd ed. New York: Oxford University Press, 2003.

Munitz, Milton K. *The Mystery of Existence: An Essay in Philosophical Cosmology*. New York: New York University Press, 1974.

O'Callaghan, John P. *Thomist Realism and the Linguistic Turn: Toward a More Perfect Form of Existence*. Notre Dame: University of Notre Dame Press, 2003.

Plotinus. *The Enneads*. Translated by Stephen MacKenna. London: Faber & Faber, 1969.

Reynolds, Blair. "Christian Mysticism as Approaching Process Theology." *Parish and Process* 1.6 (1987) 6–13.

Schleiermacher, Friedrich. *The Christian Faith*. Edited by H. R. Mackintosh and J. S. Stewart. New York: Harper & Row, 1963.

———. *On Religion: Speeches to its Cultured Despisers*. Translated by Richard Crouter. Cambridge: Cambridge University Press, 1996.

Schoonenberg, Piet J. A. M. *The Christ: A Study of the God-Man Relationship in the Whole of Creation and in Jesus Christ*. Translated by Della Couling. New York: Herder & Herder, 1971.

Sharkey, Owen. "Mystery of God in Process Theology." In *God in Contemporary Thought*, 683–725. New York: Learned, 1977.

Sokolowski, Robert. *Introduction to Phenomenology*. Cambridge: Cambridge University Press, 2000.

Stiernotte, Alfred P. "Process Philosophies and Mysticism." *International Philosophical Quarterly* 9 (1969) 560–71.

Whitehead, Alfred North. *Process and Reality: An Essay in Cosmology*. New York: Macmillan, 1929.

Wippel, John F. *The Metaphysical Thought of Thomas Aquinas: From Finite Being to Uncreated Being*. Washington, DC: The Catholic University of America Press, 2000.

Wright, George Ernest. *God Who Acts: Biblical Theology as Recital*. Studies in Biblical Theology 1/8. London: SCM, 1952.

Index

abscission, 34
absolute knowledge, 29
"absorbing," 2
activity, 2
agape, as nature of God as the
    ultimate reality, 125
analogy, 139
anamnesis, 23
angels, 26
a Patre ad Patrem, 122
Apologists, 32
Apostolic Fathers, 32
appearance, ontological priority
    of, 150
Aquinas, Thomas. *See* Thomas
    Aquinas
Archaeology of Knowledge, The
    (Foucault), 30–31
arche, 22, 33
Aristotle, 21, 23–24, 25
Arius, 19, 43–44
    criticism of, 55–56
Athanasius, 42, 43–44
Athenagoras of Athens, 33, 34
Augustine, 12, 50–54, 115, 183

Balthasar, Hans Urs von, 13
Barth, Karl, 1, 9–10, 13, 176
    arguing for free grace of God's
        Word, 63
    asymmetrical notion of mutual
        correspondence, 68
    basic rule of, 69–70

beginning from reality of rev-
    elation, 127, 136–37
coming to grips with epistemo-
    logical tension, 2
criticized for orientation to the
    past, 136
criticizing subjective method, 17
defining relation between
    immanent and economic
    Trinity, 64
denying difference between
    God's self-knowledge and
    our knowledge of God's
    revelation, 137–38
distinguishing between God's
    primary and secondary ob-
    jectivity, 3, 128, 137, 138
distinguishing between imma-
    nent and economic Trinity,
    63
on the divine revelation, 127–28
giving erroneous impression of
    two ontologically different
    Trinities, 134–35
on mode of being, 97
on mutual correspondence of
    economic and immanent
    Trinity, 65–67
pairing analogy and mystery
    with *ignoramus*, 139
position of mutual correspon-
    dence, complicated by differ-
    ent tensions, 138